BROADCASTING POLICY IN CANADA

Where do Canadian content requirements come from? What do international trade agreements mean for existing broadcasting policy and business practices? How are new media changing the face of broadcasting in Canada? *Broadcasting Policy in Canada* traces the development of Canada's broadcasting legislation and analyses the roles and responsibilities of the key players in the broadcasting system, particularly those of the Canadian Radio-television and Telecommunications Commission (CRTC).

Robert Armstrong expresses with remarkable clarity the complicated changes to issues such as Canadian content, media regulation, and tax measures to provide a comprehensive overview of policies that have created the Canadian broadcasting system as it exists today. He also discusses related issues such as the Internet, copyright, social concerns, and cultural diversity in a global media environment. *Broadcasting Policy in Canada* will serve as a valuable resource for students, policymakers, and industry players of all kinds who are affected by the CRTC's policies and decisions.

ROBERT ARMSTRONG is president of Communications Médias inc. in Montreal.

ROBERT ARMSTRONG

Broadcasting Policy in Canada

UNIVERSITY OF TORONTO PRESS
Toronto Buffalo London

© University of Toronto Press Incorporated 2010
Toronto Buffalo London
www.utppublishing.com
Printed in Canada

ISBN 978-1-4426-4096-2 (cloth)
ISBN 978-1-4426-1035-4 (paper)

Printed on acid-free, 100% post-consumer recycled paper
with vegetable-based inks.

Library and Archives Canada Cataloguing in Publication

Armstrong, Robert
   Broadcasting policy in Canada / Robert Armstrong.

   Includes bibliographical references and index.
   ISBN 978-1-4426-4096-2 (bound).   ISBN 978-1-4426-1035-4 (pbk.)

   1. Broadcasting policy – Canada – Textbooks.   I. Title.

   HE8689.9.C3A76 2009   384.540971   C2009-906071-X

University of Toronto Press acknowledges the financial assistance to its
publishing program of the Canada Council for the Arts and the Ontario
Arts Council.

  Canada Council   Conseil des Arts    ONTARIO ARTS COUNCIL
          for the Arts   du Canada   CONSEIL DES ARTS DE L'ONTARIO

University of Toronto Press acknowledges the financial support for its
publishing activities of the Government of Canada through the Book
Publishing Industry Development Program (BPIDP).

To Suzanne and Geneviève

Contents

Preface   ix

1 Introduction   3

2 History of Canadian Broadcasting Policy to 1968   20

3 History of Canadian Broadcasting Policy, 1968–1991   41

4 Structure and Change in Canadian Broadcasting   56

5 The Canadian Radio-television and Telecommunications Commission (CRTC)   76

6 Canadian Content Requirements   94

7 Public Broadcasting   112

8 Financing Canadian Content   126

9 Social Issues   143

10 Broadcasting Distribution   163

11 Distribution Carriage Arrangements   179

12 Copyright, Broadcasting, and the Internet   192

13 Canadian Ownership and Competition Policy   205

14 Broadcasting and International Trade Agreements   223

15 Conclusion   232

Appendix A Section 3 of the Broadcasting Act, 1991   247

Appendix B Schematic Overview of the Broadcasting Policy
            Framework   251

Appendix C Overview of Broadcasting Legislation, 1932–1968   252

Appendix D Summary of Canadian Content and Expenditure
            Requirements   253

Appendix E History of the Canada Media Fund   254

Appendix F Excerpts from the North American Free Trade
            Agreement (NAFTA)   257

Glossary   259

Selected Bibliography   267

Index   273

Preface

This book examines government policies related to broadcasting in Canada and the strategies in place to safeguard and strengthen the Canadian broadcasting system. The discussion also addresses related issues such as television and radio production financing, copyright, the Internet, social concerns, and cultural diversity in a global media environment.

Broadcasting is the only regulated cultural medium in Canada. The material presented here provides an introduction to broadcasting regulation, the history of broadcasting legislation and policy, and the origins and objectives of relevant government policies. The discussion is conducted with particular attention to broadcasting policy development and, while issues of political power are addressed, power relationships are not the primary focus of the book.

The Canadian broadcasting system is constantly changing and any attempt to summarize or analyse Canadian broadcasting policy at one point in time is certain to be overcome by subsequent events. This book is current to July 2009, but since broadcasting policy continues to evolve, the reader is encouraged to supplement his or her knowledge by monitoring developments in the daily press and at the Internet websites of the major Canadian broadcasting policymakers mentioned herein. All of the Canadian Radio-television and Telecommunications Commission's decisions and notices contained in this book are available on its website at http://www.crtc.gc.ca.

In preparing this book, the author wishes to acknowledge the helpful comments on specific chapters of Jane Britten, Stéphane Cardin, Charles Dalfen, Peter Grant, Randy Hutson, Nick Ketchum, Peter Miller, Kathy Robinson, Jay Thomson, and Mary Vipond. A special thanks to Andrée

Wylie, who provided detailed comments on the entire manuscript. The dedication of Ryan van Huijstee and Frances Mundy of the University of Toronto Press in guiding the manuscript through the review process is gratefully acknowledged. Two anonymous readers retained by the Press also provided useful feedback. The final text benefited from interaction with students in Communication Studies at Concordia University, where the author has been teaching courses in broadcasting policy, media policy, and media law. None of the above-mentioned is responsible for the discussion that follows.

Robert Armstrong
Montreal, 21 July 2009

BROADCASTING POLICY IN CANADA

1 Introduction

Broadcasting is a multi-billion-dollar industry in Canada that plays a fundamental role in society by providing households with a vast array of entertainment and information services. Canadians continue to patronize live events in theatres, concert halls, and sports arenas, and to gather in movie theatres to see big-budget films on large screens. But radio and television possess the advantage of reaching people directly in their homes, in their automobiles, and in the workplace. Until recently, none of the other mass media contained the bundle of characteristics – audiovisual, inexpensive, personal, accessible, and often live – that is embodied in radio and television programs. Today, these characteristics are no longer unique to conventional broadcasting. Radio and television broadcasting are increasingly being challenged by new modes of personal communications delivery that provide access to a growing array of digital sound and visual images that compete with traditional broadcasting.

What Is Broadcasting?

When we refer to *broadcasting*, what exactly do we mean? The *Compact Edition of the Oxford English Dictionary* says that *to broadcast* is

- To scatter (seeds) rather than placing in drills or rows
- To tell to many people
- To transmit by radio or television

These are commonsensical definitions. The formal definition of broadcasting that will concern us here is set out in Canada's Broadcasting Act of 1991. Section 2(1) of the Act says that '"broadcasting"' ("radiodiffusion") means any transmission of *programs*, whether or not *encrypted*, by *radio waves* or other means of telecommunication for reception by the public by means of *broadcasting receiving apparatus*, but does not include any such transmission of programs that is made solely for performance or display in a public place' (emphasis added).

For greater clarity, certain expressions that form part of this definition are also defined in section 2(1) of the Broadcasting Act and these are italicized in the paragraph above. For example, according to the Broadcasting Act, a *program* 'means sounds or visual images, or a combination of sounds and visual images, that are intended to inform, enlighten or entertain, but does not include visual images, whether or not combined with sounds, that consist predominantly of alphanumeric text.' In other words, the Broadcasting Act distinguishes between sounds or visual images and text.

Moreover, whether a program is 'encrypted' or scrambled, in other words 'treated electronically or otherwise for the purpose of preventing intelligible reception,' is irrelevant to a finding of broadcasting. Scrambling an electronic signal containing program material to permit descrambling only by paying customers (as in the case of pay television) does not remove the signal from the definition of *broadcasting*.

According to the Broadcasting Act, *radio waves* are 'electromagnetic waves of frequencies lower than 3000 GHz that are propagated in space without artificial guide,' and a *broadcasting receiving apparatus* is 'a device, or combination of devices, intended for or capable of being used for the reception of broadcasting.'

The broad nature of the definition of broadcasting in the Broadcasting Act contributes to the extensive powers exercised by Canada's broadcasting regulatory agency over the Canadian broadcasting industry. Canada's broadcast regulatory agency is responsible for putting into effect broadcasting policy, as set out in the Broadcasting Act. Canadian broadcasting policy is therefore very different from the policies governing other cultural industries such as theatrical film exhibition, sound recording, book, magazine, and newspaper publishing, and the new digital media. None of these industries is subject to government licensing or rate regulation so that, in principle, there are no government barriers to entry and anyone can engage in them, although, of course, there may be financial and institutional barriers to doing so.

Who Is the Broadcast Regulator?

A separate act of Parliament, the Canadian Radio-television and Telecommunications Act of 1976, has established that broadcasting and telecommunications throughout Canada are to be regulated by a single agency, the Canadian Radio-television and Telecommunications Commission (also known as the CRTC or the Commission). Canadian broadcasting and telecommunications are each regulated separately in accordance with distinct acts of legislation, the Broadcasting Act of 1991 and the Telecommunications Act of 1993, as amended from time to time by Canada's Parliament.

If parliamentarians were obliged to legislate the details of all of Canada's laws, the task would be nearly impossible. For this reason, Parliament and provincial and territorial legislatures often pass general laws delegating authority to the civil service (government departments or other agencies) to make specific laws called regulations. Regulations carry out the purposes of the general laws or expand on them but are limited in scope by these laws. Among other things, the Broadcasting Act empowers the CRTC to make regulations with respect to Canadian broadcasting.

But 'law' is more than a series of laws and the pursuant regulations. The judiciary branch of government (judges through a system of courts) interprets laws and regulations by relying on past judicial decisions and setting new precedents. When disputes arise over the interpretation of a law, such as the Broadcasting Act, the judiciary helps to determine which interpretation will prevail. The Supreme Court of Canada, for example, has determined that the federal government is responsible for broadcasting in Canada.

What Determines Whether the Federal or Provincial Governments Have Jurisdiction in a Particular Area of Law Such as Broadcasting?

Democratic countries usually have a legislature or parliament, which has the power to make new laws and modify or revoke existing ones. Since Canada is a federation (a collection of several provincial governments together with a central government), it has both a legislature in each province and territory to deal with local matters and a federal parliament in Ottawa to make laws for all of Canada. Laws enacted at either level are called acts, legislation, or statutes.

In a democracy with a written constitution, legislators cannot make any laws they wish. A country's constitution defines the powers and limits of powers that can be exercised by the different levels and branches of government. In many countries formed by revolution or a declaration of independence (the United States is one example), constitutional law is contained in a single document.

Canada, in contrast, became a country in the middle of the nineteenth century by an act of the Parliament of Great Britain. Consequently, the closest thing to a single constitutional document in Canada is the British North America Act of 1867 (the BNA Act, now known as the Constitution Act, 1867), by which the British colonies of Upper and Lower Canada, Nova Scotia, and New Brunswick were united in a confederation called the Dominion of Canada.

Although there is no single constitutional document in Canadian law, the Constitution Act – a part of the Canada Act of 1982 – 'patriated' or brought home from Great Britain Canada's original constitution, the BNA Act. The Constitution Act declares the Constitution of Canada to be the supreme law of Canada and includes some thirty acts and orders. The Constitution Act reaffirms Canada's dual legal system by stating that provinces have exclusive jurisdiction over 'Property and Civil Rights' and 'all Matters of a purely local and private Nature' in each province, while the federal government has jurisdiction over 'Peace, Order and good Government of Canada' as well as any 'residual' matters not expressly delegated to the provinces. This principle is the basis for the division of powers between the provinces and the federal government in Canada, including those related to media such as broadcasting.

Who Determines the Content of Legislation, Such as the Broadcasting Act?

The Constitution sets out the basic principles of democratic government in Canada and defines the powers of the three branches of government: the executive, the legislative, and the judicial.

The executive power in Canada is formally vested in the Queen or 'Crown,' but this is only a constitutional convention, as the real executive power rests with the Cabinet (in legislation, often referred to as the 'Governor-in-Council'). The Cabinet, at the federal level, consists of the prime minister and ministers of the governing political party who are answerable to Parliament for government activities. As well, federal ministers are responsible for government departments, such as the Department of Canadian Heritage and the Department of Justice. In its day-to-day activities, 'the federal government' is managed by the executive or the Cabinet.

The legislative branch of the federal government is Parliament, which consists of the House of Commons, the Senate, and the monarch or her representative, the governor general. Most laws in Canada are first examined and discussed by the Cabinet, then presented for debate and approval by members of the House of Commons and the Senate.

The Canadian Parliament, through committees of the House of Commons and the Senate, reviews the performance of government activities, including the regulation of the broadcasting industry, and makes recommendations for legislative change. The Canadian Parliament is ultimately responsible for enacting legislation that defines the laws governing broadcasting activities, such as the Broadcasting Act and, although the process is somewhat arduous, can modify the Broadcasting Act if it so desires.

Canada's Constitution also provides for courts and a judiciary, the judges who preside over cases before the courts. The role of the judiciary is to interpret and apply the law and the Constitution, and to give impartial judgments, whether they involve public law, such as a criminal case, or private (civil) law, such as a dispute over a contract. The Constitution provides only for federally appointed judges; provincial judges are appointed to office under provincial laws.

Why Is Broadcasting Regulated by Government?

Although the supply of some goods and services, such as air space for air travel, ports and harbours, and postal rates, is regulated by government, the supply of many goods and services, including some cultural activities, such as the distribution of feature films in movie theatres, is virtually unregulated. Why is broadcasting closely regulated by government while other economic and cultural activities are not?

The explanation is partly historical. In Canada, the radio frequency spectrum (like navigable waterways and air space) has historically been considered a scarce resource and use of this spectrum has been regulated by the federal government because it is available in a limited quantity.[1] This said, digital technology is, to some extent, rendering the concept of spectrum 'scarcity' less meaningful insofar as there are a growing variety of alternatives to the over-the-air distribution of broadcast signals. In the past, the scarcity of radio frequency spectrum has provided the primary justification for broadcasting regulation but, in the last few years, the presentation of Canadian content in the pursuit of cultural diversity has emerged as a central justification as well. The history of broadcasting policy in Canada up to the time of the 1991 Broadcasting Act is outlined in chapters 2 and 3, and an overview of broadcasting legislation to 1968 appears in Appendix C. As a prelude to our discussion of contemporary Canadian broadcasting policy, an outline of current trends in media penetration rates, the supply and demand for Canadian content, and broadcasting industry structure and characteristics is contained in chapter 4.

Although spectrum scarcity continues to play a role in broadcasting policy, as this book will explain, the Canadian government also uses broadcast regulation to pursue public policy objectives, such as national cultural and political sovereignty, which are not necessarily related to spectrum scarcity. What is more, there are several weaknesses in the functioning of competitive markets, or 'market failures,' that justify government regulation of the broadcasting sector.

For example, broadcast services that rely on advertising for their financing will typically seek to maximize their audiences and advertising revenues by duplicating program categories or genres as long as the audience share obtained is greater than that from other categories or genres. Thus, broadcast networks and stations may compete by converging on the same program type, such as comedies and reality shows, rather than providing alternative types, such as drama or point-of-view (POV) documentaries. In economic theory, this is an illustration of the 'principle of minimum differentiation,' which explains why bank branches sometimes cluster together or why political parties often duplicate policy proposals.

The expansion of services provided by the advent of digital technology might seem to offer a solution to this problem. But new services create another problem related to financing from advertising. The preferences of the advertiser rather than the consumer determine program choice. In most markets, individual preferences are indicated by the willingness to pay the market price. But in conventional broadcasting, the advertiser is interested in maximizing audience size and not in the intensity of individual preferences, and there is no mechanism for the viewer or listener to express such intensity. In the absence of appropriate regulatory intervention, the result is a reinforcement of the program duplication problem and 'lowest common denominator' programs.

What Is the Radio Frequency Spectrum?

As was pointed out above, the definition of *broadcasting* in the Broadcasting Act refers to the use of *radio waves*, and radio waves are in turn defined as 'electromagnetic waves of frequencies lower than 3000 GHz that are propagated in space without artificial guide.' To be more specific, a radio wave is an electromagnetic wave propagated by a vibrating antenna. Radio waves have different frequencies and, by tuning a radio receiver to a particular frequency, it is possible to capture a specific radio signal. The radio frequency spectrum is a range of frequencies that permits the communication of information via radio waves.

Different kinds of electromagnetic waves can be classified by their wavelengths and are divided into sections called bandwidths. The electromagnetic spectrum is the collection of these bandwidths and consists of gamma rays, X-rays, ultraviolet rays, visible light, infrared waves, and radio waves. As was mentioned above, the Broadcasting Act defines radio waves (or hertzian waves) as electromagnetic waves of frequencies lower than 3,000 GHz propagated in space without artificial guide. The Canadian Table of Frequency Allocations assigns the electromagnetic spectrum between 9 kilohertz (kHz) and 275 gigahertz (GHz), and is based on provisions resulting from various World Radiocommunication Conferences.[2]

Every wireless technology has its own bandwidth and there are many. For example, garage door openers and alarm systems operate at one frequency in the radio spectrum, 900-megahertz (MHz) cordless telephones at another frequency, cellular phones at still another frequency, and global positioning systems (GPS) at another frequency again.[3]

The radio frequency spectrum includes licensed frequencies for AM radio, short wave radio, citizens band (CB) radio, off-air television stations (channels 2 to 6), FM radio, and off-air television stations (channels 7 through 13). Thus, if a listener tunes to a radio station and hears an announcer say 'You are listening to 91.9 FM Montreal,' the announcer is saying the listener is tuned to a radio station that is broadcasting a frequency modulated (FM) radio signal at a frequency of 91.9 MHz. An FM radio receiver tuned to 91.9 FM will capture radio waves at this frequency and provide the listener with clear representation of the sounds transmitted by the airwaves. FM radio stations transmit in a band of frequencies between 88 MHz and 108 MHz and this band is utilized for no other purpose than to broadcast FM radio signals.

In the same way, amplitude modulated (AM) radio in Canada is confined to a band from 535 kHz to 1,705 kHz, in other words, 535,000 to 1,705,000 cycles per second. Thus an AM radio station announcer who says, 'You are listening to AM 730 Montreal' means the station is broadcasting a local AM radio signal at 730 kHz. The call letters assigned to this frequency in the Montreal area are CKAC.

Why is AM radio in a band at 535 to 1,705 kHz, while FM radio in a band at 88 to 108 MHz? These allocations are to some extent arbitrary and related to the history of broadcasting. The first radio broadcasts occurred around 1900 and frequency allocations for AM radio occurred mostly in the 1920s. FM radio was developed later in order to make accessible relatively high-fidelity and static-free music broadcasting. The Canadian Broadcasting Corporation (CBC) began FM radio operation in 1946 but FM radio did not become really popular until the 1960s. This helps to explain the higher frequencies for FM radio.

In North America, television stations were largely non-existent until after the Second World War (1946) when the Federal Communications Commission (FCC), the counterpart of the CRTC in the United States, allocated the first commercial broadcast bands for television. Canadian television broadcasting began in 1952 in order to repatriate the large number of Canadians tuning in to U.S. television broadcasts from U.S. border stations. See chapter 2.

Who Is Responsible for Spectrum Allocation?

Each country decides how to allocate its radio spectrum so as to meet domestic needs. At an international level, radio spectra are allocated among countries by the International Telecommunications Union (ITU) with a view to minimizing cross-border interference.[4] As the radio frequency spectrum is a common global resource with no national boundaries, spectrum policy and management can take place meaningfully only through bilateral agreements with neighbouring countries and via multilateral organizations such as the ITU.

Within the Canadian communications environment, use of the radio frequency spectrum is contingent on a set of spectrum and licensing policies, radio regulations, radio system standards, rules, procedures, and practices designed to maximize the economical usage of the radio frequency spectrum while minimizing the impact of one use on another. In Canada, the Department of Industry (Industry Canada) is responsible for developing national policies and goals for spectrum resource use in keeping with the Department of Industry Act, the Radiocommunication Act, the Broadcasting Act, and the Telecommunications Act, as well as ensuring effective management of the radio frequency spectrum.

Parts of the radio spectrum are licensed by Industry Canada and parts are not. For example, an important difference between cellular telephones and wireless Internet (Wi-Fi) access is that the cellular system uses part of the licensed radio spectrum while Wi-Fi access occurs in unlicensed parts of the spectrum. The economic rules governing the use of Wi-Fi are therefore different from those governing the use of cellphones. The success of Wi-Fi has directed public attention to the unlicensed spectrum outside the licensed spectrum often controlled by large corporations.

What Is the Role of the Federal Government in Determining Broadcasting Policy?

Broadcasting within Canada is a responsibility of the federal government, which has designated the CRTC as the agency responsible for regulating and supervising the Canadian broadcasting system. The Canadian government's Department of Industry (Industry Canada) determines the appropriate use of the various parts of the radio (i.e., 'broadcast') spectrum; the CRTC is responsible for issuing specific licences to stations to utilize designated frequencies for fixed periods of time not exceeding seven years.

The CRTC does not permanently alienate or sell the right to broadcast to radio and television stations and networks but instead issues renewable licences for a fixed period of time – subject to each licensee's compliance with specific regulations, conditions of licence, and policies. Some of the Commission's licensees make use of the broadcast spectrum and others do not. Before acquiring a licence, a licensee that uses a portion of the broadcast spectrum must acquire a technical certificate from Industry Canada to ensure it will be in conformity with the department's frequency allotment plan.

What Is the Broadcasting Act?

The principal agent or instrument of the Canadian government for pursuing its broadcasting policy is the CRTC and its objectives and responsibilities in applying the Canadian government's broadcasting policy are set out in the Broadcasting Act, 1991 (the Act). In the Act, the Canadian government has delegated substantial powers and authority to the CRTC to regulate and supervise the Canadian broadcasting system. The Act also sets out the mandate and organization of the CBC. The Act applies directly to three categories of broadcasting undertakings: programming undertakings (such as radio and television stations), distribution undertakings (such as broadcast cable and direct-to-home satellite operations) and networks (such as the CTV or TVA networks).

The Broadcasting Act consists of four parts.

Following the definition of certain words and expressions, Part I contains the Broadcasting Act's raison d'être in section 3 entitled a 'Broadcasting Policy for Canada.'[5] Section 3 of the Act is reproduced in Appendix A.

Part II of the Act mandates the CRTC to regulate and supervise all aspects of the Canadian broadcasting system with a view to implementing the broadcasting policy set out in section 3 of the Act. The CRTC is empowered to issue policy guidelines and statements, but the federal Cabinet is also empowered to issue to the Commission policy directions of general application on broad policy matters. Chapter 5 in this book sets out the character and responsibilities of the CRTC in more detail.

Part III of the Act governs the powers and functions of the CBC, the national public broadcaster. The CBC is the only Canadian broadcaster recognized explicitly in the Act and this, in some ways, accords a special status to the CBC. Chapter 7 examines the nature of public broadcasting and, in particular, the mandate of the CBC.

Part IV of the Broadcasting Act concerns legislative housekeeping matters and contains the repeal of the previous Broadcasting Act, related and consequential amendments to other statutes that required changes in 1991, and provisions that were transitional at the time.

The Broadcasting Act that sets out the CRTC's and the CBC's mandates is an 'objectives-based' statute (like the Telecommunications Act), with a statement of policy declared by Parliament, based on the notion that broadcasting in Canada plays an essential role in the maintenance and enhancement of Canadian sovereignty and identity. Very few Canadian statutes contain lists of objectives that are meant to guide decision-makers to give them effect and the Broadcasting Act is relatively unusual in this sense. The CRTC and the CBC are required to pay careful attention to these objectives in conducting their activities.

Who Is Responsible for Canadian Broadcasting Policy?

Canadian broadcasting policy is the responsibility of the Government of Canada, especially the Department of Canadian Heritage, rather than the provincial governments. However, since the government has delegated very broad powers to the independently constituted federal government agency, the CRTC, the Commission is a key player in broadcasting policy formulation by means of its ability to issue, renew, amend, and revoke broadcasting licences and make regulations. Some-times, the mere issuance of a new broadcast licence creates a policy precedent.

This said, the Canadian Parliament, the Cabinet, and the Department of Canadian Heritage play important roles in overseeing the activities of the CRTC. For example, the Cabinet has the ability to issue to the Commission both general policy directions (section 7 of the Broad-casting Act) and directions on specific issues that are identified in the Act (section 26). Directions on specific issues have included concerns such as the eligibility of foreign applicants to hold broadcast licences, the broadcasting of programs of urgent national importance, and the implementation of a part of the Canada-U.S. Free Trade Agreement. Upon request, or on its own initiative, the Cabinet may also set aside a CRTC decision or refer a decision back to the Commission for reconsid-eration and further public hearing. Otherwise, decisions and orders of the Commission are final and conclusive unless an appeal is upheld by the Federal Court of Appeal on a question of law or jurisdiction.

The Department of Canadian Heritage, through its minister, has the primary responsibility for advising the Cabinet on the development of government policy regarding broadcasting but there are other agen-cies and institutions that may exercise considerable influence. These include the Department of Industry, which is responsible for broadcast spectrum management, the Department of Finance whose responsibili-ties, in consultation with Canadian Heritage, include determining the budgets of the CBC, the Canada Media Fund, Telefilm Canada, and the National Film Board of Canada (NFB).[6] Furthermore, as we have said, the CBC has its own responsibilities set out in the Broadcasting Act and this allows the Corporation to establish broadcasting policy in some areas.

Appendix B of this book summarizes the relationships between the components of Canadian government in relation to broadcasting policy and identifies the major players within a schematic overview.

Do Provincial Governments Have a Role to Play in Broadcasting Policy?

The Supreme Court of Canada has determined that broadcasting lies within federal jurisdiction and provincial governments do not have a direct role to play in supervising broadcasting policy. However, section 93 of the Constitution Act, 1867 (formerly the BNA Act) gives responsibility for education to the provinces, not to the federal government. As a result, provincial 'educational' broadcasters are sometimes accorded, informally, something of a special status by the CRTC. Section 3(1)(j) of the Broadcasting Act does concede that 'educational programming, particularly where provided through the facilities of an independent educational authority [i.e., a provincial government agency], is an integral part of the Canadian broadcasting system.' But the Act is otherwise relatively quiet about educational broadcasting because 'education' is a provincial responsibility.

This said, the CRTC takes a more laissez-faire attitude toward provincial educational broadcasters than it does toward other broadcasters as long as they concentrate on broadcasting 'educational' programs as defined in two Cabinet directions to the Commission. The nature of educational broadcasting is described more fully in chapter 7 in the context of a discussion of public broadcasting.

Most of the provincial governments have also established their own production funding agencies, though these tend to direct their financing to cinema rather than to television production.

Who Finances Canadian Broadcasting?

The three conventional sources of financing for broadcasting are advertising revenues, subscriber fees, and government subsidies. Commercial broadcasters, and some public broadcasters, are financed in part by advertising revenues. Indeed, economists sometimes describe commercial broadcasting as the delivery of audiences to advertisers in return for payment (i.e., advertising revenues). Most commercial, public, and community broadcasters also receive a share of the subscription fees paid to cable, microwave, and satellite broadcasting undertakings. Finally, commercial, public, and community broadcasters receive government subsidies, to varying degrees, either directly or indirectly through tax credits and other government programs. Public donations also play a small role in the financing of broadcasting services.

The CRTC regulates and supervises the Canadian broadcasting system and encourages Canadian broadcasters to maintain, and even surpass, certain minimum levels of Canadian programming. This activity is described more fully in chapter 6. The government financing of Canadian broadcast content is accomplished through distinct organizations and mechanisms such as the Canada Media Fund and government tax credits. Although the Commission does not itself finance Canadian broadcasters or broadcasting, CRTC regulations and conditions of licence can directly influence the volume and use of production financing. For example, the Commission is able to influence the financing of Canadian programs by requiring or encouraging broadcasters to contribute to certain Canadian music and television production funds. The government financing of Canadian programs is outlined in chapter 8.

Does the CRTC Address Social Issues?

Section 3 (Broadcasting Policy for Canada) of the Broadcasting Act says that the Canadian broadcasting system 'makes use of radio frequencies that are public property' and that the Canadian broadcasting system should serve 'to safeguard, enrich and strengthen the cultural, political, *social* and economic fabric of Canada' (emphasis added).'More particularly, section 3 says that the Canadian broadcasting system should, 'through its programming and the employment opportunities arising out of its operations, serve the needs and interests, and reflect the circumstances and aspirations, of Canadian men, women and children, including equal rights, the linguistic duality and multicultural and multiracial nature of Canadian society and the special place of aboriginal peoples within that society.' How does the CRTC fulfil social objectives in establishing the requirements for its licensees? This is the subject of chapter 9.

Can the CRTC Regulate the Internet?

The transformation from analogue to digital formats is the basic technological change that is transforming the broadcasting industry at all levels. This transformation is affecting audio-visual conception and development, production, distribution, and exhibition, and the nature of social engagement through media. The transition to digital formats is creating new exhibition platforms that are reshaping the broadcasting environment and fragmenting audiences. Digital technologies offer more flexibility in conception and the possibility of fulfilling demands for highly specialized and personalized niche programming that responds to particular needs. Chapter 10 examines how cable, satellite, and digital subscriber line (DSL) technologies are affecting the distribution of Canadian broadcasting services.

Digital production is one activity. Digital distribution and retransmission is another. Does the presentation of Web pages, music, or moving pictures on the Internet constitute 'broadcasting? This question has important implications as to whether material presented on the Internet is subject to the Broadcasting Act. If Internet activities are included in the definition of broadcasting set out in the Broadcasting Act, then the CRTC can regulate and supervise Internet content. The social issues that Internet use raises (including sex role stereotyping and pornography, violence, advertising to children, and program standards generally) are potentially subject to CRTC regulations and policies. Websites could be subject to CRTC licensing, and viewing of material on such websites subject to the Copyright Act and, in certain cases, the payment of compulsory copyright licence fees. These issues are discussed in the context of the distribution issues addressed in chapters 10, 11, and 12.

Are There Ownership Restrictions in Canadian Broadcasting?

Canadian ownership constitutes a fundamental element in the Government of Canada's broadcasting policy. In fact, subsection 3(1)(a) of the section entitled 'Broadcasting Policy in Canada' says that 'the Canadian broadcasting system shall be effectively owned and controlled by Canadians.' What is a Canadian in this context? Why does the government maintain foreign ownership rules? Are foreign ownership rules sustainable in the global digital environment? These questions are addressed in chapter 13.

'Competition' policy is concerned with the degree or extent of competition in a market. According to economic theory, the extent of competition is determined by the degree to which competition approximates an ideal type: perfect competition. In a perfectly competitive market, the average return or profit to firms in the industry approximates the average return in competitive financial markets, and the firms in the industry do not possess any special leverage or advantage over consumers of the industry's products. The digitization of media, the lowering of international trade barriers, and the partial deregulation of the audio-visual sector have encouraged the convergence of certain audio-visual technologies, products, and services, the merger of companies engaged in similar audio-visual activities, and the vertical integration of creation, production, distribution, and marketing activities in Canada, the United States, and Europe. What role does the CRTC have to play in competition policy with regard to Canadian broadcasting in the digital environment and what should that policy involve? Does the CRTC have a mandate to ensure competition or to limit industry concentration in broadcasting? What is CRTC policy on industry concentration as it affects the diversity of voices in Canadian broadcasting? These questions are also addressed in chapter 13.

Will Globalization Put an End to Canadian Broadcasting Policy?

The trend toward international trade liberalization and globalization tends to reduce national identities and create pressures to eliminate policies that safeguard or strengthen cultural diversity. As a result, Canadian government policies that support the domestic audio-visual sector, such as those that favour Canadian content in broadcasting, may be at risk from the lowering of barriers to international trade and increased international economic integration. Consequently, the Government of Canada supported the establishment of a New International Instrument on Cultural Diversity that would set clear ground rules for the maintenance of policies that promote culture while respecting the rules of the international trading system and ensuring markets for cultural exports. At the General Conference of the United Nations Educational, Scientific, and Cultural Organization (UNESCO) in October 2005, a Convention on the Protection and Promotion of the Diversity of Cultural Expressions was adopted by an overwhelming majority of UNESCO's member states. This development is discussed in chapter 14.

What Kind of Regulatory Reform is Necessary?

The Conclusion of this book summarizes some of the problems raised by the current regulatory process. For example, the provision of Internet access in Canada is governed by the Telecommunications Act, which does not contain the cultural objectives of the Broadcasting Act. As the CRTC has said,

> The objectives of the *Telecommunications Act* are rooted in the concerns of access and competitiveness. They contain the objective that has been clearly enunciated by Government to 'foster increased reliance on market forces for the provision of telecommunications services and to ensure that regulation, where required is efficient and effective.'
> The objectives of the *Broadcasting Act*, by contrast, stress cultural goals

and the predominance of Canadian content within the system. The *Radio-communication Act*, which governs wireless communication and provides the authority to the Minister of Industry to set policies for wireless in the public interest, makes no reference to the cultural goals of the *Broadcasting Act*. Yet, increasingly, wireless is serving as a conduit for content similar to a cable or direct-to-home satellite. Conversely, broadcasters make significant use of radio frequency spectrum for over-the-air television and radio operations.[7]

Chapter 15 examines issues related to legislative and regulatory reform, including the Commission and board nomination process, political influence, and the question of regulatory capture.

Notes

1 The limited availability of scarce resources, such as the radio frequency spectrum, makes them susceptible to being monopolized by private interests to the detriment of the public interest. Thus governments intervene to regulate the 'natural' monopolies or near-monopolies that result from spectrum allocation to guide them in the pursuit of the public interest. Broadcasting also displays certain characteristics of what economists call 'public goods.' Public goods are commodities or services whose cost of production is unrelated to the number of consumers of the good and for which one person's consumption does not diminish the consumption of that good by another consumer. National defence is a classic example of a 'pure public good' that satisfies this definition. The 'public good' characteristics of radio frequency spectrum use provide another explanation of the need for the regulation of broadcasting.

2 Industry Canada, *Canadian Table of Frequency Allocations*, 1.

3 One megahertz represents one million cycles per second.

4 The ITU, headquartered in Geneva, Switzerland, is an international organization within the United Nations System where governments and the private sector coordinate global telecom networks and services. The ITU Radiocommunication Sector plays a vital role in the management of the radio-frequency spectrum and satellite orbits. These are considered finite natural resources and are increasingly in demand from a large number of services such as fixed, mobile, broadcasting, amateur, space research, meteorology, global positioning systems, environmental monitoring, and communication services that ensure safety of life at sea and in the skies.

5 The *Compact Edition of the Oxford English Dictionary* contains a number of definitions for the word *policy*, including reference to 'a course of action adopted and pursued by a government, party, ruler, statesman, etc.' In this book, *policy* refers to the course of action pursued by Canadian governments and their agencies, at both the federal and provincial levels, and *broadcasting policy* means policy in regard to *broadcasting* as defined in the Broadcasting Act.

6 On 9 March 2009, the Government of Canada announced the amalgamation of the Canadian Television Fund and Telefilm Canada's Canada New Media Fund to form the Canada Media Fund.

7 Canadian Radio-television and Telecommunications Commission (CRTC), *A Competitive Balance*, 7.

2 History of Canadian Broadcasting Policy to 1968

This chapter presents an overview of the development of Canadian broadcasting legislation, regulation, and policies up to the enactment of the Broadcasting Act in 1968 – the beginning of the modern era in Canadian broadcasting regulation.[1] Familiarity with the early history of Canadian institutions and policy development, especially the historical role of the CBC, provides readers with a common background and considerable insight into how broadcasting policy evolved to its current state. To help explain changes in the legal, regulatory, and policy framework, some attention is also given to the evolution of broadcasting technologies, evolving social conditions, and consumer preferences, as well as the judicial interpretation of the legislation governing broadcasting.

The British North America (BNA) Act

On 24 May 1844, Samuel Morse sent a coded message over a telegraph line between Washington and Baltimore, thereby initiating the telecommunications age. Within two years, the Toronto, Hamilton, Niagara, and St Catharine's Electro-Magnetic Telegraphy Company had established the first commercial telegraph operation in Canada. Because each country relied on a separate and distinct telecommunications technology, international messages had to be written out, in some cases translated, handed over at a country's border, and then retransmitted over the telegraph network of the neighbouring country. In the early years, national telegraph systems did not interconnect or cross national borders.

There was no mention of telephony or broadcasting in the 1867 British North America (BNA) Act, Canada's constitution (now called the

Constitution Act, 1867), because the telephone and the radio had not yet been invented. But there was a mention of the telegraph. Section 92 ('Exclusive Powers of Provincial Legislatures') of the BNA Act says that provinces may exclusively make laws in relation to 'Matters of a merely local or private Nature in the Province,' and refers expressly to 'Local Works and Undertakings *other than* ... Lines of ... Telegraphs, and other Works and Undertakings connecting the Province with any other or other of the Provinces, or extending beyond the Limits of the Province' (emphasis added). By exception, this gave jurisdiction over telegraphy to the federal government.

The successful transmission of coded telegraph messages over land-lines stimulated the search for a means to transmit live voice messages using the same telegraph network and eventually resulted in the invention of the telephone by Alexander Graham Bell in 1874 and the creation of the Bell Telephone Company of Canada in 1880.[2] The telephone established the groundwork for the subsequent invention of wireless telephony or 'radio' at the end of the nineteenth century.[3]

The invention of the radio is usually credited to Guglielmo Marconi. When Marconi was unable to obtain financing from the Italian government to pursue his research and development, he moved to England in 1897 and, with the help of the British Post Office, set up the Wireless Telegraphy and Signal Company to develop an economically viable wireless telegraph system. Marconi changed the name of his company to Marconi's Wireless Telegraphy Company in 1900 and proceeded to establish subsidiary companies in other countries. In October 1900, Marconi succeeded in sending trans-Atlantic wireless signals across the Atlantic Ocean from Cornwall, in the west of England, to St John's, Newfoundland.[4]

Marconi registered the Marconi Wireless Company of Canada in Ontario in November 1902 and with the Canadian government in August 1903. At the time, the primary objective of the Marconi Company was the construction and operation of wireless telegraph stations on ships and coastal shores to assist in commercial navigation and related ventures.[5]

Wireless Telegraphy Act of 1905

Although there was no mention of telephony or broadcasting in the 1867 British North America (BNA) Act, broadcasting appeared to lie within federal jurisdiction, and the federal government claimed regulatory responsibility for all forms of wireless telegraphy or 'radio,' as it did for telegraphy. In July 1905, the Canadian Parliament passed the Wireless Telegraphy Act that gave the Minister of Marine and Fisheries the exclusive authority to issue licences for the installation and operation of any apparatus for wireless telegraphy anywhere in Canada or on any ship of Canadian registry. Canada's Wireless Telegraphy Act was virtually identical to earlier legislation in Britain except that, in Canada, regulation of Canadian wireless operations was assigned to the Department of Marine and Fisheries, instead of the Post Office as in Britain.

Section 6 of the Wireless Telegraphy Act refers to the granting of licenses to applicants interested solely in conducting wireless 'experiments' (what were later called ham radio operations). However, the wireless telegraphy at the time consisted mostly of coded messages and was not appropriate for voice retransmission. The development of radio telephony over anything more than short distances did not become practical until the period just before the Great War of 1914. The historian Mary Vipond writes, 'The rapid growth and improvement of wireless telegraphy, increasing appreciation of its uses for navigational safety, an international radiotelegraphy agreement (the London Convention) signed by Britain and the colonies in 1912, and the advent of wireless telegraphy prompted the Canadian government to draft legislation more comprehensive than the 1905 act to cover the wireless field.'[6]

The Radiotelegraph Act of 1913

In 1913, the Canadian Parliament passed an updated Radiotelegraph Act that declared in section 2(b), 'Radiotelegraph includes any wireless system for conveying electric signals or messages including radiotelephones.' With the inclusion of radiotelephones in the Act, the federal government assumed authority over the development of all aspects of radio, including point to multipoint radio broadcasting. The Radiotelegraph Act remained in effect until the promulgation of the first legislation specifically targeting radio broadcasting in 1932.

The Radiotelegraph Act of 1913 required amateur radio operators to apply to the federal government for a call sign – the unique designation of letters that identifies a radio transmitter. While some amateur radio operators obtained call signs in this manner, many continued to create their own. Once the First World War began in 1914, the federal government suspended the ninety-five amateur licences issued up to that time and, for security reasons, ordered amateur operators off the air. In principle, responsibility for the administration of the Radiotelegraph Act lay with the Radio Branch of the Ministry of the Naval Service. But since inspectors to enforce the ban had not yet been appointed and government supervision of the airwaves was very limited, many amateur radio operators continued to operate, knowing the chances of their detection, particularly in rural areas, was unlikely.[7]

What was later to become the first commercial broadcasting operation in Canada began on 20 May 1920 when the Marconi Wireless Telegraph Company, operating with an experimental broadcast licence for Montreal radio station XWA (later called CFCF), participated in the demonstration of a musical performance in Montreal that was broadcast in Ottawa. Several months afterwards, the first broadcast of a paid radio advertisement occurred in the United States.

In April 1922, the Radio Branch of the Ministry of the Naval Service created a new class of licence for 'private commercial broadcasting' to replace the licence for experimental broadcasting that had hitherto served as a regulatory instrument. By this time, with the exception of communications within the military, non-governmental groups and individuals, including commercial broadcasters, non-profit organizations, and individual hobbyists undertook most of the radio transmitting in Canada. Radio equipment suppliers and newspapers held most of the commercial licences, but many licences never became operational, or if they did, the associated stations closed down after a short time for want of a viable economic model. On 1 July 1922, following the closing of the Ministry of the Naval Service after the end of the First World War, responsibility for the Radio Branch was transferred back to the Department of Marine and Fisheries.

Origins of Public Broadcasting

Although Canadian radio broadcasting developed overwhelmingly as a private sector venture in the 1920s, several public broadcasting initiatives occurred. In 1924, Henry Thornton, president of the Canadian National Railways (CNR), a railway network owned by the federal government, launched a radio broadcasting service for train travellers, hotel guests, and employees. The CNR's service involved a domestic network of radio stations that employed Canadian performers for concerts, talks, lectures, and other events. Anyone within range of the CNR's stations could listen to its programs.

In 1925, the University of Alberta's Department of Extension began broadcasting educational programs on CJCA, the radio station owned by the *Edmonton Journal*. These programs included short lectures by faculty members in classics, history, and politics, symphonic music recordings with commentary, and live music. In 1926, the Alberta government provided a $700 grant to build a transmitter on the university's campus, and a year later the University of Alberta established CKUA radio for educational broadcasting. Not only was CKUA the first Canadian broadcasting undertaking devoted entirely to educational programming, but it also predated the first national public broadcaster, the Canadian Radio Broadcasting Commission (CRBC), by nearly six years.

The CNR's broadcast of the proceedings on Parliament Hill on 1 July 1927 to commemorate Canada's sixtieth anniversary is said to represent the first truly national broadcast in Canada. Telephone lines provided most of the connections among the twenty-three participating stations across the country.

By international agreement, the 1927 International Radiotelegraph Conference (a forerunner of the International Telecommunications Union) initiated the allocation of frequency bands to the radio services originating with member countries. This was designed to ensure greater efficiency of operation in view of the increase in the number of radio-communication services and technical variations within each service across the member countries, including Canada. The targeted services included fixed, maritime, aeronautical, mobile, commercial, amateur, and experimental broadcasting.

The Aird Commission

In 1928, the Canadian government launched the Royal Commission on Radio Broadcasting to examine the state of the Canadian broadcasting system. Chaired by Sir John Aird, the president of the Canadian Bank of Commerce, the commission's purpose was to 'determine how radio broadcasting in Canada could be most effectively carried on in the interest of Canadian listeners and the national interests of Canada.' The commission was also instructed to 'make recommendations to the Government as to the future administration, management, control and financing thereof.'[8]

The Aird Commission's mandate appears to have been designed to address a lack of coherence and transparency that characterized Canadian radio policy up to this time. Issues of concern for the commissioners included the uneven availability of Canadian services in different parts of the country, the appropriate role of religious broadcasting, and the coherent allocation of radio frequencies, particularly in the Toronto area. By 1928, about sixty-eight radio stations and some four hundred thousand battery-operated radio receivers operated across the country, but radio stations serving the cities of Montreal and Toronto accounted for half the total radiated power of all transmitters. Private sector radio stations operated in most of Canada's major cities but use of the airwaves was not subject to uniform standards and the range of signal transmission was often limited.

Up to this time, considering the small number of listeners within most Canadian stations' contours, there does not appear to have been a generally satisfactory economic model for financing original Canadian radio programming in the private sector. As a result, entrepreneurs in Canada and the United States attempted to take advantage of the scale economies available from the networking of radio operations. During the Aird Commission's deliberations, the U.S. radio network NBC announced its intention to extend its service to Canada. In 1929, radio station CKAC Montreal joined the CBS network and, in the following year, CFCF Montreal affiliated with NBC. In Toronto, the two principal Toronto stations also joined U.S. networks: CFRB joined CBS and CKGW affiliated with the NBC Red network in 1929. As a result, the Aird Commission focused its attention on the integration of Canadian radio stations into the U.S. broadcasting system and the resulting implications for Canadian sovereignty.

It has often been said that the Aird Commission faced a choice between two alternative broadcasting models: the U.S. model of competition for audiences and revenues among privately owned stations, and the European model of publicly owned and financed broadcasting services acting as the sole provider in each respective country. The commission addressed this issue in its report of 11 September 1929 and proposed the creation of a publicly owned Canadian national broadcaster not unlike the British Broadcasting Corporation (BBC), the publicly owned broadcaster established two years earlier.

The Aird Commission's Report recommended the end of private broadcasting in Canada and the establishment of a national public radio system to be called the Canadian Radio Broadcasting Company. The commission proposed the creation of a twelve-person board of directors for the company, three federally appointed members and nine others, one from each of the nine Canadian provinces in existence at the time. To forestall a federal-provincial dispute over which level of government should regulate broadcasting, each provincial board member was to have full control over programs on the stations within his or her province. The commission believed that the physical plant and organization of broadcasting should be a federal responsibility but that broadcasting content should be a provincial responsibility. 'It is desirable ... that provincial authorities should be in a position to exercise full control over the programs or the station or the stations in their respective areas,' said the commission's report.[9]

Mary Vipond argues that 'the genesis, mandate, and personnel of the Aird commission predetermined its conclusions to an important extent':

- First, the Aird Commission's agenda was set largely by the Radio Branch of the Department of Marine and Fisheries on establishing the commission's terms of reference in 1928.
- Second, prior to their appointment to the commission, Commissioner Charles Bowman had written a series of editorials in the Ottawa *Citizen* in 1927 and 1928 advocating a public-service model for Canadian broadcasting, and Commission Secretary Donald Manson, the chief inspector of the Radio Branch, had expressed dissatisfaction with Canadian radio's status quo.
- Third, during a visit to New York before the public hearings began, the commissioners, particularly the chairman, were disturbed by NBC's assertion that Canada formed part of NBC's potential market.[10]

The Aird Commission Report stimulated a debate that addressed a variety of issues relevant to Canadian broadcasting policy today:

- The place of public broadcasting in regard to private sector broadcasting services
- The appropriate level and means of financing public broadcasting
- The place of Canadian programs relative to U.S. programs
- The subsidization of Canadian broadcasting and culture in the private sector
- The public service obligations of private sector services
- The regulation of content versus the freedom of expression and the freedom to choose
- Federal authority versus provincial authority over broadcasting

There was much support across Canada for the public broadcasting service recommended by the Aird Commission but opposition came from private broadcasters and some advertisers. The so-called European model would be more difficult to implement in Canada than elsewhere because of the variety of private sector radio stations already in existence at the time of publication of the Aird Commission's Report. The report was therefore followed by a period of intense debate and lobbying by those directly concerned, including the private sector's industry association, the Canadian Association of Broadcasters (CAB).

Although world economic growth entered into the Great Depression after the stock market crashed on 29 October 1929 (six weeks after the Aird Report was issued), the Depression did not appear to influence preparation of the bill to implement the essence of the Aird Commission's recommendations. However, economic conditions affected the political climate in Canada more generally, and Prime Minister Mackenzie King delayed the presentation of the bill in the House of Commons following a call for general elections. On 30 July 1930, the Liberal Party in power lost the elections to the Conservatives under the leadership of R.B. Bennett, who became Canada's prime minister.

In December 1930, thirty-year-old Graham Spry and twenty-six-year-old Alan Plaunt launched the Canadian Radio League and began promoting public broadcasting among influential associations such as the Canadian Clubs, the Canadian Legion, labour unions, business associations, agricultural groups, corporations, governments, and individuals. First and foremost, the Canadian Radio League aimed to encourage Prime Minister Bennett and his Cabinet to implement the concept of a public broadcasting system recommended by the Aird Commission.

About the same time, a federal-provincial jurisdictional dispute arose over responsibility for the broadcasting spectrum. In 1929, the Quebec government led by Louis-Alexandre Taschereau, passed legislation enabling it to establish a radio station and to produce programs for broadcast on other stations. In April 1931, the Quebec government passed legislation granting it exclusive licensing authority within the province. Quebec, supported by Ontario and New Brunswick, claimed that section 92 of the BNA Act referring to control over 'property and civil rights' and 'matters of a merely local or private nature in the province' conferred jurisdiction over broadcasting to the provinces. In the provinces' view, broadcasting did not constitute a 'residual' power as contemplated in section 91. The federal government responded by sending this issue to the Supreme Court of Canada by reference (i.e., without appealing a specific case) for an opinion.

In June 1931 and February 1932, the Supreme Court of Canada (by a vote of three judges to two) and the Judicial Committee of the Privy Council of Great Britain, which acted as Canada's ultimate judicial authority at the time, confirmed federal jurisdiction over Canadian broadcasting spectrum.[11] The court relied essentially on the fact that radio waves cannot be confined within a single province. Their decisions on the definition of a broadcasting 'undertaking' established that federal legislative authority extended to the regulation of the transmission of broadcast signals within Canada as well as to the reception of such signals emanating from any source outside Canada.

The Canadian Radio Broadcasting Act (1932)

In 1929, at the time of the public hearings convened by the Aird Commission, the total number of licensed radio receivers in Canada amounted to approximately three hundred thousand representing about 15 per cent of homes across a total population of 10 million. Three years later, the number of receivers and the radio receiver penetration rate of Canadian homes had approximately doubled.[12]

On the initiative of the Bennett government, the Canadian Radio Broadcasting Act of 1932 established the Canadian Radio Broadcasting Commission (CRBC) – a new entity that foreshadowed the creation of the Canadian Broadcasting Corporation (CBC) a few years later. The creation of the CRBC was intended to address a variety of problems: the uneven availability of radio signals across Canada, the absence of pan-Canadian or even interprovincial radio networks, the limited amount of Canadian programming, the lack of Canadian venture capital available to finance the start-up of radio stations, and the absence of an independent regulatory agency to supervise private sector stations.

In many ways the new Act represented a series of compromises with the vision contained in the Aird Report. The Act gave the CRBC regulatory authority over private sector radio stations in Canada, as well as the obligation to provide entertainment and information programming services to all regions of the country. While the 1932 Act envisaged the eventual nationalization of all private sector radio stations, in the interim it provided for the regulation and supervision of the existing stations and for their deployment as CRBC affiliates to carry programs produced by the public broadcaster, the CRBC.

According to the Act, the construction or acquisition of new stations by the CRBC required Parliament's approval, as did the CRBC's annual budget (which could not exceed the receipts obtaining from the Commission's licensing activities).[13] This hampered the CRBC's ability to plan and operate decisively and efficiently. One of the first actions of the CRBC was to buy the CNR's radio stations in Ottawa, Vancouver, and Moncton for $50,000. The CRBC also established or leased stations in Montreal, Chicoutimi, and Toronto, and contracted with private stations in a dozen Canadian cities to carry at least three hours a day of network programs (free of commercial advertising) as private sector affiliates of the CRBC.

But ultimately the CRBC failed to live up to expectations. In its early years, critics such as Graham Spry and Alan Plaunt of the Canadian Radio League complained that the CRBC's programming was of poor quality and its management inadequate. The Canadian Radio League believed that the public broadcasting system should be a social force for enlightenment and the promotion of Canadian identity rather than simply a source of entertainment. According to the critics, the three commissioners named to the commission did not possess enough authority under the Act or sufficient skills to adequately regulate and operate radio broadcasting in Canada. In the words of historian Mary Vipond, 'Many of the difficulties the CRBC experienced in its four years of existence probably did result from its unwieldy structure, from the political interference that resulted, and from the understandable reluctance of the government to commit itself to large capital expenditures for broadcasting in the worst years of the Depression.'[14]

Liberal opposition leader Mackenzie King accused the CRBC of serving as a Conservative political instrument because the CRBC possessed certain characteristics of a government ministry and was not truly at arm's length from Parliament.[15] When the Liberals won the 1935 federal elections, King determined that it was time to change the regulatory framework for Canadian radio broadcasting.

The Canadian Radio Broadcasting Act (1936)

Following the Mackenzie King government's election, the prime minister endorsed the Canadian Radio League's ideas for a new government-owned and -operated broadcasting corporation and assumed Parliament would approve new legislation in keeping with Alan Plaunt's proposals. However, the Minister of Transport, C.D. Howe, favoured more latitude for private sector broadcasters as well as the regulation of private broadcasters by his ministry rather than by a Crown corporation. Consequently, the Canadian Radio Broadcasting Act of 1936 that established the Canadian Broadcasting Corporation (CBC), granted the authority to regulate the radio broadcasting system, including private sector broadcasters, to the CBC while the authority to allocate radio spectrum and to license stations was accorded to the Department of Transport. To encourage dialogue between the Department of Transport and the CBC, the department was required to submit new broadcast licence applications to the CBC for its recommendations, and any decision to issue a new licence required the approval of the federal Cabinet. The new Act essentially gave effect to the vision of the Canadian Radio League.

The Canadian Radio Broadcasting Act established a CBC more similar to the BBC in Britain and, in addition, assigned to the CBC an authority to regulate private sector broadcasting that was comparable to that of the former CRBC. Section 3(1) of the new Act provided for the creation of the CBC and its governance by nine board members 'chosen to give representation to the principal geographical divisions of Canada.' And section 21 declared, 'No private station shall operate in Canada as part of a chain or network of stations except with the permission of, and in accordance with the regulations made by, the Corporation.' This dual function of the CBC as both a competitor and a regulator of private sector broadcasting provided a source of friction until legislative reform in 1958.

The CBC adopted as its first priority the establishment of an effective national distribution system for Canadian radio and established powerful new stations in Montreal (CBF) and Toronto (CBL) in December 1937. The launch of a 50,000-watt French-language CBC station in Montreal permitted the creation of separate French- and English-language CBC program schedules in Montreal and launched the French-language network of the CBC as a separate entity. The new network contributed significantly to the development of French-language radio writers and producers as well as performers and singing stars in the years that followed. French-language radio relied less on U.S. program material than its English-language counterpart and rapidly developed a distinctive style of its own.

By May 1939, the CBC owned ten high-power stations in the Maritimes, Quebec, Ontario, the Prairies, and British Columbia. This compared to about seventy-five private sector stations that, for the most part, provided relatively low-power local service, though sixty-one stations possessed an affiliation agreement with the CBC – twenty-six as full affiliates carrying CBC programs about eight hours a day and thirty-five as supplementary affiliates on a program-by-program basis. The historian Frank Peers says that radio reached 84 per cent of the Canadian population, which compares favourably to estimates by the Federal Communications Commission (FCC) in the United States, where radio reached about 61 per cent of the continental land area in the daytime and 43 per cent at night.[16]

At the same time, the creation of the CBC was not without controversy. CBC radio programming was subsidized by a licence fee on radios (initially two dollars per household) and, in return, the CBC was required to fulfil responsibilities related to national political, social, and cultural objectives. Unlike the BBC, the CBC purchased U.S. programs and competed with private sector broadcasters for Canadian talent, mass audiences, and advertising revenues. This antagonized radio station owners, including a growing number of prominent newspapers that owned and operated radio stations, including *La Presse* (Montreal) and the *Leader-Post* (Regina).

The Impact of the Second World War

At the outbreak of the Second World War in Europe in September 1939, Canada declared war on Germany and the question arose as to the contribution of Canadian radio, and particularly the CBC, to the war effort.[17] In declaring war, a position supported by all four federal political parties represented in the House of Commons, Prime Minister Mackenzie King vowed not to impose conscription (compulsory military service) as Canada had done in the First World War. Almost immediately, Quebec Premier Maurice Duplessis called provincial elections to consolidate support for his anti-war platform. Would the CBC's 'neutrality' extend to the coverage of anti-war opinions during wartime, particularly on the CBC's French-language network? And who would set policy for the CBC during wartime – the CBC's Board of Governors or the Government of Canada, specifically the Minister of Transport, C.D. Howe, who also happened to be the minister in charge of war production?

Maurice Duplessis lost the 1940 Quebec elections to Adélard Godbout and, under pressure from the opposition, Mackenzie King eventually announced a national plebiscite (referendum) on conscription

for overseas military service in January 1942. The Canadian government's direction to the CBC to limit free time on the CBC's English- and
French-language networks to the four major parties in the federal Parliament alienated many opinion leaders in Quebec. In the plebiscite on
27 April 1942, only 27 per cent of the Quebec population voted in favour
of conscription, compared to 80 per cent in the rest of Canada.[18] As a
result, the CBC earned a reputation for being a 'government tool' willing to censor certain ideas. In 1944 Maurice Duplessis' Union Nationale
regained control of the Quebec National Assembly. The CBC's role in
the conscription debate, among other issues, led to calls for a less partisan Board of Directors and coincided with the revival of a campaign by
private sector radio stations to remove the CBC's regulatory authority
over them.

At the same time, the availability of war-related news generated
considerable interest in radio as a means of information and enlightenment. In the late 1930s and early 1940s, the proportion of Canadian
households with radios expanded phenomenally, from about 33 per
cent in census year 1931 to over 75 per cent in 1941 and over 90 per cent
in 1949.[19]

The Age of Television

The end of the Second World War in 1945 coincided with the beginning of the television age. The early growth of television broadcasting
in Britain and the United States, interrupted by the war, recovered. By
June 1947, there were sixty-six television stations and eighty-one experimental television stations licensed in the United States and, by 1949,
fifty stations in operation including ten stations owned and operated
by four networks.[20] About 60 per cent of Canadians lived within a fifty-
mile radius of a U.S. off-air television transmitter and could potentially
receive U.S. television signals with a rooftop antenna. As U.S. television expanded in the late 1940s and early 1950s, Canadian households
began to access U.S. border television stations. As with the early days
of radio, the availability of imported U.S. television signals in the major
cities – particularly Montreal, Toronto, and Vancouver – created pressure to launch Canadian television broadcasting services and 'repatriate' Canadian viewers.

Television posed a dilemma for Canadian policymakers because television is a far more costly medium to develop and operate than radio.
The start-up costs of a television broadcasting undertaking are high,

operating costs, especially program production costs, are significant, and there are important economies of scale associated with operating television networks that are available only to an ownership group of many stations. From the early 1950s, U.S. networks produced relatively expensive programs and covered their costs in the domestic U.S. market. The programs spilled over into Canada via border stations and attracted Canadian viewers, particularly anglophones, who had few Canadian viewing alternatives. In this context, the issue arose as to whether the development of Canadian television should be the sole responsibility of the public broadcaster or whether private sector stations should be licensed, as was the case with Canadian radio.

The Massey Commission

On the eve of federal elections in late March 1949, the Canadian government announced an interim policy in keeping with the Broadcasting Act of 1936 that encouraged the CBC to proceed with the creation of television production centres and transmitters in Montreal and Toronto, and, in its role as the broadcast regulator, to consider applications for private sector television stations throughout the country.

Ten days later, in April 1949, the government announced a royal commission of enquiry into the arts and culture in Canada, the Royal Commission on National Development in the Arts, Letters and Sciences (the Massey Commission), to examine and make recommendations on, among other things, 'the principles upon which the policy of Canada should be based, in the fields of radio and television broadcasting.'

The Massey Commission on arts and culture reported in June 1951 and approved of the CBC's conduct sufficiently to recommend maintaining the broad outlines of the regulatory system, as it existed. With regard to television, among the Massey Commission's recommendations were the following:

- That direction and control of television broadcasting in Canada continue to be vested in the CBC
- That no private television broadcasting stations be licensed until the CBC had national television programs available
- That all private sector television stations be required to serve as outlets for such national programs
- That the finances of the radio and television systems of the CBC be maintained separately

- That the CBC exercise careful control over all television stations in Canada in order to avoid excessive commercialism and to encourage Canadian content and the use of Canadian talent
- That the whole subject of television broadcasting in Canada be reconsidered by an independent investigation not later than three years after the commencement of regular Canadian television broadcasting.[21]

The CBC began television broadcasting in French and English in Montreal (CBFT) and Toronto (CBLT) in 1952. In the years following, the CBC gradually expanded its reach by means of owned-and-operated stations and privately owned affiliates that carried a minimum amount of CBC programming as set out in an affiliation agreement. By 1955, the CBC owned and operated stations in Vancouver, Winnipeg, Toronto, Ottawa (CBOT and CBOFT), Montreal (CBMT and CBFT), and Halifax and provided certain programs to twenty-two privately owned affiliates across the country.[22] However, there was only one English-language Canadian television station in each city, and only one French-language station in those cities with substantial French-speaking populations. This was quite different from Canadian radio, where a variety of unaffiliated private sector stations coexisted with CBC radio and completely different from the United States, where several national television networks provided programming to affiliates in each city. Inevitably, political pressure developed to expand the range of choice available by licensing private sector television stations in Canada.

The Fowler Commission

In 1955, the government created a new royal commission, the Royal Commission on Broadcasting, chaired by the president of the Canadian Pulp and Paper Association, Robert Fowler, to examine the Canadian broadcasting system, including the impact of television on Canadian society, and to make recommendations to the government.

In its report of 1957, the Fowler Commission recommended that the Canadian radio and television broadcasting system continue as a single mixed system of private and public ownership but that it be regulated and controlled by a new agency representing the public interest and responsible to Parliament. According to the report, 'The choice is between a Canadian state-controlled system with some Canadian content and the development of a Canadian sense of identity, at a substantial public cost, and a privately owned system which the forces of economics will necessarily make predominantly dependent on imported American radio and television programmes.'[23] The Fowler Commission justified the regulation of broadcasting content on the basis of the scarcity of frequencies, the absence of a tradition of self-regulation that would create 'recognized standards of performance,' the influence of commercial sponsors on programming, and the pressure of U.S. economic activity.

The Fowler Commission's 1957 report on Canadian broadcasting recognized the inherent conflict of interest underlying the CBC's dual role as a broadcaster and a regulator, and recommended the establishment of a Board of Governors of Canadian Broadcasting that would regulate both the private sector and the CBC. However, this new board would be responsible to Parliament for the CBC's activities so that, in a sense, the Fowler Commission proposed retaining the regulator and the CBC together under one authority.

The Fowler Commission's report also recommended that licensing powers be retained by the Minister of Transport, who would both rule on the technical aspects of licence applications and seek the advice of the Board of Governors of Canadian Broadcasting on the economic and social aspects of the licensing decision. The Board of Governors was to hear all licence applications in a public forum and to adopt quasi-judicial procedures in this regard.

The Broadcasting Act of 1958

The Broadcasting Act of 1958 departed from the recommendations of the Fowler Commission insofar as the Act created a fifteen-member Board of Broadcast Governors (BBG) distinct from the Board of Directors of the CBC. The objects and purposes of the BBG set out in section 10 of the Act were as follows: 'The board shall, for the purpose of ensuring the continued existence and efficient operation of a national broadcasting system and the provision of a varied and comprehensive broadcasting service of a high standard that is basically Canadian in content and character, regulate the establishment and operation of networks of broadcasting stations, the activities of public and private broadcasting stations in Canada and the relationship between them and provide for the final determination of all matters and questions in relation thereto.'[24]

The new Broadcasting Act gave responsibility to the BBG for regu lating both public and private broadcasters, and for ensuring the efficient operation of national radio and television broadcasting. The BBG was not given the authority to issue new broadcasting licences but the more limited power to examine applications for new licences and make licensing recommendations to the Minister of Transport. The Act gave the power to issue broadcasting licences to the federal Cabinet. The Act also re-established a board of directors for the CBC to oversee the Corporation's operations and this board reported directly to Parliament (as it does today). Thus, although the BBG regulated all broadcasting, including the CBC's operations, the CBC's board of directors reported to Parliament, not to the regulator. In other respects, however, the new Broadcasting Act reflected the recommendations of the Fowler Commission.

Up to this time, the notion of the regulatory agency placing Canadian content requirements on private broadcasters was largely absent and, in any case, the CBC's regulations, applicable to both radio and television, were sometimes unenforced. Apart from the obligations imposed by CBC affiliation agreements, the notion of Canadian content requirements did not really exist.[25] The new Broadcasting Act established a fundamental principle by declaring that the service provided by the Canadian broadcasting system should be 'basically Canadian in content and character.' Consequently, in November 1959, the BBG issued a set of Canadian content regulations for television (to take effect in 1960) requiring that 55 per cent of all television broadcasting time be 'basically Canadian in content and character.' This minimum requirement was to be fully implemented after a two-year transitional period, with the Canadian content calculation to be averaged over four-week periods.

Inherent in these regulations were underlying principles that continue to define the framework for private sector broadcasting today:

• The airwaves are a public resource.
• Private sector broadcasting stations that obtain a licence to use the airwaves must accept certain Canadian content obligations (even if some Canadian programs incur net losses).
• To help finance these obligations, the regulator is prepared to restrict market competition to raise the average rate of financial returns of private sector broadcasters above what such broadcasters would otherwise obtain in a competitive market.

In 1960, the Government of Canada licensed the first private sector television station, CFTO-TV in Toronto, which became the flagship station of the CTV network, itself licensed in 1961 and made available in nine Canadian cities. The government also licensed CFTM-TV Télé-Métropole in Montreal that later became the flagship station of the French-language TVA network. CFTO launched on New Year's Day in 1961 and CFTM a little later in the same year.

The BBG modified its Canadian content regulations in 1962 so that 40 per cent of television programming between 6:00 p.m. and midnight would be 'basically Canadian' as well as 55 per cent of the programming over the full broadcast day. The averaging period for calculating content requirements was extended from four weeks to calendar quarters.

The introduction of private sector television stations to Canadian broadcasting in the early 1960s increased the number of U.S. programs rebroadcast in Canada, especially in prime time, and reduced the size of audiences for the CBC's Canadian programs. At the same time, a series of conflicts erupted between the CBC, private broadcasters, and the BBG over the BBG's failure to enforce its regulations and decisions. In 1964, the government rehired Robert Fowler to chair a new Committee on Broadcasting to examine the Broadcasting Act of 1958 and its impact on the Canadian broadcasting system.

The opening sentence in the Fowler Committee's report in September 1965 has become its most celebrated: 'The only thing that really matters in broadcasting is program content: all the rest is housekeeping.' Among other things, the Fowler Committee reported that the BBG appeared to be unwilling or unable to enforce broadcast stations' compliance with their commitments prior to the reissue of their licences. Promises were made by broadcasters at hearings pursuant to the Broadcasting Act but broadcast licences were granted under the authority of the Radio Act of 1938 with the result that an applicant's promise of performance could not be made a condition of the licence. As a result, the breach of a promise undertaken in regard to the Broadcasting Act could not cause the licence (granted under the authority of the Radio Act) to be revoked. According to the Fowler Committee's report, 'In fact, the program performance of the private stations – in particular the second television stations – bears little relationship to the promises made to the BBG when the licences were recommended [by the BBG]. Undertakings given to obtain the grant of a public asset have largely been ignored, and the program performance has generally fallen far short of the promises made ... A promise made by a broadcaster to obtain a licence to operate a radio or television station should be an enforceable undertaking, and not a theoretical exercise in imagination or a competitive bid in an auction of unrealistic enthusiasm.'[26]

Towards a New Broadcasting Act

In addition to the issues raised by the Report of the Fowler Committee, there was another force in play that suggested certain aspects of
the 1958 Broadcasting Act should be reconsidered. By the late 1960s,
a new phenomenon was beginning to make its appearance felt on the
Canadian television scene – cable television. Cable television or master antenna television (MATV) systems deliver television signals to
large numbers of subscribers by means of a single antenna. Instead of
each household possessing a rooftop antenna, as was the case of many
homes in the 1950s and 1960s, cable television deployed one master
antenna in a given area, collected all of the local signals in the area at
the cable 'headend,' and relayed these signals by land-based coaxial
cable to individual homes. This approach was especially attractive for
viewers living in apartment buildings, but service soon expanded to
individual homes as well. Cable television attracted new subscribers
because of the range of services available, particularly in areas border-
ing the United States, and because of the quality of reception, particularly for colour television.

Canadian cable television had its origins in London, Ontario, in
1952, but growth was slow and the Dominion Bureau of Statistics (the
forerunner of Statistics Canada) did not begin collecting data on cable
television until 1967. For that year, the bureau reported 314 systems
operating in Canada with 408,853 subscribers and 107,631 other outlets, such as apartment buildings, for a total of 516,484 subscribers. In
the late 1960s, the growth of cable television began to mushroom and
the penetration rate of Canadian households by cable exceeded that in
the U.S. (6.3 per cent in the U.S. in 1969 versus 17 per cent in Canada
in 1970).

The inadequacies of the Broadcasting Act of 1958, the rise of cable television and the issues that this raised, questions about Canadian identity and the appropriate role of Canadian content requirements, and the
report of the Fowler Committee all contributed to political pressures for
revised legislation that resulted in the Broadcasting Act of 1968.

Notes

1 See Appendix C for an overview of the legislative framework, 1932–1968.
2 In 1906, and later in 1908, amendments to the Railway Act granted the

Board of Railway Commissioners for Canada the power to regulate telephone and telegraph companies under federal jurisdiction.
3 In some of the early literature, the terms *wireless* and *radio* are synonymous
and interchangeable terms. They refer to the broadcasting of speech or
music, or to the transmission of information in a telegraph code, via electromagnetic waves travelling through space. The term *wireless* came into
use first and is of British origin, while *radio* is of American origin.
4 Newfoundland was a self-governing British colony at the time and did not
join the Canadian federation until 1949.
5 There are several accounts as to why Marconi established a company in
Canada. One explanation is that on a trip to North America to set up a
permanent trans-Atlantic receiving station, Marconi met with Nova Scotia
Liberal MP Alexander Johnston, who apparently convinced Marconi that
it would be advantageous to set up his primary North American station in
Glace Bay, Nova Scotia. Marconi received $80,000 in Canadian government
assistance for the undertaking (Vipond, *Listening In*, 6; Bird, *Documents*,
10–14).
6 Vipond, *Listening In*, 9.
7 As in Britain, the Radiotelegraph Act permitted the imposition of a licence
fee to receive signals – a disposition that was enforced intermittently on
radio owners in Canada until 1953. The licensing of radio sets in Britain
was intended to prevent unauthorized information from leaving the country, to prevent interference with naval communications, and to enforce any
international wireless agreements Britain adhered to. Licence fees applied
to television sets in the United Kingdom are still used to finance the BBC.
In 2002, each British household with a television set paid £112 for a total of
£3.2 billion (£1 = $2.31 in 2005).
8 Bird, *Documents*, 42.
9 Ibid., 44.
10 Vipond, *Listening In*, 213.
11 The Judicial Committee of the Privy Council ceased to be the court of final
appeal in Canada in 1949, but it remains so for the United Kingdom's overseas territories and Crown dependencies, and for those commonwealth
countries that have retained the possibility of appeal to Her Majesty in
Council.
12 Vipond, *Listening In*, 255.
13 The grant for the first fiscal year 1933–4 amounted to $1 million (the
equivalent of more than $15 million in 2004 dollars but still not an enor-
mous sum).
14 Vipond, 'Beginnings of Public Broadcasting in Canada.'

15 In the 1935 elections, the Conservative Party's advertising agency created a series of fifteen-minute dramatized political soap operas entitled *Mr Sage.* These programs, produced in a CRBC station studio in Toronto and highly critical of the opposition leader, infuriated Mackenzie King when they were broadcast by a temporary network authorized by the CRBC.

16 Peers, *Politics of Canadian Broadcasting*, 346, 282.

17 The Second World War resulted from the breakdown of the international security system established in 1919. Between 1936 and 1939, Nazi Germany developed an alliance with Italy (that was extended to Japan in September 1940). In the absence of allies to defend its borders, the Soviet Union signed a non-aggression pact with Germany in August 1939. Britain and France declared war on Germany two days after Germany invaded Poland on 1 September 1939. Canada declared war on Germany within a week of declarations by Britain, France, Australia, and New Zealand. Germany, Italy and, Japan subsequently invaded a series of European and Asian countries, including France in May 1940 and the Soviet Union in June 1941. The Japanese bombed Pearl Harbour in December 1941, provoking the entry of the United States into the war.

18 Peers, *Politics of Canadian Broadcasting*, 330. According to the 1941 census, 71 per cent of Canada's non-French population originated in the British Isles. See Statistics Canada, *Historical Statistics of Canada*, table A125-163.

19 Kerr and Holdsworth, *Historical Atlas of Canada*, vol. 3, *Addressing the Twentieth Century*, plate 65.

20 U.S. Bureau of the Census, *Statistical Abstract of the United States: 1950.* Washington, DC, 1950, Tables No. 540, 545.

21 Royal Commission on National Development in the Arts, Letters and Sciences 1949–1951, *Report*, 301–5.

22 Bird, *Documents*, 248–9.

23 Ibid., 254.

24 Ibid., 272.

25 Rules and Regulations set out by the CRBC in April 1933 stipulated that programs imported from foreign countries must not exceed 40 per cent of the daily schedules of Canadian programming services, but these were apparently not enforced and not reproduced in subsequent legislation or regulations.

26 Bird, *Documents*, 338–9.

3 History of Canadian Broadcasting Policy, 1968–1991

The Broadcasting Act of 1968 represents a watershed in broadcasting legislation and the beginning of the modern era in the history of Canadian broadcasting policy. The framework for broadcasting policy and regulation today, the Broadcasting Act, 1991, resembles in many ways the legislation of 1968. Among its major innovations, the Broadcasting Act of 1968 declared that the objectives of broadcasting policy could best be achieved through the regulation and supervision of the broadcasting system by a single independent public authority, the Canadian Radio-television Commission (CRTC).[1] Furthermore, the Broadcasting Act of 1968, like its successor the Broadcasting Act, 1991, was an objectives-based statute, with a statement of policy objectives declared by Parliament, based on the notion that broadcasting in Canada plays an essential role in the maintenance and enhancement of Canadian sovereignty and identity. The Broadcasting Act of 1968 defined the role of the CRTC as one of putting into effect the broadcasting policy for Canada.

The Broadcasting Act, 1968

Section 2 of the Broadcasting Act of 1968 contains the 'Broadcasting Policy for Canada' that begins, 'Broadcasting undertakings in Canada make use of radio frequencies that are public property and such undertakings constitute a single system, herein referred to as the Canadian broadcasting system, comprising public and private elements.'

In this opening statement, the Broadcasting Act of 1968 declares that radio frequencies are public property, thereby implying that persons authorized to use radio frequencies are trustees of the Canadian public and that the use of such frequencies should be governed by the public interest. Furthermore, after many years of conflict during which broadcasting by the CBC enjoyed precedence over private sector broadcasting, this declaration emphasized the unitary nature of the Canadian broadcasting system and suggests Parliament wished the public and private elements of the broadcasting system to work together harmoniously.[2]

At the same time, the Broadcasting Act of 1968 established distinct roles for the public and private elements of the system: section 2 sets out general objectives for the broadcasting system as a whole and for the national broadcasting service to be provided by the CBC. There were no distinct objectives established for private sector services. Furthermore, section 2 says, 'Where any conflict arises between the objectives of the national broadcasting service and the interests of the private element of the Canadian broadcasting system, it shall be resolved in the public interest but paramount consideration shall be given to the objectives of the national broadcasting service' (i.e., the CBC). In other words, where the objectives of the national broadcasting service and the interests of the private element of the Canadian broadcasting system entered into conflict, the objectives of the CBC were to be considered paramount.

Section 2 of the Broadcasting Act of 1968 also says that 'the Canadian broadcasting system should be effectively owned and controlled by Canadians so as to safeguard, enrich and strengthen the cultural, political, social and economic fabric of Canada.' Canadian ownership and control of 'the system' were required but not necessarily Canadian ownership and control of each and every individual element of the system (i.e., individual undertakings). Broadcasting policy should 'safeguard, enrich and strengthen the cultural, political, social and economic fabric of Canada,' but what exactly this meant and how it was to be accomplished by the CRTC became a part of an ongoing debate.

A central concept in any broadcasting legislation is the definition of broadcasting. To what does the Act apply? The 1968 Broadcasting Act defined *broadcasting* as 'any radiocommunication in which the transmissions are intended for direct reception by the general public.' *Radiocommunication* meant 'any transmission, reception of signs, signals, writing, images, sounds, or intelligence of any nature by means of electromagnetic waves of frequencies lower than 3,000 Gigacycles per second propagated in space without artificial guide.'[3]

In the years that followed, this definition of *broadcasting* led to litigation in the courts as some licensees tried to escape from the purview of the new Broadcasting Act and the new regulatory agency, the CRTC. For example, there was general agreement that the definition of *broadcasting* in the Act did not give the CRTC authority over closed-circuit 'transmitting' undertakings that made no use of over-the-air signals at any point.[4] The extent to which this exception applied to cable 'receiving' undertakings, however, was determined only by two Supreme Court decisions in 1978 that confirmed the CRTC's jurisdiction over cable. This said, the courts later interpreted 'direct reception by the public' so as to exclude the reception of pay television services that required the payment of subscription fees and the use of a set-top decoder.

One of the most important powers conferred on the CRTC in the new Broadcasting Act was the power to issue broadcasting licences, something Parliament had withheld from previous broadcasting regulators.[5] At the same time, the Act permitted the Governor-in-Council (i.e., the Cabinet) to set aside any Commission decision to issue, amend or renew a broadcasting licence, or to refer such a decision back to the Commission for reconsideration and hearing. Thus the government retained the right to set aside a CRTC decision but not to amend such a decision or to issue a licence to another applicant.

The new Broadcasting Act also permitted the Governor-in-Council to issue directions to the Commission but only on a somewhat narrow range of issues, such as the classes of applicants to which broadcasting licences could not be issued. The Government of Canada issued the first such direction almost immediately (in October 1968) in regard to the foreign ownership of Canadian broadcast licences. This direction was intended to give more precision to section 2(b) of the Act mentioned above, which began, 'The Canadian broadcasting system should be effectively owned and controlled by Canadians' by specifying that broadcasting licences could only be issued to, and amended or renewed by, Canadian citizens or eligible Canadian corporations.[6] In April 1970, the Governor-in-Council issued another direction to the CRTC, requiring that each cable system reserve at least one channel for the designated provincial educational broadcaster undertaking.

Although the Board of Broadcast Governors (BBG), created by the Broadcasting Act of 1958, had introduced Canadian content requirements for private sector broadcasters, the BBG did not enjoy much success in their implementation. See chapter 2. Beginning in 1970 under the chairmanship of Pierre Juneau, the CRTC proceeded to implement a new series of Canadian content requirements for radio and television broadcasting by means of regulations and policies. For example, in a May 1970 press release, the Commission announced that it would permit not more than 40 per cent of non-Canadian programs on television and not more than 30 per cent of television programs to come from any one country outside of Canada. The same announcement stated the Commission's intention to impose a 30 per cent Canadian content requirement on AM radio.

In November 1972, the launch of the Anik A1 satellite, capable of relaying twelve television signals, signalled the beginning of a new era of distributing or relaying broadcast and telecommunications signals by satellite. Canada thereby became the first country with a domestic satellite communications system, although the satellite transmission of broadcast signals developed relatively slowly in the years that followed. According to the *Report of the Task Force on Broadcasting Policy* (1986), 'The CBC began leasing three transponders in 1973 after being pressed to do so by the government of the day. It was Telesat Canada's only full-time broadcasting customer until 1981, when Canadian Satellite Communications Inc. (CANCOM) was licensed to provide [broadcast] service to underserved and remote areas.'[7]

Growth of Cable Distribution

As a result of the 1968 Broadcasting Act, the CRTC assumed responsibility for a range of activities previously dispersed among various government departments, including that of licensing cable systems, a responsibility formerly held by the Department of Transport.[8] At the beginning of the 1970s, almost 80 per cent of Canadian households received their television signals over-the-air, often by means of a rooftop antenna. By 1978, cable distribution had surpassed over-the-air transmission as the predominant mode of distribution.[9] As a result, issues related to cable distribution had a significant influence on the development of Canadian broadcasting policy in the years that followed.

The growth of cable distribution obliged the CRTC to develop a policy framework for cable television whose primary attraction was its ability to provide U.S. border television signals to Canadian households. The Commission's policy framework was intended to find a balance between consumer interests (consumers wanted more and better broadcast services) and the economic well-being of Canadian off-air broadcasters who provided Canadian programs, often at a loss, and whose audiences might be tempted to modify their television viewing in favour of high-profile U.S. programs. Developing an appropriate cable policy framework involved addressing issues such as requirements for local (Canadian) broadcast signal carriage versus distant (often U.S.) signal carriage, the relative priority of Canadian public and private stations, and the provision of a community channel by cable operators to give local Canadian communities access to the broadcasting system.

What is more, the growth of cable television provoked important changes in public policy in program copyright protection. For example, in the 1970s, the copyright protection of television programs covered over-the-air broadcast signal transmission but not the cable retransmission of broadcast signals. Consequently, the cable distribution of U.S. network signals in Canada, with programs that had previously been sold to off-air Canadian commercial broadcasters, threatened to reduce the audiences and revenues on which Canadian broadcasters relied.

The CRTC's first major policy statement on the cable television industry was issued in July 1971 in a document entitled *Canadian Broadcasting 'a Single System': Policy Statement on Cable Television*. As its title suggests, it emphasized integration of the cable industry into the Canadian broadcasting system and, in fact, laid the groundwork for many of the policies that would govern broadcasting distribution undertakings (BDUs) in later years.

For example, the Commission's policy statement contains the initial formulation of 'simultaneous substitution' – a requirement for cable systems to substitute, on request by a local broadcaster, a local television signal for a distant signal if and when the two signals were 'identical' (i.e., substantially comparable) and broadcast simultaneously. Thus, if a Canadian television station broadcast an hour-long U.S. program simultaneously with its U.S. network broadcast, the Canadian station was entitled to request local cable systems carrying both signals to substitute the Canadian signal, containing both the program and any advertising contained therein, for the U.S. network signal during the duration of the program.[10]

To offer some protection for Canadian television broadcasters and to stabilize the revenues they earned from the broadcast of U.S. programs (that, in principle, cross-subsidized Canadian programs in the underrepresented categories of programming), the Canadian government adopted an amendment to the Income Tax Act that discouraged Canadian advertisers from placing their advertising on U.S. border stations to reach Canadian viewers. Bill C-58 stipulated that advertising expenditures constituted eligible expenses for income tax purposes only if the associated advertising appeared on Canadian television services. In other words, expenditures made on advertising broadcast on U.S.

services did not constitute eligible deductions in Canadian corporate income tax returns.[11] This tax policy measure had the effect of discouraging the placement of Canadian advertising on U.S. services available in Canada and instead channelling such expenditures toward licensed Canadian television services.

The policies outlined in the CRTC's 1971 policy statement were initially addressed with each cable television licensee at the time of licence renewal and appropriate conditions applied to each licence to give effect to the Commission's policies. In 1976, the Commission consolidated its cable television policies and abandoned selected licence conditions in favour of the first Cable Television Regulations – applicable to all cable television licensees.

Canadian Radio-television and Telecommunications Commission Act (1976)

In the 1970s as Canadian broadcasting expanded, broadcasting and telecommunications tended increasingly to overlap as broadcasters made greater use of telephone lines, microwave towers, mainframe computers, and satellites. To improve the oversight of broadcasting and telecommunications, the Canadian government transferred the authority to regulate and supervise telecommunications from the Canadian Transport Commission to the CRTC. The Canadian Radio-television and Telecommunications Commission Act established the Canadian Radio-television and Telecommunications Commission (CRTC) in its contemporary guise. By this legislation, the CRTC recuperated all of the powers granted to the Canadian Radio-television Commission by the Broadcasting Act of 1968 as well as powers related to the regulation and supervision of telephone and telegraph companies. The CRTC Act increased the number of full-time commissioners from five to nine and allowed up to ten part-time commissioners. The full-time commissioners constituted the Executive Committee of the Commission.

The Applebaum-Hébert Report (1982)

The Applebaum-Hébert Report is the name commonly given to the report of the Federal Cultural Policy Review Committee appointed by the federal government in August 1980. This was the first government review of Canadian cultural institutions and federal cultural policy since the Massey Commission report of 1951. The Applebaum-Hébert committee's mandate was to investigate and represent the situations and needs of those 'thought to have an active interest in our culture and its institutions.' The committee's findings were largely directed towards improving means of administering arts funding, following the assignment of cultural issues to the Department of Communications in 1980. Like the Massey Commission Report, the Applebaum-Hébert Report, published in 1982, examined all of the cultural industries and was not limited to broadcasting.

The Applebaum-Hébert Report represented both a continuation of and a departure from the principles and policies outlined by the Massey Commission. Both reports emphasized the importance of arm's-length support for artists, a principle advanced by the Massey Commission in favour of creating a semi-autonomous funding agency, the Canada Council, established in 1957. The Massey Report, however, portrayed commercial culture and particularly the mass media as a threat to both traditional culture and Canadian sovereignty, while the Applebaum-Hébert Report adopted a more pragmatic approach to the cultural industries. For example, the Applebaum-Hébert committee recommended that the CBC abandon commercial advertising, close its television production facilities, and cease its television production activities in favour of acquiring programs from independent production companies.[12] The Applebaum-Hébert committee also recommended that the CRTC require private sector broadcasters to allocate substantial percentages of their programming time, production budgets, and gross revenues to original Canadian program production.

The Charter of Rights and Freedoms

When the Canadian government patriated the BNA Act in 1982, the Canadian Charter of Rights and Freedoms also became a fundamental part of the Constitution, the supreme law of Canada. The Charter takes precedence over other legislation, including the Broadcasting Act and the CRTC Act, because the Charter is entrenched in the Constitution. Hereafter, the Charter obliged the CRTC to take Charter freedoms into consideration in the course of regulating and supervising the Canadian broadcasting system.

The Charter applies to provincial legislatures as well as to Parliament. This means that when an individual who believes that Parliament or a legislature has violated his or her rights asks the courts for assistance, the courts may declare parts of a law invalid to the extent that they conflict with the Charter. In addition, courts may provide other appropriate remedies to individuals whose rights, as defined by the Charter, have been violated or infringed.

For example, section 2(b) of the Charter of Rights and Freedoms says that everyone has 'freedom of thought, belief, opinion and expression, including freedom of the press and other media of communication.' However, the Charter also recognizes that even in a democracy rights and freedoms are not absolute. Section 1 of the Charter guarantees that all the rights and freedoms set out therein are subject 'to such reasonable limits prescribed by law as can be demonstrably justified in a free and democratic society.'

Thus, freedom of expression is guaranteed but, for example, no one is free to yell 'Fire!' in a video rental outlet, to slander someone else on television, or to engage in hate propaganda on the Internet. Consequently, the Charter of Rights and Freedoms permits Parliament or a provincial legislature to limit fundamental rights if that government is able to demonstrate the limit is reasonable, is prescribed by law, and can be justified in a free and democratic society. The interests of society must be balanced against the interests of individuals.

Pay and Specialty Television Services

By the early 1980s, the licensing of the first Canadian 'pay television' services (delivered by cable distributors via a set-top decoder for a supplementary fee in addition to the basic fee) had already been delayed for several years by a reluctant CRTC. When the decision was finally made to proceed, there was little hard empirical information on how to choose the pay television services most likely to succeed, either culturally or financially. As a result, the CRTC relied on applicants' commitments and its own evaluation of experience in the United States, where pay television was booming. The CRTC conducted a public hearing in 1981 to consider the first Canadian pay television service applications, without the benefits of the hindsight we now enjoy.

In light of the success of U.S. pay television penetration in the late 1970s and early 1980s, and the expansive promises of the Canadian pay television applicants, the CRTC licensed six new services in what was presented as a head-to-head competitive model.[13] However, the licensing of so many Canadian advertising-free pay services was predicated on a false premise. The U.S. discretionary services succeeded (until a shakeout occurred in 1984) because they sold basic cable, bundled together with pay services, to first-time cable subscribers into a largely uncabled environment. Since Canadian basic cable services enjoyed a much higher level of household penetration than their counterparts in the United States, Canadian pay television was often a single service add-on, for an additional fee, to the variety of conventional services already offered by Canadian cable operators. Considering the large number of services already available on cable, many Canadian households decided that the value–price relationship of acquiring a set-top descrambler to obtain one or two additional Canadian pay services was simply too high and declined to subscribe. In the year following the launch of Canadian pay services in February 1983, Canadian pay television incurred a series of bankruptcies and amalgamations as most consumers rejected the new concept.

When, in 1983, the CRTC announced a public hearing to consider the first cable-delivered 'specialty' television service applications, it indicated that it would also be willing to allow the carriage of certain non-Canadian specialty services by cable distributors, provided that such services contributed to, and did not adversely affect, the development of the Canadian broadcasting system. This was the genesis of the Commission's 'genre protection' policy, whereby non-Canadian services that might compete directly with Canadian specialty services would not be authorized for distribution in Canada. As a result, until very recently, U.S. services such as HBO, Showtime, ESPN, and MTV were not distributed in Canada.

In the preamble to the CRTC's April 1984 decisions authorizing the first new specialty services – Action Canada Sports Network (subsequently called TSN) and MuchMusic – the Commission stated that the new services would be offered on a discretionary basis at the option of the subscriber. By definition, they would consist of narrowcast television programming and would be complementary to existing off-air and pay services.[14] With respect to advertising, the Commission noted that each specialty service would not distribute any local advertising and generally would not carry more than eight minutes of advertising material per hour.

In August 1984, the CRTC approved a restructuring of all national and regional pay licensees into two general-interest pay television licensees: First Choice (now called the Movie Network) and Allarcom Pay Television (now called Movie Central), each controlled by separate ownership groups.[15] First Choice reduced its service area from all of Canada to Eastern Canada, and the three licensees authorized to serve Ontario, the Prairies, and British Columbia amalgamated to form a single undertaking to serve Western Canada. While the Commission claimed that a competitive market environment for pay television was desirable, it effectively adopted a non-competitive or monopolistic policy that involved one licence per genre in a given geographic area.[16]

In 1985, the pay television industry began to recover with more modest ambitions and a marketing strategy that emphasized packaging with the new specialty services: TSN and MuchMusic. Rapid expansion in the volume of pay television subscribers followed for a period but, beginning in 1987, the development of extended basic cable tiers once again slowed expansion. Extended basic tiers offered by cable systems provided a negative option involving a cable filter or trap that removed the need for signal encryption or a set-top box. This dampened the growth of pay television by again isolating pay services on relatively high-cost tiers with low penetration – owing to the set-top descrambling technology required by pay television. Although specialty television services continued to enjoy considerable success, Canadian pay television subscriber penetration levels expanded slowly until the rise of digital distribution at the end of the 1990s and the beginning of a period of widespread consumer acceptance of digital set-top boxes as a concomitant of digital conversion.

Independent Television Production

In the 1970s, there was virtually no independent television production industry in Canada. A modest independent theatrical feature film industry, largely in francophone Montreal, developed in the early part of the decade, but the industry was overwhelmed, some would say undermined, by, among other things, changes in Canadian government policy relating to tax shelters (1974 to 1978) intended to encourage investment in theatrical feature films for wide audiences. The failure of the government's attempt to create a market-oriented Canadian feature film production industry led government policymakers to turn their attention to a sector where distribution is regulated and production costs are more modest and more in keeping with the size of Canadian markets, that is, television. The rise of Canadian independent television production in the 1980s is essentially attributable to three public policy changes: a tightening of the capital cost allowance for Canadian feature films (1981–7) as a result of perceived abuses by producers and packagers, the creation of Telefilm Canada's Broadcast Fund in 1983, and the adoption by the CRTC of Canadian content spending requirements for conventional broadcast services beginning in 1985.

In 1983, the federal government published *Towards a New National Broadcasting Policy*, announcing its intention to create the Canadian Broadcast Development Fund (Broadcast Fund) to finance Canadian television programs for broadcast on Canadian services. The government gave responsibility for the Broadcast Fund to the Canadian Film Development Corporation (CFDC) via a memorandum of understanding (MOU), even though, as originally conceived, the CFDC had no direct relation with the broadcasting industry. The MOU of February 1983 between the Minister of Communications and the CFDC defined eligible productions as drama and variety programs appropriate for exhibition between 7 p.m. and 11 p.m., as well as children's programs, and specified that the Broadcast Fund should be used to assist production made by private sector Canadian program producers (i.e., independent producers). The $35 million fund launched on 1 July 1983 (its financing increased to $60 million in the fifth year of operations) dwarfed the CFDC's existing theatrical feature film activities and, in 1984, the CFDC's name was changed to Telefilm Canada.[17]

In the beginning, Telefilm Canada had difficulty disbursing the financing in the Broadcast Fund for lack of eligible projects, but as the television production sector expanded and its requirements exceeded the financing in the Fund, Telefilm developed a discretionary project-by-project approach, in which an analysis of the content of the screenplay played a central role in the evaluation of proposals.

At the CRTC, beginning in 1987, the Commission extended its Canadian content expenditure approach (an approach first applied to the new pay television licensees in 1982) to conventional over-the-air television stations and networks. This involved the identification of distinct spending requirements for Canadian programs tailored to each broadcaster. Instead of relying solely on general regulations that applied to an entire class of television licences, the Commission placed more emphasis on specific conditions of licence, depending upon each licensee's strengths and weaknesses as they related to Canadian content, particularly drama.[18]

The combination of these public policy initiatives, including the subsidizing of independent production destined for over-the-air television broadcast on the supply side, and the expansion of the market for drama programming by regulation on the demand side, stimulated the emergence of the independent television production sector in Canada in the late 1980s.

Caplan-Sauvageau Task Force

In 1985, the federal government created the Task Force on Broadcasting Policy, co-chaired by Florian Sauvageau and Gerald Caplan, to address the ongoing challenges facing the Canadian broadcasting system due to audience fragmentation, changes in technology, and ongoing concerns over Canada's cultural sovereignty.

In September 1986, the Caplan-Sauvageau Task Force recommended, among other things, that

- All broadcast licensees be regarded as trustees of the Canadian public
- The CBC play a central role in ensuring that Canadians have a truly national broadcasting system, in radio and television, in English and French
- CBC funding be stable and secure for the duration of its licence period
- All American programming on CBC television be phased out as soon as possible

As for private stations, the Caplan-Sauvageau Task Force recommended that the CRTC establish more demanding conditions of licence to oblige private stations and networks to increase their expenditures on the production and broadcast of Canadian programs. The report also called for some government support and protection for the private sector, in return for which the private sector licensees (in its role as trustee of the public airwaves) should contribute to fulfilling the objectives of the Broadcasting Act.

The federal government proceeded to adopt many of the recommendations of the Caplan-Sauvageau Task Force in its revision of the existing Broadcasting Act, which became the Broadcasting Act, 1991. This is the legislation that, subject to amendments from time to time, continues to embody Canada's broadcasting fundamental policy objectives today.

Among other issues, the Broadcasting Act, 1991, attempted to address Parliament's concern or, more precisely, the Department of Communications' concern that broadcasting policy since 1968 had been primarily the responsibility of the CRTC rather than the Minister of Communications. As an independent agency with a very broad mandate, the Commission determined broadcasting policy by means of its licensing of broadcasting undertakings, regulatory decisions, and policy notices. This led to a certain rivalry between the CRTC and the Department of Communications (now the Department of Canadian Heritage) that resulted in the attribution of new powers of policy direction to the government in the Broadcasting Act of 1991.

Canada-U.S. Free Trade Agreement

One of the issues addressed by the Caplan-Sauvageau Task Force Report was the retransmission of broadcast signals by broadcasting distribution undertakings, such as cable operations. Although the Copyright Act in force at the time recognized individual radio and television programs as works subject to copyright, it did not recognize broadcast signals as having a separate and independent copyright. As a result, there was no obligation for broadcast distribution undertakings, including those relying on satellite delivery, to request permission to retransmit such signals.[19] Among other things, the Caplan-Sauvageau Task Force Report recommended recognizing the principle of a retransmission right.

In January 1989, following the signing of the Canada-U.S. Free Trade Agreement (FTA), the Canadian government amended the Copyright Act to require broadcast distribution undertakings to pay for the retransmission of works included in distant over-the-air broadcast signals. This issue is discussed further in chapter 14. The amendments pursuant to the FTA also expanded the concept of 'communication to the public' from broadcasting to include all forms of telecommunication.

Notes

1 The CRTC's responsibilities would expand to include telecommunications, and the name changed to the 'Canadian Radio-television and Telecommunications Commission' in 1976.

2 However, the Broadcasting Act, 1968, does not recognize that English- and French-language broadcasting 'operate under different conditions and may have different requirements,' a consideration that was added in the Broadcasting Act, 1991.

3 Compare this to the current definition in the 1991 Broadcasting Act, where

broadcasting means '*any transmission of programs,* whether or not encrypted, by radio waves or other means of telecommunication for reception by the public by means of broadcasting receiving apparatus, but does not include any such transmission of programs that is made solely for performance or display in a public place' (emphasis added). See chap. 1 for a discussion of the 1991 definition.

4 As a result, the provincial educational television service in British Columbia, the Knowledge Network, operated without a CRTC licence from its creation in 1980 until the revised Broadcasting Act of 1991 modified the definition of *broadcasting* to include closed-circuit systems and effectively obliged the Knowledge Network to apply for a licence. See Decision CRTC 92-684.

5 See Appendix C.

6 The October 1968 direction was subsequently revised several times over the next three years. See Bird, *Documents.*

7 Government of Canada, *Report of the Task Force on Broadcasting Policy,* 590.

8 The CRTC was given responsibility for issuing broadcasting licences subject to certification by the Minister of Transport (as of 1969, the Minister of Communications) that the applicant satisfied the relevant technical requirements of the Radio Act and regulations.

9 See Government of Canada, *Report of the Task Force on Broadcasting Policy,* table 24.1, 552.

10 As has often been pointed out, Canadian private-sector English-language television over-the-air services soon adopted the practice of filling out their primetime schedules with lucrative U.S. programs to take advantage of simultaneous substitution. This resulted in the Canadian signal, together with any advertising within, being distributed on two or more cable channels and thereby attracting larger audiences. Because they could not generally take advantage of simultaneous substitution, Canadian programs on English-language commercial television stations were relegated to the fringes of broadcasters' schedules. There have been occasional instances of Canadian broadcasters requesting simultaneous substitution in regard to U.S. or Canadian programs on a competing Canadian television station. For example, in the 1980s, simultaneous substitution occurred between CTV affiliates in the Montreal and Ottawa markets because the affiliates were owned by distinct corporate groups. However, as a result of the language difference, French-language services in Canada have never adopted simultaneous program scheduling in regard to U.S. programs.

11 The absence of U.S. corporate advertising in Canada directed at U.S. citizens virtually eliminated the threat of mirror legislation in the United States.

12 This latter recommendation was never implemented, although the CBC voluntarily abandoned the production of in-house drama, and Radio-Canada has reduced its in-house drama production to almost nothing.
13 See Decision CRTC 82-240, which sets out the initial regulatory framework for pay television.
14 See Public Notice CRTC 1984-81.
15 See Decision CRTC 84-654.
16 This approach is consistent with economic theories of program choice, suggesting that, under certain conditions, competing firms will produce program schedules of 'excessive sameness' by comparison with a single supplier or monopoly. See Owen and Wildman, *Video Economics*, chap. 3.
17 The CFDC was created by the Canadian Film Development Corporation Act in 1967 to 'foster and promote the development of a feature film industry in Canada' and it began operations in April 1968. Between 1968 and 1982, the CFDC's mandate concerned the development of a feature film industry in Canada and the provision of support to films with significant Canadian creative content. By 1982–3, the CFDC's annual operational expenses amounted to about $5 million. Memoranda of understanding with the Government of Canada governed all of Telefilm Canada's activities outside of feature film until the corporation's mandate set out in the Act was amended in 2005, at which time the title of the Act was changed to the Telefilm Canada Act.
18 In August 1979, in licence renewal Decision CRTC 79-453, the CRTC imposed a condition of licence requiring the CTV network to present 26 hours of original new Canadian drama during the 1980–1 broadcasting year and 39 hours in 1981–2. This condition of licence was appealed to the courts and, in April 1982, the Supreme Court of Canada upheld the Commission's decision (i.e., the authority of the Commission to make the decision). In CTV's subsequent licence renewal decision, Decision CRTC 87-200, the Commission imposed minimum expenditures on Canadian programming as well as other requirements, including the requirement to broadcast an average of 2.5 hours per week of regularly scheduled drama in 1987–8, rising to 4.5 hours in 1991–2.
19 CANCOM was created in 1981 to serve northern and remote communities. In 1983, the CRTC extended its so-called 3 + 1 cable television policy to satellite operations, such as CANCOM. This policy, first announced in 1971, permitted the retransmission of the three major U.S. networks (ABC, CBS, and NBC), as well as the U.S. public service network (PBS).

4 Structure and Change in Canadian Broadcasting

To understand the implications of broadcasting policy alternatives, it is essential to have some knowledge of the basic characteristics of Canadian broadcasting, how broadcasting has evolved in recent years, and the behaviour of its key contributors. This chapter provides an overview of household behaviour related to broadcasting and related media, the demand for Canadian content, and selected elements of Canadian broadcasting industry structure. The discussion in the rest of the book will refer to the figures and tables presented here.

Media Penetration Rates

Radio

Radio listening in Canada is declining. For many years, the average number of hours tuned per capita, for the age group twelve years and older, remained constant at about twenty-one hours per week. However, as indicated in figure 4.1, radio listening began to decline in the mid-1990s and this decline has continued since.

The apparent decline in radio listening since the mid-1990s may be partly attributable to radio listening on the Internet (which was poorly measured until the following decade) and partly to listening to unlicensed alternative sources of music on computers and mobile digital devices. The decline in listening over the twelve years covered in figure 4.1 appears to be concentrated among teenagers twelve to seventeen years, who on average in 2007 listened to only 7.2 hours of radio, and among women of all ages.

As suggested in figure 4.1, until recently, the average number of

FIGURE 4.1 Average weekly hours of radio tuning in Canada, 12+, 1992–2007 (hours per capita)

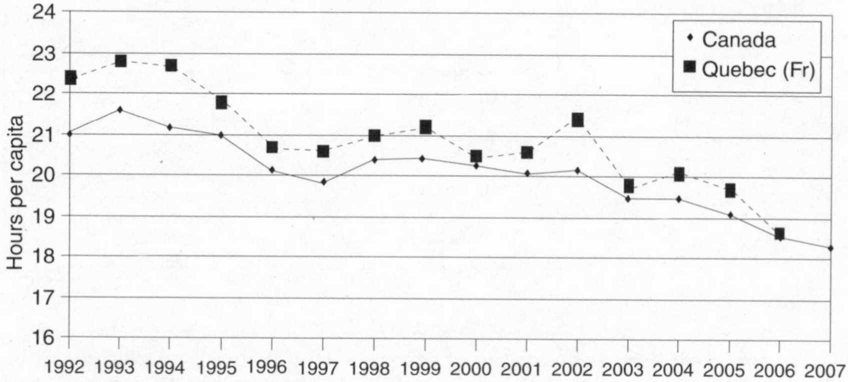

Sources: CRTC communications monitoring reports and Board of Broadcast Measurement (BBM) fall surveys

hours tuned per capita in French-speaking Quebec was higher than that of Canada (including Quebec), but the difference appears to have all but disappeared in recent years.

When the data for AM and FM radio listening per capita are separated, a decline in listening to AM stations and an increase in listening to FM stations over the last decade is apparent (see figure 4.2).[1]

The transfer of audiences from AM to FM is attributable to the quality of FM sound, the new formats adopted by FM stations, and an increase in the number and variety of FM stations available. All the same, as suggested by figure 4.1, licensed radio stations are continuing to lose audiences to unlicensed alternative sources of music on computers and mobile digital devices.

Accompanying the shift from AM to FM listening has been a shift from in-home to out-of-home listening that has persisted since at least the late 1960s. Measured out-of-home listening, which represented only 19 per cent of total listening in 1968, had increased to 51 per cent by 2004 and this trend, which appears to reflect consumer demand for portability, appears to be continuing (see figure 4.3).

The decline in in-home radio listening constitutes a dramatic change from the era when radio listening was a family experience centred on a single radio in the living room. The arrival of radios as standard equipment in automobiles, followed by the introduction of small AM-

FIGURE 4.2 AM/FM total weekly hours of radio tuning in Canada, 12+ (% of total tuning), 1995–2007

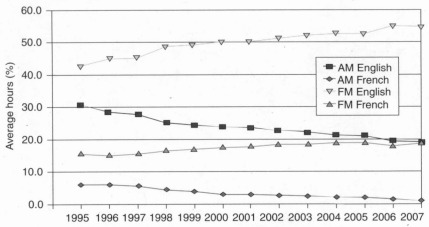

Sources: CRTC communications monitoring reports and BBM fall surveys

FIGURE 4.3 In-home share of radio listening, 1995–2004 (%)

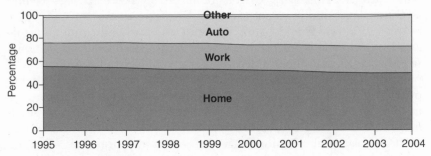

Source: BBM fall surveys

FM radios, push buttons, and higher quality stereo systems, coupled with the domination of television as the home entertainment system of choice, has increased out-of-home radio listening. These changes were also accompanied by increased radio listening in the workplace, the introduction of portable radios and headsets (such as the Sony Walkman) in the 1980s, a sustained increase in the share of listening in automobiles, the arrival of digital satellite radio, and, in recent years, the spread of new portable digital media, such as iPods and cellular telephones, with audio listening capacity.

FIGURE 4.4 Number of cable, satellite, and other wireless television subscribers in Canada, 2000–7 (millions)

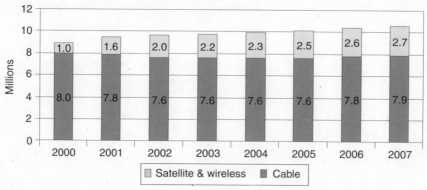

Sources: Statistics Canada 56-011-XIE, 56-209-X

Television

Television reaches about 99 per cent of Canada's 13 million households and this high penetration rate has prevailed for some time. Cable and satellite distribution undertakings enhance the broadcast experience by providing more and better listening and viewing services. Cable and satellite distribution undertakings enable the viewer to receive a variety of distant radio and television signals (including specialty and pay television), Internet services, and telephony services, in addition to providing higher quality reception of the broadcast signals originating from local off-air transmitters. The total penetration rate of cable, satellite, and other wireless services has risen steadily over the last decade. See figure 4.4, which indicates the total number of broadcast subscribers to these services since 2000 (years ending August 31).[2]

After increasing during the 1970s, 1980s, and most of the 1990s, the penetration rate of Canadian broadcast cable services declined between 1998 and 2003. As figure 4.4 suggests, part of the decline in cable television penetration was due to the growing popularity of digital satellite television services. However, in 2004 cable operators arrested the loss of television customers to satellite and wireless services and began to increase the total number of their television subscribers. This phenomenon is apparently attributable to the provision of new digital services previously unavailable from cable service providers, such as Internet access and telephony. The offer of a package or 'bundle' of digital cable

FIGURE 4.5 Number of digital TV subscribers in Canada, 2000–7 (millions)

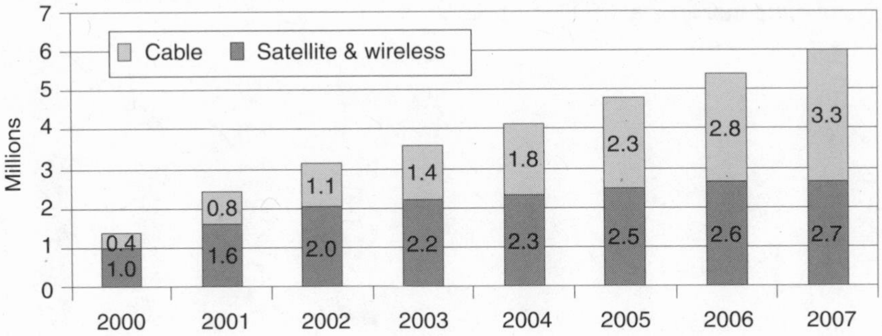

Source: Statistics Canada 56-011-XIE 56-209-X

services, both broadcast and non-broadcast, enabled terrestrial cable operators to better compete with satellite television service providers. By 31 August 2007, the total number of subscribers to television, Internet access, and telephone services offered by cable distributors had reached 14.2 million.

Digital television provides an enhanced experience and opens the door to interactive services, Internet service provision, and high-definition television (HDTV).[3] The penetration of digital cable and satellite services has been increasing rapidly in the last few years and television households are switching from analogue to digital programming services. In 2006 (year ending 31 August), for the first time, the number of digital cable subscribers exceeded the number of satellite and other wireless (MDS) subscribers (see figure 4.5).

Not only has the digital revolution affected the way in which broadcast services are distributed but it has also affected the use of playback methods. Growth in the penetration of digital video disc (DVD) players put an end to growth in the penetration of analogue videocassette (VCR) players in Canada, which ceased about 1999.

For many years, per capita viewing of television in Canada has been relatively stable. Some recent data appear to indicate a decline in television viewing, perhaps attributable to the growth in popularity of new digital media, including the Internet and mobile digital devices. It is sometimes argued that unlicensed services are directly competitive with licensed broadcast services and are negatively affecting the total volume of television viewing, particularly among those in the 12–17 and 18–34 age groups. However, at the time of publication of this book,

FIGURE 4.6 Home computer and Internet use in Canada, 2001–5 (% of households)

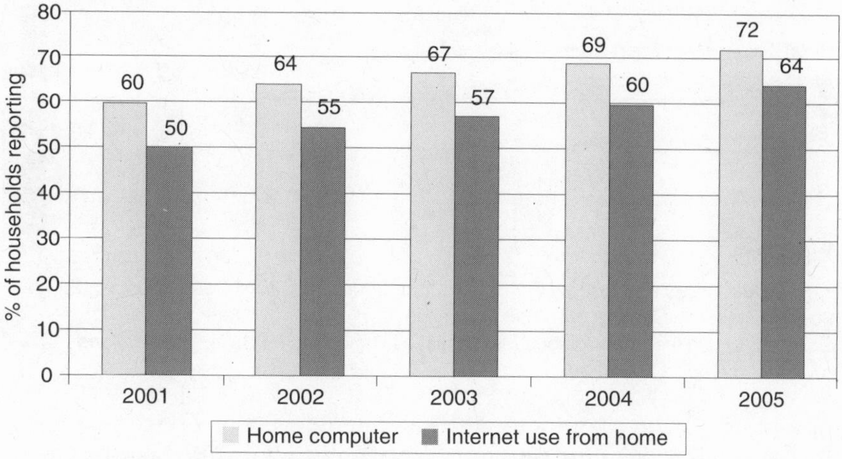

Source: Statistics Canada 62F0026MIE

the relevant data did not seem to indicate any clear trend that would as yet confirm such behaviour.[4]

New Media

The transition from analogue to digital technology is transforming the use of audio-visual media by Canadian households and institutions. This transition is reflected in the continuing increase in the share of Canadian households that own home computers and are using the Internet. As indicated in figure 4.6, on 31 December 2005, 72 per cent of Canadian households possessed home computers and 64 per cent could access the Internet.

What is more, the proportion of households reporting high-speed access to the Internet increased to 50 per cent of all households in 2005, from 43 per cent in the previous year. Only 14 per cent of households continued to use dial-up Internet access at the end of 2005.[5]

However, Internet use generally, both dial-up and high speed, varies considerably across Canada. The probability of an individual in an urban area using the Internet for personal (non-business) objectives are about one-and-a-half times those of someone doing so in un-urbanized areas. In 2005, only 58 per cent of residents living in rural and small

FIGURE 4.7 Broadband penetration of Canadian homes (%)

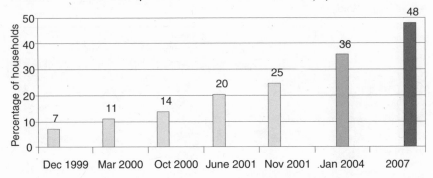

Sources: Ekos Research Associates, Statistics Canada, CRTC *Communications Monitoring Report 2008*

town areas accessed the Internet in 2005, well below the Canadian average of 68 per cent. This gap between rural and urban areas probably reflects the interaction of certain socio-economic conditions, such as income levels and education, as well as other considerations, such as the relative unavailability of high speed Internet access in remote rural areas.[6]

A continuing impediment to the streaming and downloading of video files by Internet users is the lack of high speed Internet access in Canadian homes. As indicated by the estimates of broadband penetration of Canadian homes displayed in figure 4.7, the situation is improving.

Not only are Canadians extensively using home computers to access information and entertainment, they are also using mobile digital devices. A recent portrait of Canadians' use of such devices indicates that in 2007, 65 per cent of Canadians reported owning a cellphone and 31 per cent owning MP3 players such as the iPod (of which 8 per cent were video capable).[7] These devices appear to compete directly with Canadians' consumption of traditional licensed radio and television services.

Supply and Demand for Canadian Content

Radio

Canadian commercial radio stations are required to fulfil a 35 per cent

TABLE 4.1 Fulfilment of Canadian content and French vocal music requirements by commercial radio stations, 2006 (number of stations)

Requirement	No. of stations analysed	Fulfilling requirements – all day and weekly	Fulfilling requirements – 6 a.m. to 6 p.m., M–F
35% Canadian content weekly – Canadian music	22	20	21
65% French vocal music weekly	8	6	–
55% French vocal music weekly (6 a.m. to 6 p.m.)	8	–	8

Source: CRTC *Broadcast Policy Monitoring Report 2007*, 26

Canadian content requirement for the number of musical selections aired between 6 a.m. and midnight but are not subject to any other such content requirements. See chapter 6. In addition to the Canadian content requirement, French-language commercial radio stations are obliged to program 65 per cent of their vocal music in the French language. To ensure that French-language selections are played during periods of high listening, at least 55 per cent of the popular vocal music selections broadcast between 6:00 a.m. and 6:00 p.m., Monday through Friday, must be French-language. Table 4.1 presents the results of CRTC monitoring of a limited sample of commercial radio stations for 2006 (related to licence renewals) and indicates problems of non-compliance by a few stations.[8]

Television

The number of Canadian specialty television services has increased exponentially over the last ten years, providing Canadian viewers with many more Canadian choices. Figure 4.8 indicates the growth in the number of specialty services operating over two and a half decades.

As a result of the growing availability of Canadian and non-Canadian television services, there is a continuing trend in viewing, away from the conventional off-air services toward specialty and pay services. Among English-language audiences, for example, viewing of Canadian and U.S. conventional stations is declining in favour of viewing of Canadian specialty and pay services (see figure 4.9).

According to a slightly different tabulation that focuses on the first-language of the audience rather than the language of broadcast, French-

FIGURE 4.8 Canadian specialty television services, 1980–2005

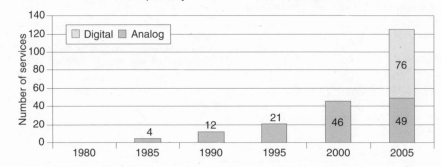

Source: CRTC statistical and financial summaries

FIGURE 4.9 Audience share of English-language station groups in Canada, 2+, 1995–2005 (% of total)

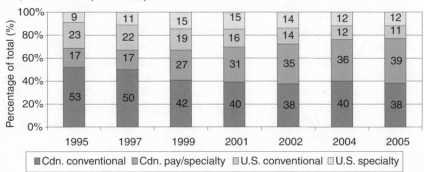

Source: Canadian Media Research Inc., *Trends in Canadian Television Audiences, New Technologies, Advertising and Programming,* 21

language audiences also shifted their preferences to French-language specialty and pay services from French-language conventional services and English-language services, both Canadian and U.S., over the last ten years.

How is the viewing of Canadian audiences distributed by program category? Figures 4.10 and 4.11 indicate the distribution of viewing for all television services (conventional, specialty, and pay) for anglophones and francophones.

As can be seen by comparing figures 4.10 and 4.11, viewing of Canadian programs by francophones is higher than that of anglophones in all categories.

FIGURE 4.10 Distribution of television viewing time, anglophones 2+, fall 2004 (% of total)

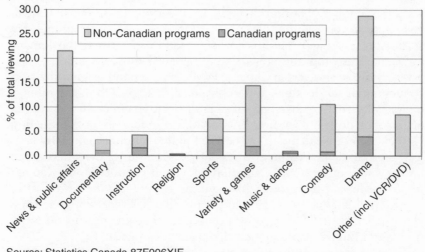

Source: Statistics Canada 87F006XIE

FIGURE 4.11 Distribution of television viewing time, francophones 2+, fall 2004 (% of total)

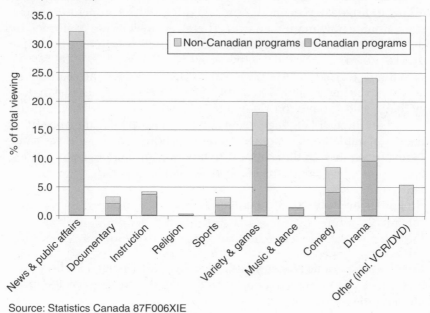

Source: Statistics Canada 87F006XIE

The issue of viewing of Canadian programs, in particular drama, is discussed further below.

As the number of authorized television services available in Canada has risen, so too has the total production of Canadian programs. The supply of Canadian programs has increased in response to the demand for Canadian programming originating with the conventional, specialty, and pay services in Canada. While the demand originating from conventional services has apparently declined, growth in the number of specialty services has had an overall positive effect on the volume of (current dollar) spending on Canadian 'independent' production. However, because many of the newer English-language specialty services present a high volume of repeat programming, their net impact on the value of 'original' Canadian television production is relatively modest. Most of the growth in spending on independent production is attributable to an expansion in the number of French-language specialty services that occurred at a date later than the expansion in the number of English-language services (see figure 4.12).

The increased presence of specialty and pay services in the Canadian broadcasting system has contributed to more choice, more fragmentation, the airing of more low-cost repeat Canadian programming, and a reduction in audiences for English-language Canadian 'priority' programs in the peak viewing hours, when U.S. entertainment programs predominate now more than ever. These conclusions are confirmed by data on the value of production of original English-language Canadian drama programs over the last few years (see figure 4.13).

In figure 4.13, a shaded distinction is drawn between the years before and after the implementation of the CRTC's 1999 off-air television policy that is said to have contributed to the decline in Canadian drama on Canadian English-language television.[9] To date, no decline appears in the comparable French-language drama production data for the same period, even though there appear to be fewer drama programs among the most popular programs in the peak viewing hours.

Broadcasting Industry Structure and Characteristics

Radio

Broadcasting Public Notice CRTC 2006-158, 'Commercial Radio Policy 2006,' identifies several economic characteristics that favour the radio industry over other media:

FIGURE 4.12 Canadian independent television production, by language, 1999 to 2008 ($ millions)

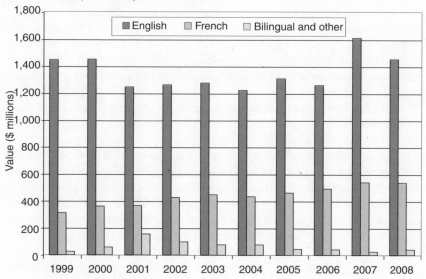

Source: CFTPA 2009 Profile

FIGURE 4.13 Value of English-language production of television drama, 1999 to 2008 ($ millions)

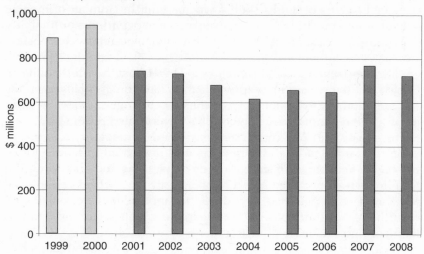

Source: CFTPA 2009 Profile

- Radio stations focus on issues of interest to the local community and generate substantial audiences and revenues from local economic activity.
- In recent years, network television has generally shifted away from local advertising to regional and national advertising, leaving the local business to radio.
- Morning and afternoon 'drive periods' provide a captive audience for radio advertising.
- Radio listening levels remain strong in the summer when television viewing diminishes.

The evolution of listening patterns and the switch from AM to FM radio tuning (see figure 4.2) have also had an influence on the structure and profitability of the Canadian radio industry. The number of FM stations has increased and the number of AM stations has declined as some AM stations have gone off the air or converted to FM broadcast. Figure 4.14 displays these trends for English- and French-language stations.[10]

One would expect the presence of more stations in a competitive market to reduce average profitability and fewer stations to increase profitability – at least in the short run. Despite the large increase in the number of English-language FM stations (from 172 to 354) over the period 1999–2007, the profitability of English-language FM stations has remained relatively stable. With an increase in the number of French-language stations (from 60 to 84) over the same period, the profitability of French-language FM stations has also remained relatively constant since 2001 (see figure 4.15).[11]

With the decline in the number of AM stations, the profitability of English-language stations improved from 2003 to 2007. However, the same phenomenon did not occur on the French-language side; the profitability of French-language stations has deteriorated seriously.

The situation in AM radio has contributed to greater industry concentration in the radio industry as owners have tried to reduce losses by seeking economies of scale through networking and takeovers. The resulting pressures gave rise to a change in the CRTC's commercial radio ownership policy in April 1998 that appears to have contributed to further concentration of ownership in the private sector radio industry[12] (see figure 4.16).

The airplay of English- and French-language music on private sector

FIGURE 4.14 Number of commercial radio stations in Canada, 1999–2007

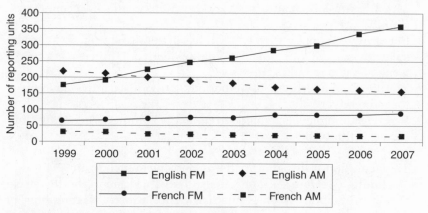

Source: CRTC Statistical & Financial Summaries

FIGURE 4.15 Profitability of radio in Canada, 1999–2007

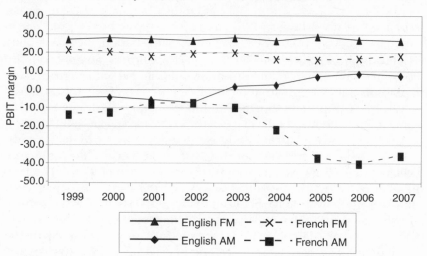

Source: CRTC statistical and financial summaries

FIGURE 4.16 Revenue share of top 5 commercial radio ownership groups (%)

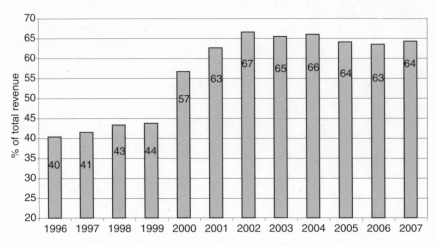

Source: CRTC statistical & financial summaries

radio is concentrated in the hands of the four international music distributors: Sony Music Entertainment, Warner Music Canada (Warner Music Group), EMI Group, and Universal Music Canada (Vivendi).

Television

Television production, whether by broadcast licence holders (i.e., 'in-house') or from independent producers unaffiliated with a broadcaster, represents a major industrial sector in Canada. Foreign location shooting is also an important source of employment for technicians as well as some lower- and middle-level creative people (see figure 4.17).

The growth in Canadian in-house and independent production indicated in figure 4.17 is related primarily to the increase in the number of licensed Canadian specialty television services in operation.[13] The total number of Canadian specialty services operating in Canada increased dramatically from 21 to 125 between 1995 and 2005 (see figure 4.8 above).

The growth in total television advertising revenues over the last decade is attributable largely to that of the specialty services. The expansion in the number of specialty services, and in viewing of these services (see figure 4.9 above), has dampened the growth of the conventional serv-

FIGURE 4.17 Value of television production in Canada, 1999 to 2008
($ millions)

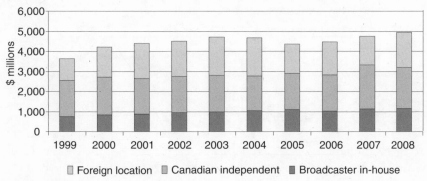

☐ Foreign location   ☐ Canadian independent   ■ Broadcaster in-house

Source: CFTPA 2009 Profile

FIGURE 4.18 Selected sources of television revenues in Canada, 1998–2008
($ millions)

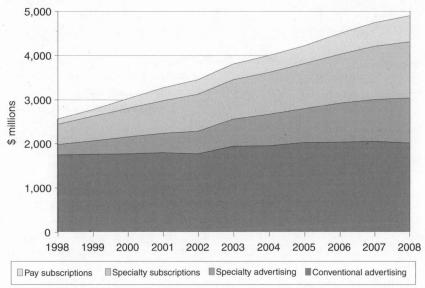

☐ Pay subscriptions   ☐ Specialty subscriptions   ■ Specialty advertising   ■ Conventional advertising

Source: CRTC statistical and financial summaries

FIGURE 4.19 Profitability of television in Canada, 1996–2008 (%)

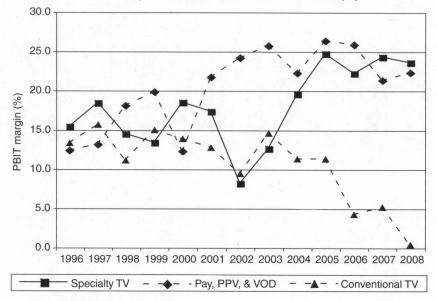

Source: CRTC statistical & financial summaries

ices. As is shown in figure 4.18, the current dollar value of advertising revenues earned by private sector conventional services, both English- and French-language services, increased slowly over nearly a decade (before declining slightly in 2008). Over the same period, subscriber fees earned by specialty, pay, PPV, and VOD services have expanded significantly. As a result, in 2007, for the first time, aggregate specialty services revenues from all sources surpassed aggregate conventional services revenues from all sources.[14]

The start-up of a number of new specialty services reduced the specialty television sector's overall profitability in the short term (i.e., during 1998 and 1999, and again in 2002 and 2003) but the sector has largely recovered[15] (see figure 4.19). By contrast, the aggregate profitability of conventional television stations and networks (including ethnic and third-language services) has declined over the last decade.

Similar results are obtained when English- and French-language services are presented separately (see figure 4.20).[16] The Télévision

FIGURE 4.20 Profitability of television in Canada, by language, 1996–2006 (%)

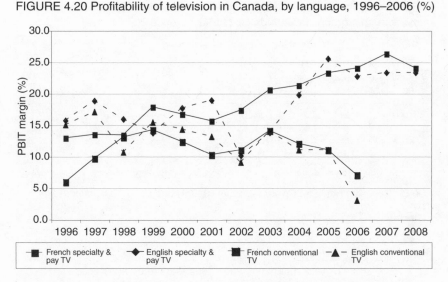

Source: CRTC statistical & financial summaries and *Monitoring Report 2007*

Quatre-Saisons (TQS) network depressed the average profitability of the French-language conventional services sector from its launch in September 1986; the service finally requested protection from its creditors in December 2007 before being transferred to new owners in June 2008.

Private sector television broadcasting is very concentrated in Canada. Thus, in 2006, CTV, CanWest Global, CHUM, Groupe TVA, and TQS earned 91 per cent of all of the conventional private sector revenues in Canada.[17] Figure 4.21 sets out the share of total revenues earned by the five largest private sector conventional television ownership groups over the last decade. The CBC, the provincial educational broadcasters, and discretionary specialty and pay services are not included in this figure.

Overall, specialty and pay television broadcasting is less concentrated than conventional television but most of the successful specialty and pay services belong to a small number of broadcasting conglomerates. Industry concentration in Canadian television and radio is discussed further in chapter 13.

FIGURE 4.21 Revenue share of 5 largest private sector conventional television ownership groups in Canada (% of total revenue)[18]

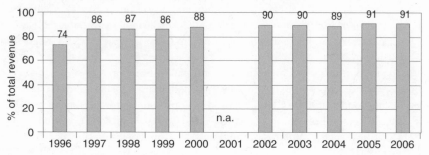

Source: Canadian Heritage, *Ownership Patterns 2001* and *CRTC Monitoring Report 2007*

Notes

1 'Other' radio tuning, principally tuning to U.S. stations, has not been included in fig. 4.2. Other tuning amounted to 4.8 per cent of the total in 2007.
2 Statistics Canada data for satellite operations include a small number of wireless operations such as multi-channel distribution systems (MDS).
3 In principle, *digital* television suggests that a digital signal is sent to the home and then displayed on a digital television receiver. However, in the current transitional stage, digital television often involves the use of a decoder that converts the digital signal to analogue format for display on an analogue television receiver.
4 See CRTC, *Communications Monitoring Report 2008*, fig. 4.3.1, 119.
5 Statistics Canada, 'Survey of Household Spending,' *Daily*, 12 December 2006.
6 See McKeown, Noce, and Czerny, 'Factors Associated with Internet Use.'
7 BBM Analytics' Media Technology Monitor 2007 survey as reported in CRTC, *Communications Monitoring Report 2008*, 171–2.
8 Unfortunately, comparable data were not reported by the CRTC in the following year.
9 Public Notice CRTC 1999-97, 'Building on Success: A Policy Framework for Canadian Television.'
10 In addition to the radio stations shown in fig. 4.14, in 2007 there were ten ethnic and Native AM stations, nine ethnic and Native FM stations, and eighty-two CBC AM and FM stations.

11 The PBIT margin is defined as profits before interest and taxes as a percentage of revenues.

12 Public Notice CRTC 1998-41, 'Commercial Radio Policy.' In 2007, the top five radio industry owners consisted of Corus, Rogers, Standard, CHUM/CTV, and Astral. Industry concentration in Canadian radio is discussed further in chap. 13.

13 The total number of Canadian conventional (off-air) private-sector television stations operating in Canada remained about constant over the last decade. Although the CRTC licensed new private-sector stations in Montreal, Calgary, Edmonton, Vancouver, and Toronto, the CBC acquired some six private sector affiliates (removing them from consideration as private sector stations).

14 Until 2006, the CRTC did not record any advertising revenues for the pay services. Beginning in 2006, with improved coverage of pay per view (PPV) and video on demand (VOD) services, the CRTC data include a small volume of advertising revenues earned by pay services (about $438,000 in 2008). Conventional, specialty, and pay television services also reported other revenues, such as program sales, but the revenues reported in fig. 4.18 account for 96 per cent of the grand total for all television revenues in 2008.

15 For example, thirteen new specialty services commenced service in 1998, three in 1999, seven in 2000, two in 2001, and forty-eight (digital services) in 2002.

16 Since 2007, the CRTC has refused to separately divulge the financial results separately for English-language and French-language conventional services.

17 In 2007, the CRTC approved the sale of the CHUM television stations to CTVglobemedia and Rogers Communications.

18 Unfortunately, data on ownership concentration were not made available in the same format for 2007. See CRTC, *Communications Monitoring Report 2008.*

5 The Canadian Radio-television and Telecommunications Commission (CRTC)

Canadian broadcasting policy is a responsibility of the Government of Canada, but the federal government has delegated considerable authority to the independently constituted regulatory agency, the Canadian Radio-television and Telecommunications Commission (CRTC). The broadcasting mandate of the CRTC is set out in the Broadcasting Act of 1991 and includes the authority to regulate and supervise all aspects of the Canadian broadcasting system. In delegating such wide powers to the Commission, the government has effectively delegated considerable policymaking powers to the Commission as well.

The CRTC's Relationship with the Government of Canada

The Canadian Parliament is the ultimate decision-maker regarding broadcasting policy in Canada. Through committees of the House of Commons and the Senate, Parliament reviews the general performance of the broadcasting industry and makes recommendations for legislation and legislative amendments. From time to time, these recommendations result in changes to the Broadcasting Act that set out the powers of the CRTC in regard to broadcasting.

On behalf of Parliament, the Department of Canadian Heritage formulates policies, proposes legislation, and designs programs to further the development of Canadian broadcasting and ultimately Canadian society. Canadian Heritage advises Parliament on broadcast regulatory issues, including the Canadian content available from broadcast services, the public's access to broadcast services, and the extent of competition among broadcasting undertakings. Canadian Heritage also advises the Minister of Canadian Heritage on government policy regarding the national public broadcaster, the Canadian Broadcasting Corporation (CBC), private television and radio stations, pay and specialty services, broadcasting distribution services (cable and satellite services), and the CRTC. In addition, Canadian Heritage develops overall policies and provides funding to organizations such as the Foundation to Assist Canadian Talent on Records (FACTOR), MusicAction, the Canada Media Fund (CMF), and the National Film Board (NFB) to assist in the financing of high-quality Canadian music and television programs (see chapter 8). Finally, in a few cases, the department provides services directly to the public, or to private sector companies, such as those provided by the Canadian Audio-Visual Certification Office (CAVCO) in relation to the certification of Canadian television programs.

In summary, the Canadian government possesses a range of policy instruments to promote its policy objectives in the realm of broadcasting. These include

- The ability to amend the legislation that establishes the framework for Canadian broadcasting, including the Canadian Radio-television and Telecommunications Act and the Broadcasting Act
- The capacity to issue a general policy direction to the CRTC as long as the direction does not affect individual decisions before the Commission
- The power to review an individual decision of the CRTC and set it aside or refer it back to the Commission for reconsideration and public hearing (but not the ability to otherwise modify such a decision)
- The provision of roughly two-thirds of the annual financing of the national public broadcaster (the CBC) that provides a wide range of radio and television services
- The power to nominate Canadians as members of the CRTC and to the Boards of Directors of the CBC and the Canada Media Fund
- The capacity to influence the nature of Canadian radio and television programming through the direct financing or subsidization of individual musical productions and programs via funding institutions and television production tax credits
- The ability to influence the definition of a Canadian program through the CAVCO

In addition to the Department of Canadian Heritage and the CRTC, the federal government agencies and institutions that may influence broadcasting policy directly include

- The Department of Industry, which is responsible for the management of Canada's radio spectrum (see chapter 1)
- The CBC, which has its mandate and structure set out explicitly in the Broadcasting Act and is therefore able to exercise a degree of autonomy that is not available to other broadcasters (see chapter 7)
- The Copyright Board, which has a mandate to establish the royalties to be paid for the use of copyrighted works entrusted to a collective administration society (see chapter 12)
- The Competition Bureau, which is responsible for the administration and enforcement of the Competition Act in Canada (see chapter 13)[1]
- The Canada Media Fund, a private-public partnership that finances television programs and includes representatives of Canadian Heritage on its Board of Directors (see chapter 8)

Canadian provincial governments also contribute to the development of broadcasting policy by authorizing educational services, such as those of Télé-Québec, TVOntario, and British Columbia's Knowledge Network, and by financing television programs through agencies, such as the Société de développement des entreprises culturelles (SODEC), the Ontario Media Development Corporation (OMDC), and British Columbia Film, among others.

Role of the CRTC

The CRTC is the independent public authority responsible for regulating and supervising Canadian broadcasting and telecommunications. Its governing statutes are the Canadian Radio-television and Telecommunications Act (CRTC Act), the Broadcasting Act, and the Telecommunications Act. The Commission reports to Parliament through the Minister of Canadian Heritage.

Generally speaking, the CRTC Act establishes the structure of the CRTC itself, while the Broadcasting Act sets out the objectives and powers of the Commission with respect to broadcasting. The primary objective of the Commission is to regulate and supervise the Canadian broadcasting system with a view to implementing the broadcasting policy set out in section 3 of the Broadcasting Act.

The CRTC is an administrative tribunal with quasi-judicial powers that behaves somewhat like a court but, in many ways, is less formal. The CRTC Act provides for up to thirteen full-time members and six part-time Commission members, who constitute its governing body. The powers of the CRTC in regard to broadcasting are identified in section 5 of the Broadcasting Act and include the power to license broadcasting undertakings, to review changes of ownership or control, to develop regulatory policies to meet the objectives of the Broadcasting Act, to resolve disputes and complaints, to monitor compliance and industry performance, and to decide on the distribution of foreign broadcasting services in Canada.

The CRTC regulates over two thousand Canadian broadcasters, including those with licences related to AM and FM radio, over-the-air television, pay and specialty television, cable distribution, direct-to-home (DTH) satellite systems, multipoint distribution systems (MDS), subscription television, and pay audio providers.[2] Regulating and supervising the activities of these services is an enormous task. In 2006, for example, the Commission processed 1,290 broadcasting applications, held numerous public hearings, discussions, and forums, issued 775 decisions, and responded to 45,740 requests for information and complaints relating to both broadcasting and telecommunications.

The CRTC's budget for the fiscal year 2008–9 (and for the following two years) was $45.9 million, of which the Commission planned to spend $24.6 million on broadcasting activities and $21.3 million on telecommunications. Licence fees levied by the CRTC on broadcasting and telecommunications licensees finance this budget. For the same year, the Commission planned to operate with a staff of 460 full-time equivalent positions (declining to 435 for 2009–10 and 2010–11), based at its headquarters in Gatineau, Quebec.[3]

Organization of the CRTC

The current structure of the CRTC is set out in the CRTC Act of 1976. In keeping with the CRTC Act, the Commission assumed the powers regarding broadcasting formerly exercised by the Canadian Radio-television Commission under the Broadcasting Act of 1968, and the powers regarding federally regulated telephone and telegraph companies formerly exercised by the Telecommunications Committee of the Canadian Transport Commission. The CRTC Act has since been amended on occasion: in 1991, for example, Bill C-40 modified the maximum number of members who could be appointed to the Commission.

The thirteen full-time and six part-time members of the CRTC are nominated by the Governor-in-Council (the Cabinet) for not more than five years at a time. The Cabinet also designates a chairperson and two vice-chairpersons. This power to nominate the members of the Commission gives the government of the day a certain power over the Commission and a certain ability to influence the Commission's overall strategic direction (see chapter 15). However, once a member of the Commission is nominated, it is relatively difficult to remove the commissioner before the end of his or her term, except for 'just cause.' In this way, the members of the Commission are protected to a large extent from day-to-day political interference, or removal if the government changes.

The chairperson is the chief executive officer (CEO) of the Commission and is responsible for directing and supervising the staff and agenda of the Commission, as well as presiding over meetings of the Commission. A majority of the full-time members, together with a majority of the part-time members, constitute a quorum of the Commission. Although the Commission makes decisions by simple majority vote, the chairperson exercises considerable power through his or her ability to name members of the Commission to public hearing panels, to direct the activities of Commission staff, and to control the CRTC's budget (including the travel budget of everybody at the Commission). In the event of the absence or incapacity of the chairperson, or if the office of chairperson is vacant, the members of the Commission may authorize one of the vice-chairpersons to exercise the powers and perform the duties and functions of the chairperson.

Objects and Powers of the CRTC

Section 5 of the Broadcasting Act sets out the principal objects (i.e., objectives) of the CRTC. The mission or overriding objective of the Commission in relation to broadcasting is established as follows: '5(1) Subject to this Act and the Radiocommunication Act and to any directions to the Commission issued by the Governor in Council under this Act, *the Commission shall regulate and supervise all aspects of the Canadian broadcasting system with a view to implementing the broadcasting policy set out in subsection 3(1) and, in so doing, shall have regard to the regulatory policy set out in subsection (2)'* (emphasis added).

The Commission is responsible for implementing each of the elements in the broadcasting policy set out in section 3(1), the heart of the Broadcasting Act's 'Broadcasting Policy for Canada' (see Appendix A), while paying attention to the 'regulatory policy' set out in section 5(2) of the Act, which is as follows:

The Canadian broadcasting system should be regulated and supervised in a flexible manner that

(a) is readily adaptable to the different characteristics of English and French language broadcasting and to the different conditions under which broadcasting undertakings that provide English or French language programming operate;

(b) takes into account regional needs and concerns;

(c) is readily adaptable to scientific and technological change;

(d) facilitates the provision of broadcasting to Canadians;

(e) facilitates the provision of Canadian programs to Canadians;

(f) does not inhibit the development of information technologies and their application or the delivery of resultant services to Canadians; and

(g) is sensitive to the administrative burden that, as a consequence of such regulation and supervision, may be imposed on persons carrying on broadcasting undertakings.

Each of these separate policy objectives has equal weight since the legislation does not indicate any order of priority among them. Furthermore, section 5(2) of the Broadcasting Act largely repeats certain elements contained in section 3(1) of the Act so that the essence of the objectives of the Commission is found in section 3(1), 'Broadcasting Policy for Canada.' Once again, there are a variety of objectives in section 3(1) and their relative importance is open to interpretation by the CRTC.

Moreover, sections 5(2)(f) and 5(2)(g) above, which can be interpreted as favouring deregulation, are not found in section 3(1). In other words, although the Commission should not inhibit the development of information technologies and should be sensitive to the administrative burden placed on broadcasting undertakings, these two objectives must be subordinated to the objectives found in section 3(1) of the Broadcasting Policy for Canada.

According to section 6 of the Broadcasting Act, in implementing its objectives, the CRTC may announce 'policies' in the form of guidelines or statements but these are not binding on the Commission in the course of its subsequent activities. Thus, when the CRTC issues, amends, renews, or revokes a broadcasting licence, it may contradict previous Commission policies and decisions without being held legally accountable. The principles of case law do not apply. In other words, although the CRTC aims to be consistent with its own policies and decisions, and usually is, it is not bound by the doctrine of precedents. This provision avoids a situation where the Commission might find itself in endless litigation over a particular decision because it contravened some obscure policy or decision announced years beforehand. It more easily allows the Commission to take specific circumstances into consideration.

Sections 7 and 8 of the Broadcasting Act establish the rules and procedures for policy directions. Provided the Cabinet issues a direction of general application on a broad policy matter to the CRTC, and the policy direction is consistent with these provisions, such a direction is binding on the Commission. In other words, the policy direction must be directed to a group of licensees and not an individual licensee (i.e., be of general application), address a broad policy matter and not a narrow issue, and direct the Commission to apply the policy within the scope of its objectives and powers as set out in the Broadcasting Act. To avoid Cabinet interference in a specific decision of the Commission, no such policy direction from the Cabinet may be made in regard to the issuance of a licence to a particular person or in respect of the amendment, renewal, suspension, or revocation of a particular licence.[4]

For example, in 1995 the federal government directed the CRTC to promote, through licensing, 'a dynamically competitive market for DTH [direct-to-home] distribution undertakings.' The direction set out the general conditions for licensing new DTH distribution undertakings and directed the CRTC to call, immediately on the coming into force of the Order, for 'licence applications to carry on DTH distribution undertakings and, thereafter, to complete the licensing process in respect of those applications at the earliest time practicable and, in the absence of the most compelling of circumstances, not later than November 1, 1995.' Further to this policy direction, the CRTC called for DTH licence applications, held a hearing, and issued decisions on 20 December 1995 (see Public Notice CRTC 1995-217, 'Introductory Statement: Licensing of New Direct-to-Home [DTH] Satellite Distribution Undertakings, and New DTH Pay-per-View [PPV] Television Programming Undertakings').

Sections 9 through 17 of the Broadcasting Act set out the powers of the CRTC that, according to section 9(1), include powers to

(a) establish classes of licences;

(b) issue licences for such terms not exceeding seven years and subject to such conditions related to the circumstances of the licensee

    (i) as the Commission deems appropriate for the implementation of the broadcasting policy set out in subsection 3(1), and

    (ii) in the case of licences issued to the Corporation, as the Commission deems consistent with the provision, through the Corporation, of the programming contemplated by paragraphs 3(1)(l) and (m);

(c) amend any condition of a licence on application of the licensee or, where five years have expired since the issuance or renewal of the licence, on the Commission's own motion;

(d) issue renewals of licences for such terms not exceeding seven years and subject to such conditions as comply with paragraph (b);

(e) suspend or revoke any licence;

(f) require any licensee to obtain the approval of the Commission before entering into any contract with a telecommunications common carrier for the distribution of programming directly to the public using the facilities of that common carrier;

(g) require any licensee who is authorized to carry on a distribution undertaking to give priority to the carriage of broadcasting; and

(h) require any licensee who is authorized to carry on a distribution undertaking to carry, on such terms and conditions as the Commission deems appropriate, programming services specified by the Commission.

Section 9(4) grants to the Commission the authority to exempt persons from Part II of the Broadcasting Act, 'where the Commission is satisfied that compliance with those requirements will not contribute in a material manner to the implementation of the broadcasting policy set out in subsection 3(1).' With this power, the Commission has exempted from regulation new media undertakings and certain mobile devices (see chapter 10).

Regulations

Much like many other legislative acts in their respective domains, the Broadcasting Act sets out a framework for broadcasting regulation in very general terms and leaves the details of broadcasting regulation to regulations and policies. In this way, the CRTC possesses a degree of autonomy in interpreting the Broadcasting Act and is not required to submit each change in regulatory detail to the House of Commons and the entire legislative process. Specifically, section 10(1) of the Broadcasting Act enables the CRTC to make regulations in regard to the following:

(a) The proportion of time devoted to the broadcasting of Canadian programs;
(b) What constitutes a Canadian program for the purposes of the Act;
(c) Standards for programs broadcast and the allocation of broadcasting time for the purpose of giving effect to the broadcasting policy set out in the Act;
(d) The character of advertising and the amount of broadcasting time that may be devoted to advertising;
(e) The time that may be devoted to the broadcasting of programs, including advertisements or announcements of a partisan political nature and the assignment of that time to political parties and candidates;
(f) The conditions for the operation of programming undertakings as part of a network and for the broadcasting of network programs;
(g) The carriage of any foreign or other programming services by distribution undertakings;
(h) The resolving of any disputes arising between programming undertakings and distribution undertakings concerning the carriage of programming originated by the programming undertakings;
(i) The submission to the Commission of such information regarding licensees' programs and financial affairs as the regulations may specify;
(j) The audit or examination of the records and books of account of licensees by persons acting on behalf of the Commission; and
(k) Such other matters as the Commission deems necessary for the furtherance of its objects.

Note that this last provision, section 10(1)(k), is very wide reaching.

Section 10(1) of the Act has permitted the CRTC to establish a distinct but complementary set of regulations in each of the following areas:

- Radio
- Television broadcasting
- Specialty television services
- Pay television
- Broadcasting distribution

- Broadcasting information requirements
- Broadcasting licence fees

These regulations may be applicable to a particular class of licences, such as broadcasting distribution undertakings, or they may be applicable to all licensees. A licensee or a person who contravenes or fails to comply with a regulation is guilty of an offence punishable on summary conviction by a court of law. Either the court can impose a fine as set out in section 32 of the Act or the CRTC can suspend or revoke the licence of the offending party as set out in section 24.

Before the Commission adopts new regulations or modifies existing regulations, it must publicize its proposal and provide a reasonable opportunity to licensees and other interested parties to make representations on the proposal. In practice, this usually involves a public hearing.

Public Hearings

The CRTC makes extensive use of public hearings to obtain the opinions of interested Canadians, including licensees and the various industry associations, on matters under the Commission's jurisdiction. In fact, the Broadcasting Act requires the Commission to hold a public hearing regarding the issue of a licence (other than a licence for a temporary network operation) and the suspension or revocation of a licence. At its discretion, the Commission can hold public hearings related to the amendment or renewal of licences, ownership transfers, complaints, and policy issues.

Public hearings are conducted by panels, named by the chairperson, each consisting of no fewer than three members of the Commission, at least two of whom must be full-time members. Such a panel may deal with, hear, and determine any matter on behalf of the Commission. Subject to certain procedural requirements, a decision of a majority of the members of a panel constitutes a decision of the Commission.

Role of Interest Groups in Decision Making

The CRTC's public hearings provide an opportunity for extensive public input into the Commission's decision making. At the Commission's public hearings on policy issues, and major decisions such as network licence renewals and large ownership transfers, a variety of industry players make their voices heard. These include industry associations, such as the Canadian Association of Broadcasters; television and film production associations such as the Canadian Film and Television Production Association and the Association des producteurs de film et de télévision du Québec; craft guilds, such as the Directors Guild of Canada, the Writers Guild of Canada, the Alliance of Canadian Cinema, Television and Radio Artists, the Société des auteurs de radio, télévision et cinéma, and the Union des Artistes; media unions, such as the Communications, Energy and Paperworkers Union of Canada and the Fédération nationale des communications; and special interest groups, such as the Canadian Conference of the Arts and the Friends of Canadian Broadcasting.

Although individual citizens may contribute, if they do so, it is usually during the written phase of a hearing. The more important oral phase of public hearings tends to be dominated by large media companies that possess broadcast licences, national industry associations, trade union federations, and other organizations that are relatively well funded. Smaller localized interest groups, particularly those from outlying regions, generally find that the specialized knowledge required to participate in the oral phase of the Commission's public hearings is beyond their means. In addition, they do not have the financial means to cover the travel expenses associated with the Commission's policy hearings, which are usually held in the National Capital Region.[5]

Within the framework of its legislative mandate, the CRTC strives to make the most enlightened decisions possible with the information at its disposal. This said, several problems arise in the search for optimal policy and licensing decisions:

- The Commission's licensees often possess specialized knowledge, including knowledge of their operations, that is not available to third parties.
- Those with the most financial resources at their disposal, including the large media companies and industry associations, are often able to hire the most competent policy advice and lobbying capacity.
- The Commission considers broadcasting programming and distribution licensees as its primary 'clients' so that its decisions and policies tend to be strongly influenced by them.

Decisions

The powers of the CRTC are very broad and include the ability to issue licences for up to seven years, subject to conditions related to the circumstances of the licensee, to amend conditions of licences, to renew, to suspend, or to revoke licences, to require distribution undertakings to give priority to the carriage of designated broadcasting services, and to require such undertakings to carry specific programming services identified by the Commission.

The CRTC may also exempt licensees from any or all of the requirements of certain parts of the Broadcasting Act or the Commission's own regulations, as long as it is satisfied that such an exemption will not inhibit the implementation of the broadcasting policy set out in section 3 of the Act. For instance, an exemption has been accorded by the CRTC to new media activities on the Internet, even though many Internet activities appear to fall within the definition of *broadcasting* contained in the Broadcasting Act. This exemption is discussed further in chapter 12.

A CRTC broadcasting decision bears a decision number that indicates the year and the chronological order in which the decision was issued (for example, Broadcasting Decision CRTC 2007-429). Typically, the decision discusses the background to the process leading up to the decision, summarizes any interventions from third parties, identifies the issues facing the Commission in arriving at the decision, summarizes the Commission's determination with respect to such issues, announces the Commission's decision, and attaches in an appendix any conditions that must be fulfilled in the course of exercising the authority granted by the decision.

In a decision, the Commission often identifies its objectives in the form of (in descending order of importance) conditions of licence, expectations, encouragements, and notes related to issues raised in the course of the decision. A licensee who contravenes or fails to comply with a condition of licence is guilty of an offence punishable on summary conviction under section 33 of the Act. Furthermore, subject to a public hearing on the issue, the Commission may suspend or revoke the licence of someone who has contravened or failed to comply with a condition of licence set by the Commission. This ability to suspend or revoke a licence does not apply to the contravention of expectations, encouragements, and other notes identified in a decision.

Appeals

If the CRTC makes a decision to issue, amend, or renew a licence, it is possible to appeal the decision to the federal Cabinet, although not if the Commission's decision involves the denial of a new licence. For example, if someone believes a licence should not have been issued to a Canadian broadcast service that proposes to use a non-Canadian satellite carrier, then that person might file an appeal to the Cabinet. Pursuant to a petition within forty-five days after the date of a CRTC decision, or on its own initiative, the Cabinet may set aside a decision or refer the decision back to the CRTC for reconsideration and hearing by the Commission. To do so, the Cabinet must be satisfied that the decision derogates from the attainment of the objectives of the broadcasting policy set out in section 3 of the Broadcasting Act. Although it can set aside a Commission decision, the Cabinet cannot otherwise modify a decision or award a licence to another party in the course of such an appeal. In other words, the ability to issue or modify broadcasting licences is limited to the CRTC.

Another forum for appeal of a CRTC decision is the Federal Court of Appeal. An appeal from a decision or order of the Commission to the Federal Court of Appeal must be based on a question of law or a question of jurisdiction, and the process must be initiated within one month of the public release of the decision or order. In such a case, if the Court agrees to hear the appeal, it will address only whether the Commission has exceeded the jurisdiction granted to it by Parliament and whether the Commission failed to use appropriate administrative procedures involved in the determination of the decision.

In essence, if a party feels that the CRTC has erred on a policy issue, then the appropriate route for appeal is by way of a request to the Cabinet to set aside or refer the decision back to the Commission for reconsideration. If a party feels that the Commission has significantly breached its own Rules of Procedure or a point of administrative law in arriving at a decision, then the appropriate route for appeal is to the Federal Court of Appeal.

Generally speaking, licensees are reluctant to appeal CRTC decisions to the Cabinet or the Federal Court of Appeal. Such appeals irritate the CRTC, with whom many licensees must collaborate on other issues, and the Cabinet appears to be reluctant to uphold the appeal of CRTC decisions so as to avoid the appearance of encouraging such appeals. To provide further insight into the CRTC's licensing, appeal, and licence revocation process, what follows is a case study of a recent appeal to the Federal Court of Appeal involving the refusal by the Commission to renew the licence of radio station CHOI-FM Québec in 2004. Such a radical sanction by the CRTC is a rare occurrence.

Case Study: Revocation of CHOI-FM Québec's Licence

The CRTC authorized Genex Communications inc. (Genex) to acquire the assets of the French-language radio station CHOI-FM Québec, formerly owned by Les Entreprises de Radiodiffusion de la Capitale inc., in Decision CRTC 97-86. In the same decision, the Commission granted Genex an initial broadcasting licence for CHOI-FM that expired on 31 August 2002.

Between 1999 and 2001, the CRTC received forty-seven complaints related to the programming broadcast by CHOI-FM. The Commission later divided these complaints into three main categories:

• Offensive spoken remarks or language
• Offensive on-air contests
• Personal attacks and harassment

The CRTC gave Genex the opportunity to respond to each of the complaints examined by the Commission, and told Genex the complaints might be the subject of further Commission analysis in the light of CHOI-FM's condition of licence relating to the Sex-Role Portrayal Code for Television and Radio Programming, and the Radio Regulations, 1986.

Between 1999 and 2001, the Commission also conducted four analyses of the station's programming. The results of each analysis were provided to the licensee, who was given an opportunity to comment on these results. All four of the analyses indicated non-compliance with the Radio Regulations that set out minimum levels for the broadcasting of French-language vocal music. In addition, an analysis of the CHOI-FM's programming during one week in July 2000 revealed that the station's logger tapes were incomplete, contrary to the Radio Regulations that require licensees to maintain logger tapes of all programming broadcast and to furnish such tapes to the Commission on request.

In Notice of Public Hearing CRTC 2001-14, the Commission called Genex to appear at a public hearing in Quebec City in February 2002 to discuss the licence renewal application for CHOI-FM. The Commission stated that it wished to discuss the licensee's apparent non-compliance with the Radio Regulations concerning the required percentages of French-language vocal music and the provision of logger tapes. In view of the number of complaints, the Commission said that it also wished to discuss with Genex the spoken word content and the quality of CHOI-FM's programming in light of section 3(1)(g) of the Broadcasting Act, which declares that 'the programming originated by broadcasting undertakings should be of high standard.' The Commission said it expected Genex to give reasons, at the hearing, why an order should not be issued compelling it to comply with the Radio Regulations.

Following the public hearing in 2002, the Commission issued Broadcasting Decision CRTC 2002-189, Short-Term Licence Renewal for CHOI-FM, in July 2002. This decision renewed CHOI-FM's licence for only two years (instead of the usual seven years) as a result of the licensee's repeated failure to comply with the Radio Regulations on abusive comment, the submission of logger tapes, the broadcast of French-language vocal music, and the condition of its licence related to sex-role portrayal. The Commission also noted Genex's failure to meet the objective that programming be of high standard as set out in section 3 of the Broadcasting Act. The Commission's decision to renew CHOI-FM's licence for two years beginning in September 2002 instead of the usual seven years effectively imposed a penalty on Genex by requiring it to reappear before the Commission about a year and a half later to renew CHOI-FM's licence once again.

In Broadcasting Notice of Public Hearing CRTC 2003-11, regarding CHOI-FM's subsequent application for licence renewal to begin in September 2004, the Commission noted the apparent failure of the licensee, on several occasions, to comply with provisions of CHOI-FM's own Code of Ethics. The Commission also noted the apparent failure of the licensee to comply with section 3 of the Radio Regulations. The CRTC therefore directed Genex to appear at a public hearing in Quebec City, and said,

> The Commission expects the licensee to show cause at this hearing why a mandatory order under section 12 of the *Broadcasting Act* (the Act) requiring the licensee to conform to the Regulations and to the condition of licence that requires the licensee to comply with the CHOI-FM Code of Ethics should not be issued.
>
> The Commission also expects the licensee to demonstrate at this hearing why the Commission should not suspend or refuse to renew the licence under sections 24 and 9, respectively of the Act.

After the public hearing, in Broadcasting Decision CRTC 2004-271 of 13 July 2004, the CRTC concluded that 'in view of the licensee's inflexible behaviour, its lack of acceptance of its responsibilities and the lack of any demonstrated commitment to rectify the situation,' Genex would not comply with the Act, the regulations, and its code of ethics, if its licence were renewed. The CRTC also concluded that the measures available to the Commission, such as another short-term renewal, the issuance of a mandatory order, or the suspension of the licence, would not overcome the problems identified. Consequently, the CRTC denied Genex's application for renewal of the CHOI-FM licence and said that CHOI-FM must cease broadcasting by 31 August 2004.

Revocation of a broadcasting licence has been resorted to on only very rare occasions and this was therefore a unusual action for the CRTC to take. Arguably, the Commission's powers of enforcement would be more complete if it were given the power to impose appropriate monetary penalties. In other words, the Commission should be able to fine a broadcaster for infractions, proportionate to the offence. At the present time, the only penalties the CRTC can impose are either relatively modest (a short-term renewal) or relatively severe (non-renewal).

According to newspaper reports, the Commission's decision concerning CHOI-FM unleashed a wave of protests. 'Fifty thousand protesters marched in the streets of Quebec City, and 7,000 took the five-hour bus ride to Ottawa and withstood a rain shower to demonstrate on Parliament Hill,' said the *New York Times*.[6] Most of the protesters supported the most controversial CHOI-FM shock jock – Jean-François (Jeff) Fillion – and called for the Commission to reverse its decision.

Following a request by Genex, the Federal Court of Appeal issued an order to the CRTC on 26 August 2004 to stay the Commission's call for applications for a broadcasting licence in Quebec City, with regard to any application to use the frequency 98.1 MHz (CHOI-FM's frequency). The stay was applicable until the Court's final judgement on the merits of Genex's appeal of the Commission's Decision 2004-271 denying CHOI-FM's licence renewal.

On 17 March 2005, Jeff Fillion abruptly left the airwaves occupied by CHOI-FM, reportedly by mutual agreement with Genex. Less than a month later, on 11 April 2005, a decision of the Quebec Superior Court awarded the former weathercaster Sophie Chiasson $340,000 in damages to be paid by Fillion, his co-hosts, and Genex for the abusive and sexist comments made on air by Fillion about her. Genex said it would appeal this decision but, in the meantime, press coverage indicated that an element of public opinion that had thereto tolerated CHOI-FM's behaviour turned against the station in the course of the Chiasson trial.

On 1 September 2005, the Federal Court of Appeal dismissed Genex's appeal after considering two basic issues: (1) Did the CRTC render an unlawful decision or err in law when it refused to renew the broadcasting licence of the French-language commercial radio station CHOI-FM, owned by Genex? (2) Did the CRTC, in making its decision, fail to comply with the principles of natural justice, the rules of procedural fairness, and its own rules of procedure?

According to the Court, Genex did not demonstrate that the CRTC failed to judicially exercise its discretion on renewal of licences. Genex 'was unable to establish a breach of the principles of natural justice, the standards of procedural fairness and the CRTC's own rules of procedure which would amount to an error of law warranting our intervention. It was also unable to demonstrate a jurisdictional error or such material error in law as would make decision 271 on non-renewal [Broadcasting Decision CRTC 2004-271] unreasonable and require that it be set aside,' said the Court.[7]

On 31 October 2005 Genex filed an appeal of the Federal Court's decision to the Supreme Court of Canada. On 14 June 2007, the Supreme Court dismissed the application for leave to appeal with costs to the respondent, the attorney general of Canada.

Before the Supreme Court responded to the appeal, Radio Nord Communications inc. (now called RNC MEDIA inc.) agreed to purchase CHOI-FM's equipment and other assets from Genex for $9 million and, in May 2006, Radio Nord filed an application with the CRTC for a new broadcasting licence to carry on a French-language FM radio programming undertaking in Quebec City, with a view to continuing the operation of radio station CHOI-FM on the 98.1 MHz frequency. In October 2006, in Broadcasting Decision CRTC 2006-600, the Commission approved Radio Nord's application.

Notes

1 The purpose of the Competition Act is to maintain and encourage competition in Canada in order to promote the efficiency and adaptability of the Canadian economy, to ensure that small and medium-sized enterprises have an equitable opportunity to participate in the Canadian economy, and to provide consumers with competitive prices and product choices. See chap. 13.
2 The Commission also regulates over eighty telecommunications carriers.

3 CRTC, *2008–2009 Estimates*.
4 As discussed further below, the Cabinet may also hear appeals of a particular CRTC decision and set a decision aside or refer it back to the commission for reconsideration and hearing, either pursuant to an appeal or on its own initiative.
5 The commission is trying to address this problem by increasing its use of tele-conferencing but an appearance by tele-conference is not a perfect substitute for actually appearing at an oral hearing.
6 Krauss, 'Bad Mouth or Free Mouth.'
7 http://decisions.fca-caf.gc.ca/en/2005/2005fca283/2005fca283.html.

6 Canadian Content Requirements

Making Canadian content available to Canadians is a cornerstone, some would say the raison d'être, of the Broadcasting Act. Historically, the development of Canadian broadcasting policy has focused primarily on ensuring the availability of Canadian content within the broadcasting system. Today, the intent of government policy is also to maintain access to a diversity of voices and to ensure that Canadian views are well represented. Considering Canada's relatively open borders and close proximity to the United States, the CRTC's requirements for Canadian programming are designed to safeguard and strengthen Canadian cultural diversity while respecting individual freedom of choice.

Section 3(1) of the Broadcasting Act sets out very general requirements for Canadian programming that include the following objectives:

(e) each element of the Canadian broadcasting system shall contribute *in an appropriate manner* to the creation and presentation of Canadian programming;

(f) each broadcasting undertaking shall make maximum use, and *in no case less than predominant use*, of Canadian creative and other resources in the creation and presentation of programming, *unless* the nature of the service provided by the undertaking, such as specialized content or format or the use of languages other than French and English, renders that use impracticable, in which case the undertaking shall make the greatest practicable use of those resources; [Emphasis added]

Section 3(1)(e) of the Broadcasting Act effectively says that each element must contribute to the creation and presentation of Canadian content but that this contribution may differ from one licensee to another and need not be the same for all. Section 3(1)(f) of the Act goes further and requires each licensee to make 'predominant' use of Canadian content (i.e., devote more than 50 per cent of its programming resources to Canadian resources) except where the nature of the service makes this impractical. As a result, the CRTC requires over-the-air television broadcasters to devote at least 60 per cent of their total schedules from 6 a.m. to midnight to Canadian programs but allows many specialty and pay television services to devote less than 50 per cent of their program schedules to Canadian content – presumably because it believes such a requirement would be 'impracticable.'

This said, the Broadcasting Act does not contain a definition of what constitutes 'Canadian creative resources,' 'Canadian programming,' or a 'Canadian program.' The definition of these concepts has been left to the discretion of the CRTC.

To fulfil the objectives of the Broadcasting Act, the CRTC has established requirements to ensure the development and presence of Canadian content within the broadcasting system. These typically take the form of

- Regulations that apply to entire classes or broad categories of licences
- Conditions of licence that represent binding obligations on individual licensees
- Expectations, encouragements, and notes recorded by the CRTC in licensing decisions related to individual licensees' specific commitments
- Policies of a more general nature that reflect the Commission's overall strategy

These requirements have been developed over the last forty years and have come to be known and largely accepted, sometimes grudgingly, by radio, television, and distribution undertakings. When a licence to operate a broadcast service is granted or renewed, the licensee essentially enters into a form of contractual agreement with the CRTC whereby it agrees to abide by the Commission's requirements, including its Canadian content requirements, in return for the privilege of holding the licence. If the licensee does not respect its agreement with the CRTC, the Commission may impose certain sanctions, including more onerous conditions of licence and a reduced licence term or, in more extreme cases, may call the licensee to a hearing and suspend or revoke its licence. These latter, rather draconian measures are rarely applied but, as we saw in chapter 5 with regard to CHOI-FM in Quebec City, the revocation or non-renewal of a broadcast licence can occur.

The CRTC has established Canadian content requirements for

- The financing of Canadian television programs and Canadian talent
- The development and production of high quality Canadian radio and television programs and music
- The broadcast of a minimum number of Canadian programs and music on radio and television
- The provision of Canadian programming services by Canadian distribution undertakings

In this chapter, we will examine the CRTC's Canadian content requirements for radio, television, and distribution undertakings. A résumé of Canadian program and expenditure requirements is set out in Appendix D later in this book. The financing of Canadian programs is addressed in chapter 8. In addition to the CRTC's requirements, the Government of Canada has established certain rules with respect to the Canadian ownership and control of broadcasting licences. These rules are discussed in chapter 13.

Requirements for Radio

Canadian radio stations are licensed in one of several distinct categories or 'classes' of licence and each has somewhat different Canadian content requirements. The main categories are:

- Commercial stations
- Not-for-profit stations
- Campus stations
- Community stations
- Native stations
- Ethnic stations
- Stations owned and operated by the CBC

Radio programs are divided into different 'content categories' for which Canadian or 'local' requirements also differ. These content categories are:

- Category 1: Spoken Word (e.g., news and open-line programs)
- Category 2: Popular Music (e.g., pop, rock, dance, easy listening)
- Category 3: Special Interest Music (e.g., concert, world beat, jazz, blues)
- Category 4: Musical Production (e.g., musical themes and bridges)
- Category 5: Advertising (e.g., commercial announcements)

The Spoken Word content of most radio stations is 'local,' rather than imported from non-Canadian sources, and therefore assumed to be Canadian. With this in mind, the CRTC's primary approach to ensuring the availability of Canadian content on radio has been to require stations to play specific minimum levels of Canadian music. The Commission's intention is not to restrict unnecessarily Canadian radio stations in what they wish to air, but rather to ensure that Canadian radio listeners have access to a wide variety of musical alternatives that includes Canadian music. As a result, historically, radio has played an important part in promoting Canadian artists and Canadian music. Indeed, the success of Canadian music at home and abroad is attributable, in part, to the encouragement of Canadian talent through the CRTC's music requirements for Canadian commercial radio.[1] The Commission also requires broadcasters to make annual contributions toward the development of Canadian music talent.

How much airtime must be dedicated to Canadian songs on licensed Canadian radio stations?

- All radio stations must ensure that 35 per cent of their Popular Music (Category 2) selections are Canadian each week.
- Commercial radio stations must ensure that 35 per cent of the musical selections aired between 6 a.m. and 6 p.m., Monday through Friday, are Canadian.
- In addition, at least 25 per cent of the musical selections from subcategory 31 (Concert Music) and at least 20 per cent of subcategory 34 selections (Jazz and Blues) aired during each broadcast week by commercial radio stations must be Canadian.[2]
- Ethnic radio stations must ensure that at least 7 per cent of the musical selections they air each week during ethnic programming periods are Canadian.

The CRTC's Radio Regulations also require that Canadian selections be reasonably distributed throughout the broadcast day to ensure that

Canadian music selections are played during periods of high listening and not just in low listening periods. Canadian commercial radio's recent success in fulfilling the CRTC's requirements is indicated in table 4.1.

French-language radio stations must ensure that at least 65 per cent of the popular vocal music selections broadcast each week are in the French language. As well, at least 55 per cent of the popular vocal music selections broadcast between 6 a.m. and 6 p.m., Monday through Friday, must be in the French language.

Definition of Canadian Music

What distinguishes 'Canadian' music as opposed to any other country's music? How does the CRTC distinguish between a Canadian and a non-Canadian musical selection?

Four elements, called the MAPL system, determine whether or not a song qualifies as Canadian. The MAPL system refers to the four elements in the Radio Regulations used to qualify musical selections as Canadian as determined by the CRTC in the course of a long public hearing process. The MAPL system is designed to assist the development of all aspects of the Canadian music industry while remaining sufficiently simple for the radio industry to implement and for the Commission to monitor.

The primary objective of the MAPL system, which is cultural, is to encourage increased exposure of Canadian musical performers, lyricists, and composers to Canadian audiences. The secondary objective, an industrial objective, is to strengthen the Canadian music industry, including both its creative and technical components.

How does MAPL system work? To qualify as 'Canadian' a musical selection must generally fulfil at least two of the following conditions:

- **M** (music): the music is composed entirely by a Canadian
- **A** (artist): the music is, or the lyrics are, performed principally by a Canadian
- **P** (production): the musical selection consists of a live performance that is recorded wholly in Canada, or performed wholly in Canada and broadcast live in Canada
- **L** (lyrics): the lyrics are written entirely by a Canadian

In four special cases a musical selection may qualify as Canadian content without necessarily fulfilling the above criteria. For example, if the musical selection was recorded before January 1972 and meets one of the conditions, it will qualify as Canadian.

It should be noted that the MAPL definition of Canadian content is relatively objective and does not rely on an analysis of the content of the music in question. This approach to Canadian content recognition facilitates its application and is the approach adopted by the CRTC for television programs as well.

Requirements for Television

Pursuant to the Broadcasting Act, the CRTC has established a range of Canadian content requirements for television programming undertakings:

- Exhibition requirements for overall levels of Canadian content aired over the broadcast day and in the evening hours
- Spending requirements for overall levels of Canadian content and for particular licensees in particular program categories
- Exhibition requirements for the broadcast of 'priority' Canadian program categories for certain players, such as large multi-station ownership groups
- Incentives for certain program categories of Canadian content, such as 150 per cent time credits

In addition to these requirements, Parliament has set out objectives for the CBC directly in the Broadcasting Act that include the mandate to provide distinctly Canadian radio and television services to Canadians.

The definition of a Canadian program constitutes a fundamental building block in the CRTC's regulatory framework for television. Among other things, the CRTC relies on the definition of a Canadian television program to help determine the role of the classes of television programming undertaking and the volume of Canadian programs each player will contribute to the broadcasting system.

Definition of a Canadian Television Program

Who is to say what is, and what is not, a Canadian television program? The current method of defining Canadian television productions has been developed over more than forty years. During this time, the definition of a Canadian television program has evolved as the demands placed on the definition have changed. Today, the definition of a Canadian program provides a foundation for Canadian television broadcasting (and, in many ways, for the development of the Canadian theatrical feature industry as well). The basic definition of a Canadian program helps to determine how much Canadian programming broadcasters will deliver and how this programming will be financed.

What does the CRTC recognize as a Canadian television program? The CRTC will normally accept any one of the following as Canadian:

- Programs produced in-house by a licensee of the CRTC
- Independently produced programs that satisfy the CRTC's own certification system
- Programs certified by the Canadian Audio-Visual Certification Office (CAVCO), a division of the Department of Canadian Heritage
- Programs produced internally by the National Film Board of Canada (NFB)
- Programs certified pursuant to one of the international co-production treaties negotiated by the Department of Canadian Heritage (and called official co-productions to distinguish them from other kinds of domestic and international co-productions).

Thus the CRTC recognizes a broad range of programs as Canadian, only some of which are formally certified. Essentially, formal certification is reserved for independent productions, including international co-productions among two or more partners.[3]

For independent television and theatrical feature film productions, the Canadian program certification requirements established by CAVCO are essentially the industry benchmark. A central element in CAVCO certification is the use of a points system that recognizes the number of Canadian creative elements in the production (director, screenwriter, lead performers, production designer, director of photography, music composer. and picture editor.)

To be certified as Canadian by CAVCO, a program (other than a co-production) must achieve six points for creative elements out of a possible ten points. In addition to this requirement, a Canadian producer must control the production and be the principal decision-maker, the Canadian producer must hold world rights to the production for at least twenty-five years, and the Canadian producer must ensure that at least 75 per cent of total production expenses are paid to Canadian production elements. CAVCO certification is necessary for a production to obtain federal or provincial tax credits.

The CRTC's own certification process has been substantially harmonized with that of CAVCO but differences remain. These include the CRTC's recognition of co-ventures (described below) and the absence of any CRTC requirements with respect to copyright and distribution rights in the Commission's definition of a Canadian program.[4]

As with the MAPL system for recognizing Canadian music, one of the main characteristics and advantages of both the CAVCO and the CRTC approach to certification is its relatively objective nature resulting from the use of quantitative measures of Canadian production elements. This quantitative approach does not involve an analysis of scripts or of program content that would require a more subjective, discretionary, or qualitative evaluation. Administration of the CAVCO and CRTC certification processes is therefore comparatively straightforward and does not require highly sophisticated analysis (except in unusual circumstances), and the result is not usually disputed (except insofar as the certification criteria themselves are ambiguous).

CAVCO's definition of a Canadian production is probably the most rigorous of the certification processes identified above and essentially provides a floor on which other elements in the Canadian broadcasting system depend. However, the CAVCO process is used primarily to determine eligibility for the Canadian Film or Video Production Tax Credit. Independently produced information, sports, and game shows, among others, are not eligible for this tax credit and producers of these programs seldom seek CAVCO certification because of the administrative burden that accompanies the processing of a CAVCO application. Independent producers of such programs normally seek CRTC certification instead.

Programs produced internally by Canadian broadcast licensees (information, sports, some entertainment programs, promotional programming and interstitials) and programs produced by the NFB almost always exceed the minimum requirements established by CAVCO and the CRTC. These types of program receive Canadian content recognition without formal certification.

Table 6.1 indicates the relative importance of in-house production and independent production in 2007–8.

There are at least two ways for producers to bypass some of the rules established by CAVCO, including the basic six-point requirement, and obtain Canadian certification with fewer Canadian production elements than CAVCO or the CRTC would ordinarily allow:

TABLE 6.1 Volume of qualifying Canadian television production, 2007–8

	$ millions	%
Programs produced in-house by a licensee of the CRTC	1,155	36.2
Programs certified by CAVCO or the CRTC	2,032	63.8
TOTAL	3,187	100.0

Source: Canadian Film and Television Production Association, 09 Profile

- Certification as a CRTC co-venture
- Certification as an official international co-production

For the CRTC, a co-venture is a co-production with a non-Canadian partner that does not fulfil the requirements of the official co-production treaties. Such co-ventures qualify for certification as Canadian by the CRTC even though they do not meet CAVCO's requirements for the Canadian producer's control of the production (and are therefore not eligible for tax credits).

For instance, Canadian co-ventures destined for U.S. television services may require a U.S. co-producer as a condition imposed by the U.S. partner. As long as the Canadian producer controls at least 50 per cent of the total budget, and the production meets the CRTC's other certification criteria, this kind of co-venture will be certified as Canadian by the Commission. A co-venture involving a co-producer from a commonwealth or French-speaking country may also be certified as Canadian even though the program attains only five points (instead of six) and 50 per cent (instead of 75 per cent) of service and post-production costs are paid to Canadians.

The Government of Canada has negotiated international co-production treaties that target both industrial and foreign policy objectives, with approximately fifty-five countries over the last four decades. As a result of the ad hoc nature of the negotiations conducted by Canadian Heritage, and despite Telefilm Canada's efforts to introduce common policies in the administration of the co-production treaties, the treaties tend to differ from one to the next. Although a program that is certified as an official Canadian co-production must have a Canadian producer or co-producer, the point system for Canadian productions does not necessarily apply and, in some cases, the value of Canadian production elements can contribute as little as 10 per cent of the total value of all production elements, and the co-production may still qualify as Canadian. The value of Canadian production elements can even fall to zero in the special case of 'twinning' a foreign production with an all-Canadian production. If Canadian Heritage certifies a program as an official co-production, it is recognized as a Canadian program by the CRTC.

The net result of the CRTC's overall Canadian content recognition process is to identify a broad range of programs that contribute to the objectives of the Broadcasting Act – with a minimum of administrative burden. A second result of the recognition process, formal certification, contributes to the determination of eligibility for financial assistance provided by Canadian governments (see chapter 8).

However, the CRTC recognition process, including formal certification, does not, and is not intended to, distinguish between industrial-type programs and more culturally distinct Canadian programs, or between inexpensive game shows and high-quality drama. Instead, the various government agencies, including the CRTC and the government funding institutions, establish their own incentives and criteria to accomplish policy objectives in such areas. These incentives and criteria supplement the recognition process for a Canadian production and target the Canadian government's more cultural objectives.

Exhibition and Spending Requirements for Television

The CRTC has established separate exhibition and spending requirements for recognized Canadian programs for conventional, specialty, and pay television services.

The Television Broadcasting Regulations require private sector conventional television stations and networks to devote 60 per cent of their programming between 6 a.m. and midnight to Canadian programs and 50 per cent in the evening broadcast period between 6 p.m. and midnight. The CBC is required to broadcast 60 per cent in both periods but generally exceeds this percentage by a very wide margin. Conventional television stations and networks are not usually required to fulfil spending requirements. Regulatory requirements for expenditures on Canadian programming by conventional stations and networks were removed by the CRTC effective 1 September 2000.

However, requirements for specialty and pay television services continue and vary from one licensee to the next. Exhibition requirements for specialty, pay, and pay-per-view (discretionary) television services are determined by the CRTC case by case. The Commission's exhibition requirements are based on such considerations as the nature of the service proposed by the applicant, the availability of Canadian programming falling within the designated format, and the applicant's other plans and commitments. The Commission also takes into account the applicant's proposed wholesale distribution fee and the type of carriage that the service would receive. These requirements for discretionary services are set by condition of licence (see Appendix D).

The Commission's exhibition requirements depend on the nature of the service offered and its status as an analogue, Category 1, or Category 2 digital specialty service. The analogue specialty services typically have the highest Canadian content requirements, ranging from 100 per cent to 15 per cent. Category 1 services are required to devote at least 50 per cent of the broadcast year, and of the evening broadcast period, to the exhibition of Canadian programs. The Canadian content obligations for Category 2 services are much lower. Category 2 services are required to devote at least 35 per cent of the broadcast day, and of the evening broadcast period, to the broadcast of Canadian programs by the end of the third year of operation. Each ethnic service is required to ensure that it devotes not less than 15 per cent of the broadcast day, and of the evening broadcast period, to the broadcast of Canadian programs (see Appendix D).

In Broadcasting Public Notice CRTC 2004-2, 'Introduction to Broadcasting Decisions CRTC 2004-6 to 2004-27 Renewing the Licences of 22 Specialty Services,' the Commission adopted a graduated approach to setting Canadian programming expenditure requirements that services licensed in 1996 are required to fulfil. These requirements are based upon the average profitability of each service over the licence term that ended in August 2004.[6] For example, licensees whose historical profitability levels were in the 20 per cent to 24 per cent range are required to increase their minimum annual expenditures on Canadian programming by an increment of three percentage points over the amounts specified in their existing conditions of licence. Increments of four and six percentage points were required of licensees whose historical profitability levels were between 25 per cent and 29 per cent, and 35 per cent and 39 per cent, respectively.

Requirements for 'Priority' Television Programs

On conventional English-language services, Canadian news and sports programs are generally able to cover their costs of production through the sale of advertising in the programs.[7] However, higher cost Canadian entertainment programs (drama, variety, and children's programs as well as long-form documentaries) would not cover their costs without government regulation and subsidies. As a result, these categories of programs are often under-represented in television schedules, particularly during the prime time evening hours on the private sector networks. In their place, the commercial English-language broadcasters generally schedule lower cost programs, including U.S. programs that can also benefit from simultaneous substitution opportunities.[8]

French-language television broadcasting in Canada is different from English-language broadcasting in a number of ways. French-language entertainment programs benefit from a 'star system' that is maintained by the local media, with the result that domestic drama and variety programs are capable of outperforming U.S. programs in many situations. However, even on the French-language side, Canadian point-of-view documentaries and children's programs are a rarity on the private sector conventional (off-air) stations. What is more, with a few exceptions, French-language programs do not travel well outside of Quebec, so their costs must be fully amortized at home. Unlike some English-language programs, only occasionally are French-language television programs able to attract audiences and revenues abroad.

Since the production costs of French-language programs must be amortized entirely in the domestic market, their production values are often more limited, squeezing costs to a lower level than the costs of English-language programs.[9] In French as well as in English, the volume of high-quality entertainment programs that can cover their own costs without government financing is limited. As a result, French-language conventional, specialty, and pay television broadcasters often supplement their schedules with inexpensively acquired U.S. and other foreign programs in the form of drama series, game shows and feature films, original music videos, etc., dubbed into the French language.

To encourage both English- and French-language private sector broadcasters to broadcast programs in the under-represented categories, the CRTC has instituted regulations, conditions of licence, and policies that create a demand for Canadian programs in the under-represented or 'priority' program categories. In other words, the CRTC has designated certain under-represented television program categories as 'priority' programs: these are drama, music and dance, and variety programs, long-form documentary programs, certain regionally produced programs, and Canadian entertainment magazine programs.[10] For example, the largest multi-station groups (CTV, Global, Rogers, and TVA) are currently required to broadcast over the broadcast year, on average, at least eight hours per week of 'priority' Canadian programs during the 7 p.m. to 11 p.m. viewing period. Other conventional broadcasters have lighter 'priority' Canadian program requirements that are set out by condition of licence, case by case.[11] In Broadcasting Notice of Consultation CRTC 2009-411, 'Policy Proceeding on a Group-Based Approach to the Licensing of Television Services and on Certain Issues relating to Conventional Television,' the Commission proposed, for discussion at a public hearing in November 2009, a revised approach to the obligations of multi-station ownership groups, that would take effect 1 September 2010.

The Scheduling and Promotion of Canadian Programs

Once high-quality programs are produced, it is important they be appropriately scheduled and promoted. Apart from the CBC-owned services, the scheduling and promotion of Canadian programs on many English-language television services, particularly in the peak viewing hours, takes second place to U.S. programs.

The scheduling of Canadian programs on English-language television in the peak viewing hours presents a conundrum for Canadian television policymakers, including the CRTC. In order to protect the territorial integrity of Canadian rights to U.S. programs obtained by Canadian broadcasters, the CRTC obliges Canadian broadcasting distribution undertakings to undertake the simultaneous substitution of U.S. programs licensed by Canadian private sector broadcasters. In effect, this allows the creation of multiple distribution channels for the same U.S. program – all containing Canadian advertising spots supplied by the Canadian broadcaster that has requested the substitution. Simultaneous substitution is accompanied by Canadian network promotion of the U.S. programs, and waves of publicity from the U.S. entertainment industry's machinery (*Entertainment Tonight, Access Hollywood, TV Guide*, U.S. magazines sold in Canada, Canadian newspapers, etc.) that cannot be matched for Canadian programs.

In building their program schedules, the major English-language private sector Canadian television networks first fill out their weekly schedule with simulcast U.S. programs that are broadcast in line with U.S. schedules to take advantage of simultaneous substitution opportunities. They then place their weekly Canadian 'priority' programming around the simulcast U.S. programs in the leftover slots of their schedules.

Simultaneous substitution provides important revenue opportunities for Canadian television services that they use, in part, to finance Canadian programs that cannot cover their costs. At the same time, simultaneous substitution often results in the placement of Canadian programs in the less desirable parts of the schedule, especially during prime time. In an environment of second-best scheduling and limited promotion, it is very difficult for Canadian 'priority' programs with their comparatively limited production budgets (e.g., C$1 million per hour for drama) to attract audiences comparable to the high-budget U.S. programs (e.g., C$3–5 million per hour), with their high-profile stars and media promotion, that are aired on Canadian private sector conventional services.

The recent Review of the Regulatory Framework for Broadcasting Services in Canada commissioned by the CRTC and released in August 2007 raises a number of questions about the continued usefulness of simultaneous substitution in pursuing Canadian content objectives. [12]

Has the CRTC's 1999 Television Policy Achieved Its Objectives?

In 1999, the CRTC established certain regulatory measures designed to encourage private sector television broadcasters to air more 'priority' programming in the peak viewing hours,[13] which include

- Exhibition requirements for the broadcast of 'priority' Canadian television program categories for certain players, including eight hours of priority programming per week during the peak viewing period (7 p.m.–11 p.m.) for large multi-station ownership groups
- Incentives related to certain television program categories, such as the 150 per cent time credit for ten-point Canadian drama programs, for selected licensees

These new requirements have been in place since 2000–1 and do not seem to have been successful. Between 2000–1 and 2005–6, in total, the production of original independently produced Canadian programs (i.e., 'priority' programs for the most part) appears to have remained about constant or declined, especially in the drama category. Only in 2006–7 and 2007–8 were there any signs of improvement (see table 6.2).

In the words of Dunbar and Leblanc,

The available data strongly suggests that the existing regulatory incentives and obligations with respect to English language Canadian drama programming are not effective. Snapshots of the schedules for OTA [over-

TABLE 6.2 Volume of Canadian independent television production by category, 1998–9 to 2007–8 ($ millions)

	1998–9	1999–2000	2000–1	2001–2	2002–3	2003–4	2004–5	2005–6	2006–7	2007–8
Fiction	991	1,087	867	876	860	749	832	806	954	933
Children's	368	388	370	358	300	290	280	276	379	250
Documentaries	254	186	260	287	313	374	387	395	481	424
Magazines	71	97	131	145	128	133	143	144	130	156
Variety & arts	73	83	104	111	127	159	125	120	143	149
Other	28	28	33	26	56	24	47	53	90	120
TOTAL	1,785	1,869	1,765	1,785	1,802	1,730	1,814	1,794	2,177	2,032

Source: Canadian Film and Television Production Association, 09 Profile

the-air] stations in specific markets suggest that the amount of Canadian drama that is being broadcast during peak time in the regular season by English language commercial OTA television services is very limited. Priority programming obligations appear to be largely satisfied by the broadcasting of entertainment magazines and reality television programming, and by scheduling priority programming during lower viewing periods, such as Friday and Saturday nights and the summer period.[14]

Distribution Requirements for Canadian Distribution Undertakings

To help ensure that each element of the Canadian broadcasting system contributes to the presentation of Canadian programming as the Broadcasting Act requires, the CRTC requires that broadcasting distribution undertakings, such as cable and satellite systems, include certain Canadian services and give them priority positioning. For example, section 17(1) of the Broadcasting Distribution Regulations stipulates that the channel listing or menu of a Canadian cable distribution undertaking must provide the following Canadian television services and give them priority over non-Canadian television services in the following order:

- The programming services of all local television stations owned and operated by the CBC
- The educational television programming services that are the responsibility of an educational authority designated by the province in which the licensed area of the undertaking is located
- The programming services of all other 'local television stations'[15]
- The programming services of a 'regional television station' owned and operated by the CBC, unless the licensee is already distributing, under paragraph (a), the programming services of a local television station owned and operated by the CBC[16]
- The programming services of all other 'regional television stations,' unless the licensee is distributing, under the provisions above, the programming services of a television station that is an affiliate or member of the same network

Class 1 and Class 2 cable distribution undertakings must distribute the above programming services on the undertaking's basic band of services. The regulations for satellite services are similar but somewhat different.

Furthermore, the CRTC has established certain 'linkage' rules for the provision of Canadian specialty and pay services by Canadian distribution undertakings. For example, the larger (Class 1) cable licensees are required to carry the following services on a 'dual status basis,' that is, as part of the basic service, unless the operator of that service consents to its distribution as a discretionary service. Such 'dual status' services include CBC Newsworld, Vision TV, YTV, MuchMusic, VRAK-TV, MétéoMédia / The Weather Network, TV5, and Le Réseau de l'information (RDI).[17]

Any current discussion of distribution and linkage rules for the provision of Canadian specialty and pay services by distribution undertakings is complicated by the fact that the Canadian broadcasting system is currently in a transitional period.[18] Many of the CRTC's existing distribution and linkage rules will change in the process of the conversion to a predominantly digital environment. See chapter 11 for a fuller discussion of the Commission's distribution carriage arrangements now and in the future.

Notes

1 Bryan Adams, Isabelle Boulay, Céline Dion, les Cowboys Fringants, Angèle Dubois, Angela Hewitt, Diana Krall, k.d. lang, Avril Lavigne, Shania Twain, Rufus Wainwright, et al.

2 For a complete review of commercial radio requirements, see Broadcasting Public Notice CRTC 2006-158, 'Commercial Radio Policy.'

3 Applications for official international co-production status are administered by Telefilm Canada and, if acceptable, certified by Canadian Heritage.

4 See Public Notice CRTC 2000-42, 'Certification for Canadian Programs – A Revised Approach 17 March 2000.'

5 The data in table 6.1 are approximate insofar as they are for two different reporting years ending 31 March 2008 and 31 August 2008. See Canadian Film and Television Production Association, *09 Profile*, 10.

6 The CRTC measures profitability in terms of profits before interest and taxes (PBIT) calculated as a percentage of total revenues, and called the 'PBIT margin.'

7 Canadian news and sports on specialty services are very popular, but it is more difficult to draw general conclusions about the profitability of individual programs on specialty services because they also receive a share of cable and satellite subscriber fees that is determined by the overall subscriber penetration rate of the service. In other words, the total value of any given program on a specialty service is more than simply the advertising revenue that it generates.

8 Simultaneous substitution is a provision in the CRTC's Broadcasting Distribution Regulations that entitles Canadian broadcasters to request cable and satellite distributors to substitute a local signal in place of a distant signal, while the two signals are identical. This provision is widely used by Canadian English-language broadcasters to protect their programs rights within Canada by substituting their version of a U.S. program (including the Canadian advertising in the program) for the version broadcast on a U.S. network and to thereby obtain simultaneously multiple windows and audiences for the advertising in a single program.

9 For example, French-language television makes more use of téléromans (primetime soaps) as well as primetime variety and interview programs than does English-language television.

10 A description of many of these requirements is set out in detail in Public Notice CRTC 1999-97, 'Building on Success – A Policy Framework for Canadian Television, 11 June 1999.'

11 For a more complete description of 'priority programs' and the current obligations of multi-station ownership groups, see ibid.

12 Dunbar and Leblanc, *Final Report*.

13 See Public Notice CRTC 1997-97.

14 Dunbar and Leblanc, *Final Report*, xiii.

15 According to the Television Distribution Regulations, a 'local television station,' in relation to a licensed area of a distribution undertaking, means a licensed television station that has a Grade A official contour that includes any part of the licensed area or, if there is no Grade A official contour, has a transmitting antenna that is located within fifteen km of the licensed area.

16 A 'regional television station,' in relation to a licensed area of a distribution undertaking, means a licensed television station, other than a local television station, that has a Grade B official contour that includes any part of the licensed area.

17 See Broadcasting Public Notices CRTC 2005-45, 'Distribution and Linkage Requirements for Class 1 and Class 2 Licensees,' and Broadcasting Public Notice CRTC 2005-46, 'Linkage Requirements for Direct-to-Home (DTH) Satellite Distribution Undertakings.'

18 See Broadcasting Public Notice CRTC 2006-23, 'Digital Migration Framework,' and Broadcasting Public Notice CRTC 2008-100, 'Regulatory Frameworks for Broadcasting Distribution Undertakings and Discretionary Programming Services.'

7 Public Broadcasting

What is public broadcasting? The term covers a wide variety of activities undertaken by a range of different types of organization. Whereas commercial broadcasting is generally concerned with delivering audiences to advertisers and generating net revenues or profits, public broadcasting is characterized by non-profit objectives, often government ownership, and the provision of some form of broadcast service 'in the public interest.' Public broadcasting constitutes one of the policy instruments that governments use to try to correct some of the market failures generated by a broadcasting system that relies extensively on commercial activities.

A basic problem with public broadcasting is the 'principal-agent' problem. Viewers and listeners (the principals) may not adequately transmit their preferences to the public broadcaster (the agent), with the result that the public broadcaster's management tends to substitute its own preferences for those of the public. Alternatively, governments may try to intervene directly to express the 'will of the people.' In many countries, arm's-length arrangements are devised to limit political interference in editorial functions while retaining some public accountability for use of tax revenues. With regard to cultural issues, public broadcasters sometimes promote 'high' culture, which may result from the capture of the broadcaster by special interests or, alternatively, from the pursuit of cultural diversity or merit programming.

The Canadian Broadcasting Corporation (CBC), the British Broadcasting Corporation (BBC), France 2 and France 3, RAI in Italy, the Australian Broadcasting Corporation (ABC), and the Public Broadcasting System (PBS) in the United States, as well as the Canadian educational broadcasters Télé-Québec, TVOntario, TFO, the Saskatchewan Communications Network (SCN), and the Knowledge Network (Knowledge) in British Columbia are all public broadcasters of one form or another. Some public broadcasters, such as the CBC/Radio-Canada and Télé-Québec, sell commercial advertising in their television programs, and their revenue-seeking strategies at times influence their motives and behaviour. Others, such as the BBC and France Télévisions, do not air commercial advertising.[1] Public broadcasters such as PBS in the United States are non-governmental, non-profit organizations that provide services comparable to that of government-owned public broadcasting services.

In an international study of public broadcasting for the BBC, the consultants, McKinsey & Company, identified three different types of clusters based on public broadcasters' strategy:

- A focus on distinctiveness over market share (e.g., the Australian Broadcasting Corporation and PBS)
- A focus on market share over distinctiveness (e.g., the Italian public broadcaster, RAI)
- Some form of equilibrium between the two[2]

In Canada, recently, it is arguable that CBC English- and French-language television and radio are favouring audience share over distinctiveness.[3] Is this what Parliament intended or Canadians desire? Because the CBC is financed predominantly by government grants paid for by taxpayers, almost every Canadian has an opinion on the mandate and strategies of the CBC.

As described in chapter 2, the CBC was responsible for regulating and supervising all of Canadian broadcasting until the creation of the Board of Broadcast Governors (BBG) in 1958. Even today, the CBC is very different from other Canadian broadcasters, as a result of its place in the history of broadcasting, its designation as a Crown corporation, its mandate as Canada's national public broadcaster, and the fact that its objectives and powers are explicitly set out in the Broadcasting Act. This gives the CBC a special status in its relationship with the broadcast regulator, the CRTC, that no other broadcaster enjoys.

The Mandate of the CBC

The major elements of the CBC's mandate are found in sections 3(1)(l) and (m) of the Broadcasting Act:

(l)   the Canadian Broadcasting Corporation, as the national public
       broadcaster, should provide radio and television services incorpo-
       rating a wide range of programming that informs, enlightens and
       entertains;
(m) the programming provided by the Corporation should
       (i)   be predominantly and distinctively Canadian,
       (ii)   reflect Canada and its regions to national and regional audi-
              ences, while serving the special needs of those regions,
       (iii) actively contribute to the flow and exchange of cultural expres-
              sion,
       (iv)   be in English and in French, reflecting the different needs and
              circumstances of each official language community, including
              the particular needs and circumstances of English and French
              linguistic minorities,
       (v)   strive to be of equivalent quality in English and in French,
       (vi)   contribute to shared national consciousness and identity,
       (vii) be made available throughout Canada by the most appropriate
              and efficient means and as resources become available for the
              purpose, and
       (viii) reflect the multicultural and multiracial nature of Canada;

Section 46(1) (Objects and Powers) of the Broadcasting Act states that
the CBC 'is established for the purpose of providing the programming
contemplated by paragraphs 3(1)(l) and (m).' However, the CBC cannot
interpret this mandate in isolation from the CRTC because section 46(1)
goes on to say that this mandate should be pursued 'in accordance with
the conditions of any licence or licences issued to it by the Commission
and subject to any applicable regulations of the Commission.'
    The mandate for the CBC is distinct from, though certainly comple-
mentary to, the overall objectives set out for the Canadian broadcasting
system as a whole in sections 3(1)(a)–(k) of the Act. What happens if a
conflict arises between the objectives set out for the CBC and the interests of another broadcaster? The Broadcasting Act answers this question in section 3(1)(n): 'Where any conflict arises between the objectives
of the Corporation set out in paragraphs (l) and (m) and the interests
of any other broadcasting undertaking of the Canadian broadcasting
system, it shall be resolved in the public interest, and where the public
interest would be equally served by resolving the conflict in favour of
either, it shall be resolved in favour of the objectives set out in para-

graphs (l) and (m).' In other words, in the event of such a conflict, the public interest and the objectives of the CBC take precedence over the interests of any other broadcaster.

In 2007, the House of Commons Standing Committee on Canadian Heritage conducted a review of the role of the CBC in the Canadian broadcasting environment that resulted in a report in February 2008 entitled *CBC/Radio-Canada: Defining Distinctiveness in the Changing Media Landscape.* The Standing Committee report recommended maintaining the current provisions of the statutory mandate of the CBC/Radio-Canada as set out in sections 3(1)(l) and (m) of the Broadcasting Act, except for adding the role of new media to the existing mandate. However, the committee also recommended the ratification of a seven-year memorandum of understanding between the Government of Canada and CBC/Radio-Canada, setting out the respective responsibilities of the signatories. These would include governance structure, funding over the seven-year duration of the agreement, advertising revenues, regional programming, and partnerships with other broadcasters.[4]

The Organization of the CBC

Not only does the Broadcasting Act contain the CBC's mandate but it also establishes the broad lines of how the Corporation should be organized. Thus Part III of the Act sets out, albeit in very general terms, the CBC's governing structure and how the Corporation should manage its operations.

In a preamble to Part III, section 35(2) specifies that the articles in the Broadcasting Act referring to the CBC should be 'interpreted and applied so as to protect and enhance the freedom of expression and the journalistic, creative and programming independence enjoyed by the Corporation in the pursuit of its objects and in the exercise of its powers.' This can be taken as a form of assurance for the CBC that Parliament intends to respect the arm's-length relationship that federal government agencies are reputed to possess in their relationships with government.

There follow articles that establish the structure and powers of the Board of Directors of the CBC. According to the Broadcasting Act, the Board of Directors should consist of twelve people appointed by the Governor-in-Council, including a chairperson and a president. Each director is appointed to hold office during good behaviour for a term not exceeding five years. A director must be a Canadian citizen and must not be engaged in broadcasting or in the production or distribution of broadcast programming.

The Board of Directors is responsible for the management of the CBC's businesses, activities, and other affairs. Ultimately, the CBC is accountable, through the Minister of Canadian Heritage, to Parliament for the conduct of its affairs. The chairperson of the Board presides at meetings of the Board and performs the duties and functions of the office on a part-time basis. The president of the CBC is the chief executive officer (CEO) of the Corporation and has supervision over and direction of its work and staff.

Under the direction of its president and Board of Directors, the CBC operates two conventional television networks (in English and French), four Canadian radio networks (in English and French), Radio Canada International, and seven specialty services – Newsworld, le Réseau de l'information (RDI), Bold (Country Canada), SportsPlus, Galaxie, the Canadian Documentary Channel (82 per cent ownership), and ARTV (61 per cent ownership). The CBC also holds a 40 per cent participation in the satellite radio operation Sirius Canada.

The English- and French-language activities of CBC Radio and CBC Television are managed by distinct management teams in Toronto and Montreal with oversight from the Corporation's head office in Ottawa. The total revenues for the CBC in 2007–8 amounted to over $1.7 billion, of which about 57 per cent came from parliamentary appropriations, 19 per cent from television advertising and program sales, 9 per cent from specialty service fees, and the remaining 15 per cent from other sources.[5]

The mandate and structure of the CBC outlined in the Broadcasting Act are very general. In concrete terms, how does CBC management fulfil this mandate? Some of the answers to this question are provided by the corporate documents published by the CBC on its website.[6]

In what way do the mandate and structure of the CBC affect what appears in the CBC's schedules? It is of interest to compare the schedules of CBC television with that of other broadcasters across the country. Generally speaking, the CBC's television schedule is dominated heavily by Canadian programs, while English-language private sector stations often place Canadian programs in the periphery of their schedules.[7] For example, in the 2007–8 broadcast year, the CBC said CBC Television aired 80 per cent Canadian programming over the full broadcast day, and 81 per cent in the peak viewing period of 7:00–11:00

p.m. For Radio-Canada, the corresponding shares were 79 per cent over the broadcast day, and 89 per cent in the peak viewing period.[8]

The CBC and the CRTC

By comparison with other broadcasters, the powers of the CRTC with respect to the CBC are, to some extent, limited by certain aspects of the Broadcasting Act. The CRTC has been given the mandate to 'regulate and supervise all aspects of the Canadian broadcasting system with a view to implementing the broadcasting policy set out in subsection 3(1) [of the Act].' However, in keeping with the history of the CBC (see chapters 2 and 3), the Broadcasting Act also sets out the objectives, powers, and structure of the CBC distinctly and separately. As a result, the CBC is empowered in certain ways that private sector broadcasters are not.

Furthermore, according to section 9(1)(b) of the Broadcasting Act, the CRTC is responsible for issuing Canadian broadcast licences, including those of the CBC, subject to conditions of licence 'related to the circumstances of the licensee.' However, section 23 of the Act requires the CRTC to consult with the CBC in regard to any condition that the Commission proposes to attach to a licence of the Corporation. If no agreement can be reached on the proposed condition, the CBC may refer the condition to the Minister of Canadian Heritage for consideration and determination.

What is more, section 24(2) of the Broadcasting Act says that no licence in connection with the operation of any radio or television station owned and operated by the CBC may be suspended or revoked by the CRTC except with the consent of the Corporation. Although the revocation of a CBC licence may never have been contemplated by the CRTC, sections 23 and 24(2) provide the CBC, the national public broadcaster, with a margin of autonomy from the CRTC that private sector broadcasters do not enjoy.

Does the CRTC's regulatory framework give special status to Canadian public broadcasting generally? The answer is, some, but not very much. For example, as was indicated in chapter 6, the priority list of services for broadcasting distribution undertakings (BDUs) generally accords a higher priority to the programming services of all local television stations owned and operated by the CBC and a higher priority to provincial educational television programming services than to all other television services. But otherwise, the Commission tries to treat all of its licensees on a relatively equal footing. This sometimes leads to disagreements with those who believe that the CBC is 'more equal than the others' and should not be subject to the same rules as private sector broadcasters.

The last complete statement of the CRTC's view of the CBC is set out in Public Notice CRTC 2000-1, 'A Distinctive Voice for All Canadians: Renewal of the Canadian Broadcasting Corporation's Licences.'

Provincial Educational Broadcasters

The CBC constitutes Canada's national public broadcaster. Who are the other public broadcasters? Essentially, they are the provincial educational broadcasters: Télé-Québec, TVOntario (TVO), TFO (the French-language counterpart of TVO), the Saskatchewan Communications Network (SCN), and the Knowledge Network in British Columbia.[9]

As indicated in chapter 2, the courts have determined that broadcasting is a federal responsibility. However, section 93 of the Canadian Constitution Act says that responsibility for education lies with the provinces. Educational broadcasting constitutes a kind of divided jurisdiction or shared responsibility between the two levels of government, and provincial educational broadcasters are therefore accorded something of a special status by the CRTC. In effect, the Commission adopts a somewhat more hands-off attitude toward provincial educational broadcasters than it does toward other broadcasters as long as they are broadcasting primarily 'educational' programs.[10]

The Broadcasting Act contains only one mention of educational broadcasting, in section 3(1)(j), which declares that 'educational programming, particularly where provided through the facilities of an independent educational authority, is an integral part of the Canadian broadcasting system.' However, the Canadian government has issued two directives to the CRTC that elaborate on its intentions with regard to educational broadcasters.

In one directive, the Canadian government provides a special status for the designated provincial educational broadcasting services by ensuring that such services are carried by most BDUs. Since 1970, the Commission has not been authorized to issue or renew a BDU licence unless at least one channel of the BDU has been reserved for the provincial educational broadcasting service (providing such status is requested by the provincial authority).[11]

The 1970 directive also sets out a definition of 'educational' programming:

(a) programming designed to be presented in such a context as to provide a continuity of learning opportunity aimed at the acquisition
or improvement of knowledge or the enlargement of understanding
of members of the audience to whom such programming is directed
and under circumstances such that the acquisition or improvement
of such knowledge or the enlargement of such understanding is subject to supervision or assessment by the provincial authority by any
appropriate means; and

(b) programming providing information on the available courses of
instruction or involving the broadcasting of special education events
within the educational system.

A second Canadian government directive in regard to educational
broadcasting requires that provincial educational authorities be independently incorporated, presumably to avoid a situation where a federal government agency would be directly instructing a provincial
government on how to behave.[12]

There are other television broadcasters that provide educational programming, including the CBC, as well as a number of non-commercial
radio stations that were initially licensed as educational broadcasting
stations. For example, Canal Savoir is a non-profit French-language
service specializing in higher education that is broadcast off-air in
Montreal and carried on many distribution undertakings throughout
Canada but it is not designated as an 'educational authority' by the
Quebec government. As examples of provincial government educational authorities, the following discussion examines the mandate and
operations of Télé-Québec and TVOntario.

Télé-Québec

Télé-Québec is organized in accordance with the Loi sur la société de
télédiffusion du Québec (last modified in 2007). This legislation specifies that Télé-Québec is an agency of the Quebec government and is to
be administered by a Board of Directors consisting of eleven members,
including a chair of the Board and a president, nominated by the government. The other directors on the Board are also nominated by the
Quebec government, after consultations with the milieu undertaken by
the Minister of Culture and Communications. The chair and president
of Télé-Québec are appointed for a term of no more than five years and
the other members of the Board for terms of no more than four years.

Chapter 2 of the Loi sur la société de télédiffusion du Québec sets out the mandate and powers of Télé-Québec. Its mandate is to operate an educational and cultural television undertaking that ensures, by any means of distribution, the accessibility of its services to the public. Télé-Québec is entitled to produce and distribute audio-visual programs as well as their ancillary products and related documents. Télé-Québec's activities should develop a taste for learning, favour the acquisition of knowledge, promote art and culture, and reflect regional realities and the diversity of Quebec society.

In its recent licence renewal application for the period ending 31 August 2016, Télé-Québec committed to broadcast an average of eight hours each week of priority programming during the prime-time programming period (between 7 p.m. and 11 p.m.), conditional upon the funding that it formerly received from the Canadian Television Fund being maintained throughout the new licence term.[13] This is identical to the requirement for the large multi-station private sector ownership groups, which, at the time of writing, are required to broadcast an average of eight hours of priority programming each week.

One of the characteristics of public television broadcasters generally, and Télé-Québec in particular, is their attention to programming for children and youth. Public television services are the major providers of children's programming among the general interest (off-air) services.[14] For English-language services, this situation is largely attributable to the safeguards surrounding advertising directed to children, endorsed by the CRTC and the Canadian Association of Broadcasters and codified in the Broadcast Code for Advertising to Children to which all private sector broadcasters adhere. Private sector broadcasters tend to consider the Broadcast Code for Advertising to Children as a disincentive for the financing of children's programming. In Quebec, advertising directed to children is subject to more stringent restrictions than in the rest of Canada in the form of the provincial Consumer Protection Act, which effectively prohibits advertising to children except in exceptional circumstances. The issue of advertising to children is examined in more detail in chapter 9.

During the year 2006–7, Télé-Québec aired an average of fifty-four hours per week of children's and youth programming, which constituted 42 per cent of its total program schedule. Télé-Québec's children's and youth programming is generally aired in the 7 a.m. to noon and in the 3:30 p.m. to 7 p.m. periods.

In Broadcasting Decision CRTC 2006-698, the Commission approved amendments proposed by Télé-Québec to its own advertising code of conduct, including amendments to increase the maximum amount of advertising it may broadcast from 8 to 12 minutes per hour and to remove the prior restriction prohibiting the broadcast of more than 800 minutes of advertising material per week. The implementation of this change has resulted in Télé-Québec drawing closer to the program format utilized by commercial broadcasters.

For the broadcast year ending 31 August 2009, Télé-Québec expected to receive $66.2 million in government grants, $2.4 million in program sales, and another $9.1 million in advertising revenues for a total of $77.7 million. Télé-Québec attracts an average of about 3 per cent of the total French-speaking television audience in the province.

TVOntario (TVO)

TVOntario (TVO), the public educational television service in Ontario, is the trade name of the Ontario Educational Communications Authority, a Crown agency that reports to Ontario's Minister of Training, Colleges, and Universities and, on certain issues, to the Minister of Education as well. TVO is Canada's oldest educational television service, and reaches over 98 per cent of Ontario with some 215 off-air transmitters.

TVO is the creation of the Ontario Educational Communications Authority Act, which sets out the objectives, powers, and structure of the service. The Act specifies that the 'Authority' consists of not more than thirteen members, including the chair, who are appointed by the Lieutenant-Governor-in-Council (the Ontario Cabinet) for not more than three years at a time. The primary objective of TVO is 'to initiate, acquire, produce, distribute, exhibit or otherwise deal in programs and materials in the educational broadcasting and communications fields.' In the course of its most recent licence renewal application, TVO declined to commit to broadcast any specific amount of priority programming.[15]

TVO does not broadcast commercial advertising and received $37.5 million in funding from the Government of Ontario and $11.2 million in other revenues (including membership and corporate donations) for a total of $48.8 million in 2007–8. In a manner similar to PBS in the United States, TVO is partly funded by donations from the public, including viewer contributions encouraged by on-air funding drives.

As with most of the provincial educational services, children's and youth programming plays a very prominent role in TVO's schedule.

During February 2008, for example, children's and youth programming occupied the entire schedule up to 7 p.m. (and up to 3:30 p.m. on
weekends).

TVO operates an English-language service while the Government of
Ontario's French-language service, the Office des télécommunications
éducatives de langue française de l'Ontario, formerly a division of
TVO, now operates as a distinct and independent entity, TFO.[16]

The Community Television Channel

The Community Television Channel also provides a form of public
service, albeit at the local or regional level. This said, section 3(1)(b)
of the Broadcasting Act refers to the 'private, public and community
elements' of the broadcasting system as if the community elements
formed a distinct category. In the past, the CRTC has required cable
television undertakings to provide access to their local communities via
a channel dedicated to community service. In this context, the CRTC's
1991 Community Channel Policy stated that, among other things,

- The role of the community channel should be *primarily of a public
  service nature*
- The programming of the community channel should complement
  the programming provided by conventional broadcasters
- The community channel should foster the development of programming that reflects the community and promotes active participation
  by its citizens [emphasis added]

In 1997, the CRTC established a revised regulatory framework for
broadcasting distribution undertakings (BDUs) addressing the issue of
their contributions to Canadian programming.[17] The CRTC's revised
framework responded in part to the rise of alternative modes of broadcast distribution, such as microwave and satellite delivery, and undertook to generalize the BDU regulations so that they would apply to
all broadband, subscription-based, distribution undertakings (whether
using wireline, satellite, or wireless technologies), and not just to coaxial cable distribution undertakings.

The regulations introduced in 1997 require that all distributors contribute a minimum of 5 per cent of their gross annual revenues derived
from broadcasting activities to the creation and presentation of Canadian programming. For the purposes of meeting the 5 per cent total con-

tribution requirement, all Class 1 terrestrial distribution undertakings having 60,000 or more subscribers are permitted to allocate up to 2 per cent of their gross annual revenues derived from broadcasting activities to local expression in the form of a community channel. The balance of the 5 per cent total contribution must be remitted to an independently administered production fund (see chapter 8).[18]

In October 2002, the CRTC announced a new policy on community-based media.[19] The new framework replaced the existing policies for the community channel and addressed such issues as

- The definition of local programming
- Citizen access and training
- Advertising and sponsorship
- Licensing and ownership
- Limitations on self-promotion

Large cable companies are not required to operate a community channel, although many of them choose to do so. However, as noted above, they are entitled to reduce their required contribution to Canadian production funds by up to 2 per cent if they elect to make an equivalent contribution to local expression, such as operating a community channel. For example, Videotron in Montreal operates Canal Vox subject to the CRTC's community channel policy.

Cable companies can use community channels to distribute public service announcements and some commercial messages, as long as they fulfil specific criteria that are outlined in section 27 of the CRTC's Broadcasting Distribution Regulations.[20] Cable companies may not use community channels to distribute promotions for their retail Internet services. Small cable companies that serve communities without local radio or television service are entitled to distribute a maximum of twelve minutes of commercial messages during each clock hour of community programming.

Notes

1 The BBC Charter stipulates that the BBC cannot air commercial advertising on any media in the United Kingdom, but the BBC does air advertising outside the United Kingdom on services such as BBC Canada. The five public networks operated by France Télévisions do not air commercial

advertising between 8 p.m. and 6 a.m. and will cease all commercial advertising by the end of 2011.

2 McKinsey and Company, *Public Service Broadcasters around the World*.

3 CBC management sometimes says that the term *Radio-Canada* is the French-language equivalent of *CBC* and each refers to the entire Corporation but, in popular usage, *the CBC* designates the Corporation's English-language operations and *Radio-Canada* designates its French-language operations.

4 One of the advantages of a memorandum of understanding, as opposed to changes to the Broadcasting Act, is that the legislator would not be tempted to undertake a wholesale revision of the Act – a potentially long, drawn out process.

5 CBC/Radio-Canada, *Annual Report 2007–2008*, 2:19.

6 http://cbc.radio-canada.ca/docs/index.shtml

7 See http://www.friends.ca/Resource/schedules.asp on the website of the Friends of Canadian Broadcasting for a cross-Canada comparison of the CBC's English-language television program schedules with those of private sector stations, including the stations of CTV, Global, and Citytv.

8 CBC/Radio-Canada, *Annual Report 2007–2008*, 2:3.

9 ACCESS – The Educational Station is the designated provincial educational authority in Alberta. It is privately owned by CTVglobemedia.

10 Some provincial broadcasters also appear to claim jurisdiction over 'cultural' programming, another area of provincial interest, but the CRTC has not formally recognized such jurisdiction.

11 Direction to the CRTC (Reservation of Cable Channels).

12 Direction to the CRTC (Ineligibility to Hold Broadcasting Licences).

13 See Broadcasting Decision CRTC 2009-444, 'CIVM-TV Montréal and its Transmitters – Licence Renewal.'

14 About 10 per cent of Canadian households do not subscribe to cable or satellite distribution undertakings and therefore do not have access to the children's programming available from specialty and pay television services. Public television helps to provide children's programming to them.

15 See Broadcasting Decision CRTC 2008-207, 'TVO (CICA-TV Toronto and Its Transmitters) – Licence Renewal.'

16 See Broadcasting Decision CRTC 2008-143, 'TFO – Licence Renewal.'

17 Public Notice CRTC 1997-25, 'New Regulatory Framework.'

18 Note that in Broadcasting Public Notice CRTC 2008-100, 'Regulatory Frameworks for Broadcasting,' the commission announced that it intended to increase the required contribution to Canadian programming by licensed terrestrial and DTH undertakings from 5 to 6 per cent of the

gross revenues derived from broadcasting activities. . In Broadcasting Regulatory Policy CRTC 2009-406, 'Policy Determinations Resulting from the 27 April 2009 Public Hearing,' the contribution was raised to 6.5 per cent. Licensed BDUs will be required to direct the additional 1.5 per cent, estimated to be approximately $100 million in the first year, to a new fund, to be known as the Local Programming Improvement Fund (LPIF), that is designed to improve the quality of local programming in regional markets. At the time of writing, the Commission had not yet introduced amendments to the BDU *Regulations* to implement the LPIF.

19 Broadcasting Public Notice CRTC 2002-61, 'Policy Framework for Community-Based Media.'

20 In Broadcasting Decision CRTC 2008-234, the commission issued a short-term licence renewal of two years to Shaw Cablesystems and Videon Cablesystems (both owned by Shaw) for, among other things, the repeated failures of Shaw to comply with the regulations concerning the community channel.

8 Financing Canadian Content

The CRTC regulates and supervises the Canadian broadcasting system and encourages Canadian broadcasters to maintain, and even surpass, certain minimum levels of Canadian programming. However, the Commission does not itself finance Canadian programs. The public financing of Canadian broadcast content is accomplished through distinct government programs and organizations such as tax credits and the Canada Media Fund (CMF). This said, the CRTC is able to influence the financing of Canadian programs by requiring or encouraging broadcasters to contribute to recognized Canadian music and television production funds. The CRTC also indirectly influences the financing of Canadian programs by means of its Canadian content requirements (see chapter 6) that, in effect, generate an important part of the demand for Canadian programs in the under-represented categories of programming.

This chapter outlines how both the Ministry of Canadian Heritage and the CRTC influence the financing of Canadian music and television programs. It also provides an introduction to the policies and operations of the Foundation to Assist Canadian Talent on Records (FACTOR), MusicAction, the Canada Media Fund, and Telefilm Canada, and an overview of government tax credits.

The Broadcasting Act makes relatively few references to broadcast 'production' since the primary concern of the Act is the transmission or 'broadcasting' of programming. However, section 3 of the Act (see Appendix A) does say,

- Each element of the Canadian broadcasting system shall contribute in an appropriate manner to the *creation* and presentation of Canadian programming

- Each broadcasting undertaking shall make maximum use, and in no case less than predominant use, of Canadian creative and other resources in the *creation* and presentation of programming, unless …
- The programming provided by the Canadian broadcasting system should include a significant contribution from the Canadian *independent production* sector (emphasis added)

Radio Broadcasters' Contributions to Canadian Talent Development

As part of their licence renewal applications, all licensees of private commercial radio stations are required by the CRTC to make an annual financial commitment to Canadian Content Development (CCD).[1] The Commission believes that well-designed CCD initiatives to support, promote, train, and develop Canadian musical and spoken-word talent increase the supply of and demand for high-quality Canadian music in a variety of genres and enlarge the supply of spoken-word material for broadcast.

Broadcasting Public Notice CRTC 2006-158, 'Commercial Radio Policy 2006,' sets out each radio station's basic annual contribution to CCD:

- Stations with total revenues in the previous broadcast year of less than $625,000 make a fixed contribution of $500
- Stations with total revenues in the previous broadcast year between $625,000 and $1,250,000 make a fixed contribution of $1,000

Stations with total revenues exceeding $1,250,000 in the previous broadcast year must contribute $1,000 plus 0.5 per cent of the portion of the previous year's total revenues that exceeds $1,250,000.

To ensure the continuity of funding for the two principal organizations, no less than 60 per cent of the basic annual CCD contribution must be forwarded to FACTOR or MusicAction. The remaining amount may be directed to any eligible CCD initiative, at the discretion of the licensee. Aside from FACTOR and MusicAction, additional eligible parties include

- National, provincial, and territorial music industry associations
- Schools and educational institutions that are accredited by provincial authorities
- Initiatives, including talent contests, for the production and promotion of local music and local musical artists, particularly emerging artists

- Independent parties dedicated to producing new spoken-word content that would otherwise not be produced for broadcast
- Audio content initiatives that would further advance the fulfilment of specific objectives of the Canadian broadcasting system as outlined in the Act, such as a community radio fund, Native radio, and other specialized audio broadcasting services

In Broadcasting Public Notice 2006-158, 'Commercial Radio Policy 2006,' the Commission estimated that, if the revised CCD policy had been applied to the 2004–5 broadcast year, $4.1 million would have been generated from the new basic annual CCD contribution as opposed to $2.8 million under the previous regime.

In the same public notice, the Commission also announced that applicants for new licences, licence renewals, and transfers of ownership or control of radio stations would be asked to make specific commitments to provide airplay for and to promote emerging Canadian artists and music. Following the public process in each case, the Commission could decide to impose conditions of licence.

Radio Ownership Transfers

Financial commitments to projects related to Canadian content development are also frequently included as part of the benefits package proposed in applications to the Commission for authority to transfer the ownership or control of existing radio stations or in applications for licences to operate new radio stations. The CRTC considers that all such contributions are important to help ensure a sufficiently large pool of Canadian music and other Canadian creative material is available for radio broadcast.

According to the Commission's 1998 commercial policy statement, set out in Public Notice CRTC 1998-41, 'Commercial Radio Policy,' 'Because the Commission does not solicit competing applications, the onus is on the applicant to demonstrate that the application filed is the best possible proposal under the circumstances and that the benefits proposed in the application are commensurate with the size and nature of the transaction.' The Commission therefore requires applicants involved in a transfer of ownership or control of a profitable radio programming undertaking to commit to undertake clear and unequivocal benefits (to the Canadian broadcasting system) representing a minimum direct financial contribution to eligible third parties associated with Canadian content development of 6 per cent of the value of the transaction.[2]

FACTOR

The Foundation to Assist Canadian Talent on Records (FACTOR) was founded in 1982 by CHUM Limited, Moffat Communications, and Rogers Broadcasting Limited, in conjunction with the Canadian Independent Record Producers Association and the Canadian Music Publishers Association.

FACTOR is a private non-profit organization that provides financial assistance for the growth and development of the English-language Canadian independent recording industry. FACTOR administers the voluntary contributions from sponsoring radio broadcasters and two components of the Department of Canadian Heritage's Canada Music Fund Council's programs.[3] FACTOR has been managing federal funding since the inception of the department's Sound Recording Development Program in 1986.

FACTOR's financing is provided through programs that assist Canadian recording artists and songwriters to create music and produce music videos. FACTOR also provides financial assistance for domestic and international tours and showcases, and supports Canadian recording companies, distributors, recording studios, music video production companies, producers, engineers, and directors – the various facets of the infrastructure required for Canadian artists and 'labels' to advance their presence on international markets. FACTOR currently provides more than $14 million annually to support the Canadian music industry.

MusicAction

MusicAction is a non-profit organization founded in August 1985 at the initiative of Quebec radio, music, and show business professionals. The primary objective of MusicAction is to encourage the development of French-language music via the production and distribution of recorded works. MusicAction administers public and private funding to encourage the growth and consolidation of the Canadian independent sound recording industry. Proposals for French-language vocal music, classical music, world music, and instrumental music receive MusicAction's support. English-language vocal music proposals are referred to FACTOR.

The Department of Canadian Heritage, via the Canada Music Fund

Council's programs, contributed $5.9 million to MusicAction, and private sector radio broadcasters contributed another $2.1 million in 2008–9. This allowed MusicAction to disburse about $7 million to the music industry during the year.[4]

Financing Television Programs

Generally speaking, the per capita costs of producing Canadian television programs are much higher in Canada than in other countries, because of Canada's relatively small population, which supports not one, but two broadcasting industries, one in each of the two official languages.[5] Given the pervasive nature of the U.S. entertainment industry's supply of television programs, and Canada's open borders, geographical proximity, and common language with the United States, Canadian government support of high-quality English-language Canadian television programming is essential to the maintenance of a distinct English-language broadcasting environment. It is equally important for French-language Canadian television programming because of the small francophone population – less than a quarter of Canada's total population. Without government financing, Canada's broadcasting system would be unable to provide a significant number of Canadian television programs that contribute to Canadian identity and cultural diversity, or to maintain a standard of quality comparable to that of other industrialized countries, particularly in the under-represented or 'priority' program categories (drama, documentaries, variety, and children's programming).[6]

Canadian television programs are produced by broadcasters in their own studios (in-house production), by related or affiliated production companies, or by production companies of which broadcasters have no ownership control (independent production). Independent production companies provide an important part of Canadian television production and receive the great majority of direct government funding to do so.

As mentioned above, section 3 of the Broadcasting Act requires that the programming provided by the Canadian broadcasting system 'include a significant contribution from the Canadian independent production sector.' However, the Act does not define what constitutes a 'significant' contribution or what even constitutes 'independent' production. When the Act came into force in 1991, 'independent' production companies apparently referred to those production companies that had no ownership ties to any television broadcaster but, as a result of

TABLE 8.1 Value of television financing from selected government financing mechnisms, 2007–8

Year ending 31 March 2008	$ millions
Federal tax credits (television only)	216
Provincial tax credits (television only)	317
Canadian Television Fund (contributions from Canadian Heritage)	120
Canadian Television Fund (CRTC-mandated BDU contributions)*	122
Independent TV production funds (CRTC-mandated BDU contributions)	43
TOTAL	818

Sources: Canadian Film and Television Production Association, 09 Profile, 46; Canadian Television Fund, Annual Report 2007–08, 13
*Broadcasting distribution undertakings (BDUs). Total BDU contributions to the CTF in 2007–8 amounted to about $165 million but only the portion of total financing that was allocated to productions that completed production during the year is indicated in table 8.1.

subsequent cross-media ownership convergence, the meaning of 'independent' or non-related production has been broadened by the CRTC. When considering applications for new services or for transfers of ownership or control since the mid-1990s, the Commission has examined problems arising from the vertical integration of broadcasters and 'independent' production companies, case by case. In the last few years, the CRTC has defined an 'independent' production company as a production company in which a CRTC licensee, and any company related to a licensee, owns or controls, directly or indirectly, in aggregate, less than 30 per cent of the equity of the production company.[7]

Independent production usually involves the pre-production financing of programs with a combination of presales to broadcasters, foreign distribution advances, tax credits, and other sources of government financing, including that provided by the Canada Media Fund. Typically, at least 80 per cent of the financing of each program is in place (i.e., secured by commitments from third parties) before the producer commences the principal photography of the production.

To ensure that a supply of Canadian television programs in the 'priority' program categories is available, the Canadian government, together with the provincial governments, has established a range of funding instruments with varying objectives. All of these instruments are intended primarily to assist independent productions and rely on the certification process of the Canadian Audio-Visual Certification Office (CAVCO) or that of the CRTC, in addition to their own criteria, to help attain their objectives. Considerable resources are disbursed via these funding mechanisms, as is indicated by the rough tabulation in table 8.1 which relates to completed productions in the year 2007–8.

Each of these funding instruments relies on the CAVCO or CRTC Canadian content certification process (with additional requirements) to establish eligibility for access to its financing. The various government funding agencies do not attempt to define Canadian programs or content per se, but they do use the definitions of a Canadian program developed by CAVCO and the CRTC as a building block in establishing eligibility criteria for their own funding decisions. Since resources are limited and the demand for financing is high, the administrators of each of these sources of financing establish additional criteria, over and above simple recognition as a Canadian program, in order to ration the available financing among the competing applicants.

For example, the Canadian Film or Video Production Tax Credit provided by the federal government is available to a wide range of film and television projects in the under-represented or 'priority' program categories, many of which are industrial in nature and do not pursue distinctly Canadian cultural objectives. Access to the federal tax credit for Canadian programs requires CAVCO certification, which normally includes, among other criteria, six Canadian content points. Productions that do not meet CAVCO's requirements (or their equivalent), and are not in the 'priority' program categories, can sometimes be recognized as Canadian productions by other means, such as CRTC certification, but they will not be eligible for financing from the major financing mechanisms assisted by governments, such as the Canada Media Fund.

There are exceptions to the general rules. For instance, the Canadian portion of the total budget of an 'official' international co-production may be eligible for the federal tax credit even though the international co-production itself has not attained six Canadian content points (see chapter 6 for the definition of an 'official' international co-production). In this case, the Canadian portion of the co-production's budget would be required to satisfy CAVCO's eligibility rules for the production to benefit from the tax credit.

At the other end of the scale, the Canadian Television Fund (CTF), directed at television programs in the 'priority' categories, requires CAVCO certification, ten Canadian content points, and numerous additional criteria that are outlined further, below. Since the eligibility criteria for CTF financing are more stringent than those for the federal tax credit, fewer projects are eligible for CTF financing than for the tax credit.

Depending on their nature and objectives, independent television projects can make use of financial structures that rely on one or possibly more of these sources of government financing – together with other public and private sector sources of funds. Public sector and para-public CTF or CMF financing typically account for more than 50 per cent of the total budgets for all CAVCO-certified programs aired on public sector English-language and French-language services, both public and private. Federal and provincial tax credits and agency financing, such as that of the CTF or CMF, are therefore central to the production of distinctly Canadian programs in the under-represented or 'priority' program categories.

Cultural vs Industrial Objectives

One of the issues raised by federal and provincial government policy as it applies to the financing of Canadian television programs is the extent to which the policy pursues 'cultural' objectives as opposed to more 'industrial' objectives. Cultural objectives typically concern the program content itself, whereas industrial objectives are related to such economic considerations as employment, advertising revenues generated (which are dependant on the size of audiences), program sales revenues, and export value. The Canada Media Fund and the Société de développement des entreprises culturelles du Québec (SODEC) pursue both 'cultural' and 'industrial' objectives, while the federal and provincial tax credits, especially the production services tax credits (see below), are examples of funding mechanisms or policy instruments that pursue primarily 'industrial' objectives.

Another related policy issue concerns 'discretionary' versus 'automatic' funding. 'Discretionary' funding involves a minimum of discretionary judgement on the part of fund administrators, such as an evaluation of the originality of a concept, the quality of a script, or the presence of Canadian themes and subject matter. 'Automatic' financing is provided to any production that fulfils objective (often quantifiable) criteria such as the number of Canadian content points and the share of the total budget paid to Canadian residents. For this reason, 'automatic' financing is not subject to the sometimes 'arbitrary' judgement of the fund administrators. Whoever fulfils the published requirements automatically qualifies for financing from the fund – whether or not the program content itself is meritorious.

Consequently, the fulfilment of cultural objectives often requires discretionary funding, whereas the fulfilment of industrial objectives can be accomplished by automatic funding. One of the problems with automatic funding is that it is difficult for the government to control or limit in advance the total amount of funding that will be provided in a given fiscal year, since demand for automatic funding is open-ended and, to some extent, unpredictable at the beginning of the fiscal year. This is the case with tax credits: the government does not know in advance how much the tax credit program is going to cost, unless it places a ceiling on the program's financing and leaves latecomers out in the cold. Another problem with automatic funding is that access often depends on quantitative, as opposed to qualitative, criteria. Quantitative criteria are to some extent arbitrary and may favour the larger, more established companies with track records and success with quantitative measures, such as audience ratings, relative to new companies or companies that produce innovative programs with less audience appeal. The major problem with discretionary production funding is that it bestows discretionary powers on fund administrators when, as William Goldman has said about Hollywood studio production, 'Nobody knows anything.'[8] Arbitrary decision-making can result.

There is a wide variety of funding available to Canadian television and film productions, although, of course, there is never enough to satisfy demand. An extensive list of national and provincial funding sources is published annually in the trade magazine Playback.[9] The following discussion examines five sources of television funding:

• The Canadian Television Fund (to be integrated into the Canada Media Fund in 2010)
• Telefilm Canada
• Provincial funding agencies
• 'Private sector' funds
• Federal and provincial tax credits

The Canadian Television Fund

The Canadian Television Fund is a non-profit corporation with a budget of about $289 million in 2008–9 that was financed by the federal government ($120 million), by Canadian distribution undertakings in keeping with requirements set out by the CRTC ($161 million), and by investment revenues ($8 million).[10] The Department of Canadian Heritage, the Cable Production Fund (a creation of the CRTC and Canadian cable companies in 1994), and Telefilm Canada created the CTF in 1996 (see Appendix E). For the year 2009–10, the CTF is administered in accordance with a contribution agreement with Canadian Heritage. Generally speaking, the CTF establishes policy for access to its funding and, by contractual agreement, Telefilm Canada administers the allocation of CTF funding. The CTF is scheduled to be superseded by the Canada Media Fund as of 1 April 2010.

In June 2007, following a temporary refusal by Shaw Communications and Videotron earlier in the year to make their required contributions to the CTF, the CRTC released a Task Force Report on the Canadian Television Fund.[11] Among other things, the CRTC Task Force recommended that the existing objectives of the CTF be broadened to include more support for Canadian television programs that succeed with Canadian audiences and that the Commission amend its BDU Regulations so that the funds contributed by BDUs are allocated to a more flexible and market-oriented private sector funding stream. However, the CRTC proposals met with considerable opposition from interested parties, including the CTF.

As a result of this opposition, the Commission felt compelled to conduct a public hearing in February 2008 to consider the recommendations of the CRTC Task Force Report. Shortly after the hearing, the Minister of Canadian Heritage announced that the government had asked the CRTC to report and make recommendations on the Canadian Television Fund pursuant to section 15 of the Broadcasting Act, by which the Governor-in-Council can request the CRTC to make reports. Among other things, the government reminded the Commission that the Canadian Television Fund operated under the terms of a Contribution Agreement with the Department of Canadian Heritage that 'gives effect to the Government's policy and terms and conditions for the entire Canadian Television Fund program,' and expressed a 'need to ensure appropriate alignment between the Commission's regulatory policies and the Government's policies in respect of the Canadian Television Fund.'[12]

In its June 2008 report on the CTF to the Minister of Canadian Heritage, the CRTC made several recommendations in line with those of the Commission's Task Force Report but limited its own actions to relatively modest measures such as amending the Broadcasting Distribution Regulations to make mandatory the monthly contributions of companies that distribute broadcasting services, 'once the Department of Canadian Heritage has resolved the major issues.'[13] The challenge to the CRTC's authority by Shaw and Videotron is discussed further in chapter 15.

For 2009–10, the CTF is managed under the auspices of the Canada Media Fund by a seven-member Board of Directors named by the Department of Canadian Heritage and the Canadian Coalition for Cultural Expression.[14]

The CTF allocates its financing in keeping with five funding streams:

- Broadcaster Performance Envelope Stream ($242 million in 2007–8)
- Development Financing Stream ($9 million)
- French-language Projects outside Quebec Stream ($8 million)
- Aboriginal-Language Projects Stream ($3 million)
- Versioning Assistance Stream ($1.5 million)

The categories of programming financed by the Broadcaster Performance Envelope Stream, by far the most important of the five funding streams, include Canadian-made drama, documentaries, children's and youth programming, variety shows, and performing arts programs. For the year 2009–10, the Broadcaster Performance Envelope Stream has four essential requirements for project eligibility:

1. The project speaks to Canadians about, and reflects, Canadian themes and subject matter.
2. The project will be certified by the CAVCO and has achieved ten out of ten points (or the maximum number of points appropriate to the project) as determined by the CTF using the CAVCO scale.
3. Underlying rights are owned, and significantly and meaningfully developed, by Canadians.
4. The project is shot and set primarily in Canada.

The first requirement allows CTF administrators to disqualify projects that have no identifiable Canadian content on the screen, even though they meet all of the fund's other requirements. CTF financing is oversubscribed and this requirement allows CTF administrators to reject some projects that would otherwise qualify, thereby permitting the CTF to respect its overall budget.[15]

With regard to official treaty co-productions, the four essential requirements are interpreted to treat the co-production partner as Canadian. Accordingly, the terms *Canadian* and *Canadians* in requirements 1 and 3 above, and the term *Canada* in requirement 4 are deemed to include the co-production country. The ten-out-of-ten points referenced in requirement 2 must be attained by citizens of Canada or the co-producing country.

There are many essential requirements that characterize CTF policy that are not discussed in detail here. For example, eligible productions must have a licence fee agreement with a Canadian broadcaster that meets CTF requirements, including the appropriate threshold for the category of program in question. CTF contributions then consist of 'licence fee top-ups' and equity investments over and above this commitment by the broadcaster(s) proposing to air the production. Generally, the first participation of the CTF is in the form of a licence fee top-up to a maximum of 20 per cent of the production budget. Amounts in excess of 20 per cent, if approved, are in the form of an equity investment.

A 'licence fee top-up' is essentially a cash grant to the producer, while an equity investment involves the producer conceding to the CTF a copyright ownership interest or share in the television production and a claim on any net revenues that may result. The value, if any, of equity investment in a production is subject to a standardized recoupment schedule that sets out how revenues from the production will be divided among the concerned parties (distributors, producers, investors, etc.).

On 9 March 2009, the Government of Canada announced the amalgamation of the CTF and Telefilm Canada's Canada New Media Fund to form the Canada Media Fund. Following public consultations to determine its policies and procedures, the official launch of the CMF is planned for 1 April 2010. In the interim, the CTF and the Canada New Media Fund are continuing in keeping with their existing modus operandi. See chapter 15 for a discussion of the political history of the government's announcement.

Telefilm Canada

Telefilm Canada is a federal cultural agency dedicated primarily to the development and promotion of the Canadian film, television, and new media industries. Telefilm Canada reports to the Ministry of Canadian Heritage.

Telefilm has its origins in the Canadian Film Development Corporation (CFDC), created in 1967, with a mandate to finance Canadian theatrical feature films. In 1983, the federal government established the Canadian Broadcast Program Development Fund to finance Canadian television programs and assigned responsibility for administering this fund to the CFDC. In 1984, the CFDC changed its name to Telefilm Canada to signal the importance of this new responsibility. Until the year

2006–7, Telefilm played a central role in the disbursement of financing to the Canadian independent television production sector. However, this changed and Telefilm has become a secondary player in television insofar as Telefilm no longer exercises significant policy- or decision-making powers in the broadcasting sector. Telefilm's former Broadcast Fund, at one point renamed the 'Equity Investment Program (EIP)' of the Canadian Television Fund, is now completely integrated into the CTF.

However, by contract, Telefilm administers the distribution of financing of the CTF subject to oversight by the CTF. All of Telefilm's other activities relating to theatrical feature films, new media, promotion, and festivals lie outside the responsibility of the CTF.

At the time of writing, Telefilm Canada also manages the Canada New Media Fund (CNMF). The CNMF was created in 1998 to encourage the creation and development of Canadian interactive digital content. In 2007–8, the CNMF provided $11.5 million in financial assistance to seventy-one projects. As mentioned above, the Government of Canada is in the process of amalgamating the CTF and the CNMF to form the CMF.

Provincial Funding Agencies

There are a number of provincial government funding agencies. Apart from tax credits, their contributions to television production (as opposed to theatrical film production) are very modest. This said, typically they do assist in script and concept development for television productions. Here are a few examples of such agencies:

- La Société de développement des entreprises culturelles du Québec (SODEC)
- Ontario Media Development Corporation
- British Columbia Film
- Manitoba Film and Sound Recording Development Corporation
- Nova Scotia Film Development Corporation

For example, the SODEC provides financial assistance to Quebec-based productions that use Quebec-based production elements, primarily theatrical feature films and other cultural activities. Its assistance to television programs is limited to the development phase and to documentary production. The SODEC's participation in Quebec tax credits is discussed below.

'Private Sector' Funds

Most of the 'private sector' sources of financing are the result of requirements by, or formal commitments to, the CRTC – a government agency. Thus to call them private sector funds is misleading. Sources of financing mandated by the CRTC include contributions by broadcasting distribution undertakings to the CTF and a range of funds created as a result of commitments undertaken by private sector licensees of the Commission at licence renewal time or as a result of ownership transfer benefits in order to obtain some benefit from the Commission. The Corus Fund, Astral's Harold Greenberg Fund, le Fonds Cogeco, le Fonds Vidéotron, and Rogers Telefund are a few examples of what are sometimes called 'private sector' funds. These funds were created voluntarily in order to satisfy certain CRTC requirements and are now formalized in CRTC conditions of licence. The financing for these funds originates with private sector companies, but in the absence of the CRTC's codification of these companies' commitments, the funds would not exist.

Federal and Provincial Tax Credits

Tax credits have come to play a fundamental role in financing Canadian television programs in the under-represented categories of programs and they represent an interesting example of 'automatic' financing as opposed to 'discretionary' financing.

Tax credits, as the name suggests, allow private sector companies to reduce their tax liability. To encourage the employment of domestic labour, tax credits are typically calculated on the basis of eligible salaries and wages. For example, the federal government's tax credit currently amounts to 25 per cent of eligible salaries and wages expended on the production, up to 60 per cent of the total cost of production. Thus the federal tax credit can contribute up to 15 per cent of a producer's total production budget.

The CAVCO co-administers the Canadian Film or Video Production Tax Credit and the Film or Video Production Services Tax Credit with the Canada Revenue Agency. The objective of the Canadian Film or Video Production Tax Credit (CPTC) is to encourage Canadian programming and to develop the economic basis for an active domestic production sector. The CPTC requires CAVCO certification. The Film or Video Production Services Tax Credit (PSTC) is designed to enhance

FIGURE 8.1 Sources of financing for English-language independent Canadian television production, 2007–8

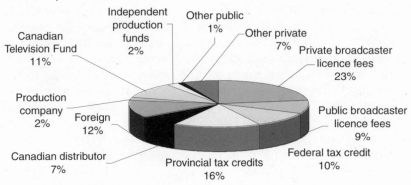

Source: CFTPA 09 Profile

Canada as a location of choice for non-Canadian film and video productions employing Canadians, as well as to strengthen the domestic production industry and secure investment from non-Canadian productions. At the time of writing, the PSTC is available at a rate of 16 per cent of qualified Canadian labour expenditures as opposed to 25 per cent for the CPTC.

The Quebec production tax credit (Crédit d'impôt remboursable pour la production cinématographique et télévisuelle), administered by the SODEC, covers 29.2 per cent of eligible Quebec labour costs, up to a ceiling that varies according to certain criteria (14.6 per cent of the total cost of production for most television programs, 19.7 per cent for one-off documentaries, 24.3 per cent for regional productions, and so on). The SODEC also administers a production services tax credit for location shooting (Crédit d'impôt remboursable pour services de production cinématographique et télévisuelle) covering 20 per cent of qualified Quebec labour How do all these sources of financing play out in the average production budget? Figures 8.1 and 8.2 give some indication.[16]

Figures 8.1 and 8.2 show that English-language and French-language production financing are, in some ways, quite different. For example, English-language production more frequently resorts to foreign pre-sales than does French-language production and the foreign sales potential also leads to more substantial Canadian distribution advances.

FIGURE 8.2 Sources of financing for French-language independent Canadian television production, 2007–8

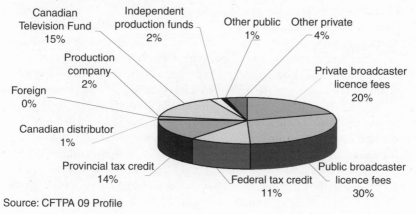

Source: CFTPA 09 Profile

Notes

1 In Broadcasting Public Notice CRTC 2006-158, 'Commercial Radio Policy 2006,' which set out a revised policy for Canadian commercial radio, the commission replaced the pre-existing term *Canadian talent development* (CTD) with *Canadian content development* (CCD).

2 See chap. 13 for a discussion of the CRTC's requirements for ownership transfers.

3 The Canada Music Fund comprises eight programs, of which two are administered directly by Canadian Heritage, the Support to Sector Associations Program, and the Policy Monitoring Program.

4 Part of the difference between revenues and disbursements is attributable to administrative costs. See MusicAction, *Annual Report 2008–2009*, http://www.musicaction.ca/musicaction/ra.asp.

5 Canada is also the home of ethnic, third-language, and Aboriginal radio and television programming (see chap. 9).

6 See chap. 6 for a formal definition of *priority* programs.

7 See, for example, Decision CRTC 2001-458, 'Licence Renewals for the Television Stations Controlled by Global,' para. 42.

8 Goldman, *Adventures in the Screen Trade*, 39.

9 The last such listing was in the 2 March 2009 issue. See also Standing Committee, House of Commons, *Our Cultural Sovereignty*, Appendix 9.

10 Canadian distribution undertakings contribute to the CTF as a result of requirements set out in the CRTC's Broadcasting Distribution Regulations.

At the time of writing, the regulations require that all distributors contribute a minimum of 5 per cent of their gross annual revenues derived from broadcasting to the creation and presentation of Canadian programming. To meet the 5 per cent total contribution requirement, all Class 1 terrestrial distribution undertakings having sixty thousand or more subscribers are permitted to allocate up to 2 per cent of their gross annual revenues derived from broadcasting to local expression in the form of a community channel. The balance of the 5 per cent total contribution must be remitted to an independently administered production fund. If so desired, 20 per cent of the 5 per cent may be contributed to another independent production fund instead. In July 2009, the CRTC announced its intention to increase distributors' contribution to 6.5 per cent, with the additional 1.5 per cent to be allocated to a distinct Local Programming Initiatives Fund (unrelated to the CTF). See Broadcasting Regulatory Policy CRTC 2009-406, 'Policy Determinations Resulting from the 27 April 2009 Public Hearing.'

11 See Broadcasting Public Notice CRTC 2007-70, 'Call for Comments on the Canadian Television Fund (CTF) Task Force Report.'

12 Order in Council P.C. 2008-289, 14 February 2008.

13 *CRTC Report to the Minister of Canadian Heritage on the Canadian Television Fund*, 5 June 2008, 4.

14 The CCCE is a loose association of cable and DTH satellite companies.

15 The financing in the assigned envelopes is administered by broadcasters themselves, and the excess demand for BPE financing is thereby managed by them rather than by the CTF.

16 The data in figs. 8.1 and 8.2 lump together, under the rubric 'Other private,' voluntary private sector investment together with contributions from CRTC-mandated 'private sector' funds (see the discussion above).

9 Social Issues

Section 3 (Broadcasting Policy for Canada) of the Broadcasting Act says that the Canadian broadcasting system 'makes use of radio frequencies that are *public* property' and that its programming provides a *'public* service essential to the maintenance and enhancement of national identity and cultural sovereignty.' What is more, the Canadian broadcasting system should serve 'to safeguard, enrich and strengthen the cultural, political, *social* and economic fabric of Canada' (emphasis added). This latter statement is very general. What is meant by *social* in this context and to what extent does the CRTC address *social* as distinct from cultural, political, and economic issues?

An exhaustive discussion of social issues related to broadcasting would require a book-length treatment. To focus the examination of such issues here, the discussion is limited to the treatment of certain social issues by the CRTC ('social' issues not always being easy to distinguish from 'cultural' issues).

Social Issues in the Broadcasting Act

In general, the Commission addresses social issues selectively, where such issues can be justified clearly by reference to the Broadcasting Act. Specifically, section 3(1) of the Broadcasting Act says,

(d) the Canadian broadcasting system should ...
  (iii) through its programming and the employment opportunities arising out of its operations, serve the needs and interests, and reflect the circumstances and aspirations, of Canadian *men, women* and *children*, including *equal rights*, the *linguistic duality* and

multicultural and multiracial nature of Canadian society and the special *place of aboriginal peoples* within that society ...

(g) the programming originated by broadcasting undertakings should be *of high standard* ...

(k) a range of broadcasting services *in English and in French* shall be extended *to all Canadians* as resources become available ...

(p) programming accessible by *disabled persons* should be provided within the Canadian broadcasting system as resources become available for the purpose. [Emphasis added]

How does the CRTC address these social objectives in its regulation and supervision of the Canadian broadcasting system? Generally speaking, the Commission's activities related to social objectives fall into three broad categories:

• Ensuring that a minimum volume of programming is 'accessible' to specific social groups
• Seeking to ensure that all broadcast programming is 'of high standard' and thereby respects certain community standards with regard to language and images
• Improving the 'employment opportunities' of under-represented social groups in Canadian broadcasting operations, both on-air and off-air

English and French Linguistic Minority Communities

Ensuring that a minimum volume of programming is accessible to minority language groups is one of the objectives of the CRTC's social agenda. Section 3(1)(k) of the Broadcasting Act, cited above, appears to say that, where financial and technical resources are available, English and French services must be provided to all Canadians, including linguistic minorities in remote areas. Section 3(1)(m) is more specific and says that CBC programming should 'be in English and in French, reflecting the different needs and circumstances of each official language community, *including the particular needs and circumstances of English and French linguistic minorities*' (emphasis added).

In Broadcasting Public Notice CRTC 2008-100, 'Regulatory Frameworks for Broadcasting Distribution Undertakings and Discretionary Programming Services,' the Commission announced new access rules for minority language services. As of 31 August 2011, the Commission intends to impose a single rule stipulating that all licensed terrestrial (cable) broadcasting distribution undertakings (BDUs) be required to distribute one minority-language Category A or Category B service for every ten majority-language services they distribute. Direct-to-home (DTH) satellite undertakings will continue to be required to distribute all Category A services.[1]

In June 2008, pursuant to section 15 of the Broadcasting Act that permits the Government of Canada to give directions to the CRTC, the government requested the Commission to seek comments from the public and to report no later than 31 March 2009 regarding

- The availability and quality of English- and French-language broadcasting services in English and French linguistic minority communities in Canada
- Any deficiencies and challenges in those communities in the provision of official-language broadcasting services
- Measures to encourage and facilitate access to the widest range of official-language broadcasting services possible and to ensure that the diversity of English and French linguistic communities across Canada is reflected in the Canadian broadcasting system.[2]

In its final report to the government, the CRTC concluded that official-language minority communities have appropriate access to television services and that the CBC and community radio stations play a 'most important role' in official-language minority communities. The Commission also determined that community reflection in programming available via the Canadian broadcasting system can be improved. In the medium and long term, the Commission offered the opinion that new media represent the best solution for ensuring access to a maximum number of services and for allowing a better reflection of official-language minority communities within the Canadian broadcasting system.[3]

Ethnic, Third-Language, and Aboriginal Programming

The CRTC licenses ethnic radio and television broadcasting services to increase the variety of programming offered by the broadcasting system in view of the multicultural and multiracial nature of Canadian society. According to Public Notice CRTC 1999-117, 'Ethnic Broadcasting Policy,' the Commission defines *ethnic* programs as programs, including cross-cultural programming, directed specifically to a culturally or racially distinct group other than one that is Aboriginal Canadian, or from France or the British Isles. Ethnic programming may be in any language or combination of languages, including English and French.

In principle, ethnic programming may be aired on any broadcast service, including services dedicated specifically to such programming. For example, television services such as the over-the-air service CJNT-TV Montreal, and the specialty television service Telelatino, are considered ethnic stations or networks that provide ethnic programming.[4] Generally speaking, spectrum scarcity limits the number of over-the-air stations in each market so that each over-the-air ethnic station is required to serve a variety of ethnic groups within its service area. This restriction does not apply usually to specialty and pay services that may target one ethnic or language group.

The CRTC requires Canadian over-the-air ethnic television stations to air at least 60 per cent of each broadcast month, and ethnic radio stations, at least 60 per cent of each broadcast week, to ethnic programming. The remainder of an ethnic station's programming may consist of non-ethnic (i.e., English- or French-language) programming in order to generate advertising revenues to cross-subsidize its ethnic programming, if necessary. At least 50 per cent of all programming broadcast by ethnic stations must be third-language programming (i.e., programming in languages other than English, French, or those of Aboriginal Canadians).

The CRTC does not limit the volume of ethnic programming that Canadian non-ethnic stations may air in the official languages, English and French. However, to provide a measure of protection for ethnic stations, the Commission does limit the volume of third-language programming by non-ethnic stations to no more than 15 per cent of their schedules, unless the station has prior approval from the Commission. Campus radio stations and certain community radio stations are allowed to provide up to 40 per cent of their schedules in the form of third-language programming. For radio, where the programming is often predominantly musical, the spoken-word component of the program determines the ethnic group served.

The CRTC requires usually that Canadian ethnic television stations broadcast the same minimum Canadian content levels as non-ethnic private television stations, that is 60 per cent Canadian content over the total broadcast day and 50 per cent during the evening broadcast period. The Commission may, however, vary these requirements by condition of licence. The detailed Canadian content requirements for ethnic radio stations are contained in Public Notice CRTC 1999-117.[5]

As a general rule, Canadian BDUs seek to carry a wide range of programming, including ethnic services, to retain their existing subscribers and attract new ones. The CRTC permits non-Canadian services to be distributed by BDUs, provided the distributed services are included in the Commission's eligibility list. This list is revised and supplemented from time to time by the Commission. Until 2004, the CRTC generally did not allow BDUs to carry non-Canadian specialty programming services that were considered by the Commission to be totally or partially competitive with Canadian discretionary services.[6]

However, under pressure from Canadian Heritage and the BDUs, the Commission announced a revised policy for third-language services in Broadcasting Public Notice CRTC 2004-96, 'Improving the Diversity of Third-Language Television Services: A Revised Approach to Assessing Requests to Add Non-Canadian Third-Language Television Services to the Lists of Eligible Satellite Services for Distribution on a Digital Basis.' The Commission's revised approach placed greater emphasis on expanding the diversity and choice in television services available to third-language ethnic communities in Canada and less emphasis on protecting existing licensed Canadian services.

The CRTC has also licensed a variety of Aboriginal radio and television services. For example, there are more than 250 native radio stations across Canada in rural areas, small towns, and reserves, most of which are exempt from the regular licensing process. Native Communications Inc. serves much of Manitoba with a province-wide network of Aboriginal radio stations.

In February 1999, the Commission licensed the Aboriginal Peoples Television Network (APTN), which targets both Aboriginal and non-Aboriginal viewers. According to the Commission, APTN offered clear and significant commitments to 'offer a high-quality, general interest television service with a broad range of programming that reflects the diverse perspectives of Aboriginal peoples, their lives and cultures' and to 'provide a much-needed, positive window on Aboriginal life for all Canadians, whether living in the North or in the South.'

Furthermore, in its initial licensing decision, the Commission declared that it was vitally important that APTN's unique service be available to all Canadians. Thus, in Public Notice CRTC 1999-70, 'Order Respecting the Distribution of the Aboriginal Peoples Television Network,' pursuant to it powers in section 9(1)(h) of the Act to issue mandatory orders, the Commission required Class 1 and Class 2 cable and multipoint distribution undertakings as well as direct-to-home (DTH) satellite distribution undertakings to distribute APTN's signal as part of their basic service.

Cultural Diversity

The CRTC considers that English- and French-language radio and television services reach millions of Canadians and that the major broadcasting programming undertakings exert a strong influence on how Canadians of all racial and cultural backgrounds perceive one another and their place in society. As a result, the Commission has broadened its perspective on ethnic, third-language, and Aboriginal programming and encouraged all major services to become more proactive on general issues related to cultural diversity.

In response to the report of the Canadian Association of Broadcasters (CAB), *Reflecting Canadians: Best Practices for Diversity in Television*, in July 2004, which concluded among other things that Aboriginal peoples, Asian Canadians, and visible minorities were under-represented on-air, the CRTC

- Requires broadcasters to address such under-representation in their corporate plans
- Obliges the CAB to report annually on the implementation of initiatives to address the challenges of cultural diversity at an industry-wide level
- Requested that the CAB develop and file an action plan to examine issues surrounding the presence, portrayal, and participation of persons with disabilities in broadcasting[7]

With regard to persons with disabilities, the CAB implemented an action plan and submitted its final report to the CRTC in September 2005. In December 2005, the CAB filed a task force report entitled *CAB Review of Industry Codes: Broadcasting Public Notice CRTC 2005-24.*[8] In this report, the CAB submitted that the Canadian broadcasting system would be best served by the development of an expanded portrayal code that would replace the Sex-Role Portrayal Code. According to the CAB, most of the proscriptive provisions contained in the Sex-Role Portrayal Code are as applicable to the portrayal of other minority concerns as they are to gender issues. The CAB therefore submitted that these provisions should be revised to include industry standards concerning the depiction and portrayal of ethnocultural and Aboriginal groups – and persons with disabilities. In Broadcasting Public Notice CRTC 2008-23, 'Regulatory Policy: Equitable Portrayal Code,' the Commission approved a revised Equitable Portrayal Code along these lines. See below.

Since much of the discussion concerning cultural diversity in broadcasting has been directed to images on television, the CAB has also developed a specific approach to diversity on radio, which was endorsed by the CRTC in 2007.[9]

The Role of Self-Regulation

The CRTC relies to a considerable extent on self-regulation by broadcasting licensees to address the social policy concerns raised by the Broadcasting Act. This self-regulation often consists of industry initiatives as well as broadcast content standards and codes of conduct developed by industry organizations, such as the CAB and Advertising Standards Canada.

The Canadian Broadcast Standards Council (CBSC) is a non-governmental organization created by the CAB to administer program standards established by its members, Canada's private broadcasters. Advertising Standards Canada (ASC) is an industry association that regroups 170 advertisers, advertising agencies, media organizations, and suppliers to the advertising sector. Through Clearance Services, ASC administers program standards established by its members and provides Canadian companies with an independent, fee-based advertising copy review service to help advertisers to comply with pertinent laws and regulations.

The Commission itself addresses complaints that are related to broadcasters who are not CBSC members and with issues that do not fall within the parameters of the codes administered by the CBSC. Of the complaints received by the Commission in the year ending 31 March 2008, about 27 per cent were referred to the CBSC.[10]

Broadcasting codes of conduct related to social issues play an important role in setting out certain industry standards and guidelines for programming and advertising content. Through such codes, broadcasters agree to conduct themselves in certain ways on issues such as advertising to children, gender portrayal, and violence on television. In this way, broadcasters commit to respect certain interests of the population they serve, while maintaining their own responsibility to respect editorial and journalistic freedom. The Commission believes that delegating responsibility to the broadcasting industry itself to develop rules and monitor their effectiveness increases the understanding of social issues and generates greater acceptance and adherence by licensees than if the Commission were to unilaterally impose specific solutions. It also reduces considerably the burden on the CRTC of administrating complaints related to social issues.

However, the CRTC remains involved in the development, review, approval, and enforcement of broadcast codes. If a societal issue cannot be resolved by the self-regulating mechanisms in place, the Commission usually possesses sufficient authority to address the problem. In some ways, 'self-regulation' should be considered as a form of 'co-regulation' rather than unfettered self-regulation by broadcasting licensees.

This said, there is relatively little systemic monitoring of licensees by the CRTC or the broadcasting industry's self-regulatory agencies on social issues unless a specific problem is brought to the Commission's attention. The CRTC and the self-regulatory institutions function largely on a complaints basis and generally do not take action on a specific problem issues unless and until a formal complaint is filed or they are directed or encouraged to do so by the Canadian government.

Advertising to Children

In May 2007, the CRTC announced a phasing out of the twelve-minute-per-hour ceiling on advertising by conventional television broadcasters. In Broadcasting Public Notice CRTC 2007-53, 'Determinations regarding Certain Aspects of the Regulatory Framework for Over-the-Air Television,' the Commission announced that it would increase the twelve-minute-per-hour limit on traditional advertising to 14 minutes per hour in peak viewing periods (7 p.m. to 11 p.m.) effective 1 September 2007. The limit was increased to fifteen minutes per hour for all viewing periods effective 1 September 2008, and eliminated altogether as of 1 September 2009. Advertising on specialty services is determined by a condition specific to each specialty service's licence.

To what extent does the CRTC concern itself with the interface between advertising and children? Aside from particular conditions and expectations attached to specific broadcasting licences, the Commission generally requires broadcasters to adhere to two industry codes related to advertising content – The Broadcast Code for Advertising to Children and The Code for Broadcast Advertising of Alcoholic Beverages. Both codes address the potentially negative social effects of advertising to children and are complementary to federal and provincial laws and regulations governing advertising, including any regulations and procedures established by the CRTC, Industry Canada, and Health Canada.

The CAB first established its Broadcast Code for Advertising to Children in 1971, and the code has undergone several revisions since then. Beginning in 1974, the CRTC made adherence to the code a condition of licence for originating television stations and, beginning in 1977, for licensees of FM radio stations. The Commission approved a revised Broadcast Code for Advertising to Children that came into effect on 1 July 1993.

The Broadcast Code for Advertising to Children applies to commercial messages that are carried in children's programs and in programs adjacent to children's programs or commercial messages directed at children. For the purposes of this code, *children* refers to persons younger than twelve years of age. The Code is designed to complement the general principles for ethical advertising outlined in Advertising Standards Canada's Canadian Code of Advertising Standards, which applies to all advertising.

According to the preamble in the Broadcast Code for Advertising to Children, 'The purpose of the *Code* is to serve as a guide to advertisers and agencies in preparing commercial messages which adequately recognize the special characteristics of the children's audience. Children, especially the very young, live in a world that is part imaginary, part real and sometimes do not distinguish clearly between the two. Children's advertising should respect and not abuse the power of the child's imagination.'

The Broadcast Code for Advertising to Children addresses issues such as factual presentation, product prohibition, avoiding undue pressure, scheduling, price and purchase terms, and comparison claims. Furthermore, no station or network may carry more than four minutes of commercial messages in any one half-hour of children's programming or more than an average of eight minutes per hour in children's programs of longer duration.

For commercial broadcasters, the enforcement body for the code is the Children's Advertising Section of Advertising Standards Canada's Children's Clearance Committee. Broadcasters are required to obtain approval for their commercial messages from the Children's Advertising Section prior to broadcast, unless the message is 'local' (i.e., carried in one market only). In this latter case, the broadcaster remains responsible for ensuring that the advertising conforms to the code.

The CBC (which is not a member of the CAB) is required, by condition of licence, to adhere to the standards for children's advertising set out in the Corporation's own Advertising Standards Policy, Advertising Directed to Children Under 12 Years of Age, as this policy is amended from time to time and approved by the CRTC. At a minimum, CBC stations adhere to the standards set out in the CAB's Broadcast Code on Advertising to Children. The CBC is also required, by condition of licence, to forgo broadcasting any commercial message during any child-directed programming, and any child-directed commercial message between programs directed to children of preschool age. For the purpose of this condition of licence, programs directed to children and scheduled before noon during school-day morning hours are deemed to be programs directed to children of preschool age.

The Code for Broadcast Advertising of Alcoholic Beverages also contains certain requirements that relate to advertising seen by minors (i.e., persons under the legal alcohol drinking age). Following a Federal Court ruling that invalidated the CRTC's prior regulations prohibiting the broadcast advertising of spirits-based beverages containing more than 7 per cent alcohol by volume, the Commission strengthened the Code for Broadcast Advertising of Alcoholic Beverages and placed greater responsibility on the industry itself to meet certain standards through self-regulation.

The current regulatory framework for alcoholic beverage advertising is intended to balance freedom of expression with the responsibility of broadcasters for the content they broadcast. Although pre-clearance of advertising material is no longer required, the Commission nonetheless continues to require adherence to the Code for Broadcast Advertising of Alcoholic Beverages. Today, Advertising Standards Canada reviews alcoholic beverage advertising copy upon the request of broadcasters and alcoholic beverage manufacturers.

In regard to minors, the Code for Broadcast Advertising of Alcoholic Beverages says that commercial messages must not

- Attempt to influence non-drinkers of any age to drink or to purchase alcoholic beverages
- Be directed at persons under the legal drinking age, associate any such product with youth or youth symbols, or portray persons

under the legal drinking age or persons who could reasonably be mistaken for such persons in a context where any such product is being shown or promoted

- Portray the product in the context of, or in relation to, an activity attractive primarily to people under the legal drinking age
- Contain an endorsement of the product, personally or by implication, either directly or indirectly, by any person, character or group who is or is likely to be a role model for minors because of a past or present position of public trust, special achievement in any field of endeavour, association with charities and/or advocacy activities benefiting children, reputation or exposure in the mass media

Thus the Code for Broadcast Advertising of Alcoholic Beverages, though it is not generally targeted at minors, supplements the Broadcast Code on Advertising to Children in regard to the consumption of alcohol.

Quebec Consumer Protection Act

In most of Canada, self-regulation by broadcasters of advertising directed to children is considered to be adequate for their protection. However, the Quebec government has established a tighter legal framework for children's advertising. Article 248 of the Quebec Consumer Protection Act says, 'Subject to what is provided in the regulations, no person may make use of commercial advertising directed at persons under thirteen years of age.'[11] This blanket prohibition is rendered slightly more flexible in article 249, which establishes whether or not an advertisement is directed at persons younger than thirteen years of age. According to the Regulations respecting Application of the Consumer Protection Act that give effect to the Act, certain exceptions to the blanket prohibition are permitted.

In practice, the net effect of the Quebec Consumer Protection Act is to ban commercial advertising from programs broadcast from within Quebec. However, programs broadcast and received in Quebec from the rest of Canada (where the Broadcast Code for Advertising to Children applies) or from the United States (where there are no such restrictions on advertising) are not affected. Since nearly all English-language children's programs distributed in Quebec originate outside the province, English-language programs are largely unaffected by the Quebec government's legislation.

As a result of the Quebec Consumer Protection Act's ban on advertising in children's programs, most privately owned French-language television services that rely on advertising, such as the conventional networks, TVA and V, consider children's programs unprofitable and do not broadcast them. Ultimately, the Consumer Protection Act has the effect of limiting French-language children's television programs broadcast in Quebec to publicly funded services, such as Radio-Canada and Télé-Québec, as well as to specialty services that obtain subscriber fees for their financing irrespective of any commercial advertising they may carry, such as VRAK-TV.[12] The Consumer Protection Act has attained its objective of banning advertising to children younger than thirteen years of age, at least in French-language broadcast programs, but it has also had the (presumably unintended) effect of reducing the total volume of French-language children's programming available in Quebec.

Canadian Broadcast Standards Council (CBSC)

The Canadian Association of Broadcasters established the CBSC in 1989. In addition to participating in the creation and revision of the industry codes it administers, the CBSC makes information available about the codes, oversees a complaints resolution process, renders 'non-binding' decisions where necessary, and undertakes to inform its members about emerging social trends.

Whereas Advertising Standards Canada is responsible for industry codes related to advertising content, the CBSC is responsible for the administration of several codes related to program content:

- CAB Equitable Portrayal Code
- CAB Voluntary Code regarding Violence in Television Programming
- Radio Television News Directors Association of Canada (RTNDA) Code of (Journalistic) Ethics
- CAB Code of Ethics

As was mentioned previously, one problem with the self-regulatory codes is that only actions that provoke complaints are reviewed. The CRTC and the CBSC encourage members of the public to address their complaints, in the first instance, to the broadcaster, cable company, satellite service, or other service provider responsible for the program or service concerned. If the result is unsatisfactory, members of the public are advised to address the CBSC, which can then issue a 'non-bind-ing' decision. If the result is still unsatisfactory, the complaint may be addressed by the CRTC.

The CRTC says it is not a board of censors and it does not have the authority to instruct broadcasters, in advance, on what they can broad-cast, nor can it act pre-emptively to disallow a program before it has been broadcast. As part of the ground rules for complaints, the Com-mission says it must receive a complaint from a member of the pub-lic within four weeks of the broadcast. After twenty-eight days, radio and television services are no longer required to retain their broadcast logger tapes, and without a recording of the program in question, it is possible that neither the CRTC nor the broadcaster can address the concern.

Sex-Role Stereotyping and Equitable Portrayal

What Canadians see and hear on television and radio influences their outlook and behaviour. Sex-role stereotyping in broadcasting refers to the way that men and women are portrayed or represented in programs and commercial messages on radio and television.

The CRTC believes that self-administered industry rules and guide-lines effectively assist broadcasters and advertisers in reducing sys-tematic discrimination based on gender from their programs and commercial messages. Until March 2008, the CRTC required all broad-casters in Canada to adhere to the Sex-Role Portrayal Code for Televi-sion and Radio Programming.

Following Commission review, revisions by the CAB, and a public process, the CRTC approved a new more encompassing Equitable Por-trayal Code as proposed by the CAB and set out in Broadcasting Public Notice CRTC 2008-23, 'Regulatory Policy: Equitable Portrayal Code.' This public notice amended the Sex-Role Portrayal Code for Television and Radio Programming by replacing it with the Equitable Portrayal Code. All licensees that, by condition of licence, had been governed by the Sex-Role Portrayal Code have been governed since by the Equitable Portrayal Code. However, the application of the condition of licence is suspended as long as the licensee remains a member in good standing of the Canadian Broadcast Standards Council.

In its statement of intent, the CAB's Equitable Portrayal Code estab-lishes that 'broadcasters shall strive to present equitable portrayal. This code is intended to overcome unduly negative portrayal and stereotyping in broadcast programming, including commercial messages, based on matters of race, national or ethnic origin, colour, religion, age, gender, sexual orientation, marital status or physical or mental disability.'

Among others, the Equitable Portrayal Code addresses the following issues:

- Equitable portrayal
- Human rights
- Negative portrayal
- Stereotyping
- Stigmatization and victimization
- Derision of myths, traditions, or practices
- Degrading material
- Exploitation
- Language and terminology
- Contextual considerations

The Canadian Broadcast Standards Council administers the Equitable Portrayal Code and address questions or complaints from the public about Canada's private broadcasters' programming. For its part, the CBC is required, by condition of licence, to adhere to its own Guidelines on Sex-Role Portrayal, as amended from time to time and approved by the Commission and, at a minimum, to the CAB's Sex-Role Portrayal Code for Television and Radio Programming. In either case, if a complainant is not satisfied with the proposed resolution of a complaint, the CRTC will get involved.

As was demonstrated in the case study of CHOI-FM related in chapter 5, however, the simple existence of a social code and its acceptance, in principle, by broadcasters does not mean that discrimination, or even defamation, based on gender has disappeared from Canadian broadcasting.

Violence in Television Programming

The CRTC's Policy on Violence in Television Programming is set out in Public Notice CRTC 1996-36, 'Policy on Violence in Television Broadcasting,' and consists of three elements:

- Industry codes of conduct

- Instruments that enable adults, including parents, to make informed viewing choices (rating systems, on-screen icons, and the V-chip)
- Media literacy, education, and public awareness

There are at least four industry codes of conduct that relate to violence on television:

- The CAB's Voluntary Code regarding Violence in Television Programming administered by the Canadian Broadcast Standards Council
- The Pay Television and pay-per-view programming code regarding violence
- The industry code of programming standards and practices governing pay, pay-per-view, and video-on-demand services
- The Radio Television News Directors Association of Canada Code of Ethics administered by the Canadian Broadcast Standards Council

At the time of licence renewal or upon issuance of new licences, the CRTC requires the licensees of conventional television stations, networks, and specialty programming undertakings, including those of the CBC, to comply with the CAB's Voluntary Code regarding Violence in Television Programming as a condition of licence. The Commission generally suspends the application of this condition of licence for television licensees who are members in good standing of the CBSC. Similarly, the Commission requires pay television and pay-per-view services to adhere to their industry codes related to violence as a condition of licence.[13]

The CAB's Voluntary Code regarding Violence in Television Programming addresses a number of issues such as program content, children's programming, program scheduling, program classification, viewer advisories, news and public affairs programs, and violence against women, specific groups, animals, or in sports programming. Among other provisions, the code forbids programming that contains gratuitous violence, that is 'material which does not play an integral role in developing the plot, character or theme of the material as a whole,' and programming that sanctions, promotes, or glamorizes violence, and says that 'programming which contains scenes of violence intended for adult audiences shall not be telecast before the late evening viewing period, defined as 9 pm to 6 am.'

Not everyone is satisfied with the effectiveness of the CAB's Voluntary Code regarding Violence in Television Programming. For example, on 30 January 2007, Bloc Québécois MP Bernard Bigras presented Bill C-327, a private member's bill related to violence on television, which was debated in the House of Commons. The bill was reintroduced into the following session of Parliament on 16 October 2007 and aimed to amend the Broadcasting Act to add regulations regarding violence in television programming aimed at children under the age of twelve.

While the CRTC agreed with the objectives of Bill C-327, it did not see the necessity of the provisions that called for prescriptive regulation in lieu of industry self-regulation supported by conditions of licence. This said, the CRTC would like to possess greater powers of enforcement, including the ability to fine a broadcaster for an infraction, which the Commission is not currently able to do in such circumstances.[14] For its part, the CBSC affirms that the codes it administers are effective and claims that most violence in media today originates in video games, DVDs, and the words of popular music, rather than in television broadcasting. According to the CBSC, no legislative change is necessary.

Employment Equity

Generally speaking, the CRTC does not involve itself in issues relating to employment or working conditions in broadcasting, with a few notable exceptions. For example, the Commission usually declines to address issues related to unionization, layoffs, or working conditions at broadcasting undertakings, even if a Commission decision may have a direct impact on such conditions. However, the Commission does address certain gender equality issues in the workplace.

Employment equity in large broadcasting operations falls under the ambit of the federal government's 1995 Employment Equity Act and is not enforceable by the CRTC.[15] As part of changes to the Employment Equity Act, the Government of Canada amended the Broadcasting Act to remove jurisdiction from the CRTC for matters related to employment equity for broadcasters who employ one hundred or more employees. Broadcasters with fewer than one hundred employees are still subject to the Commission's 1992 Employment Equity policy. This policy, as amended in Public Notice CRTC 1997-34, 'Amendments to the Commission's Employment Equity Policy,' requires such licensees to provide information related to their employment equity practices and initiatives at the time of licence renewal and in their annual returns forms.

The CRTC's Policy Respecting On-Air Presence forms part of its policy on employment equity, as well as its policy on gender portrayal, and complements its approach to self-regulation and education.[16] The Policy Respecting On-Air Presence targets four designated groups: women, Aboriginal persons, disabled persons, and members of visible minorities. The Commission generally expects that the presence in broadcasters' programming of members of these four groups will reflect Canadian society. In any initial licence application and in licence renewal applications, broadcast licensees with a total of twenty-five or more employees are expected to respond to questions regarding the on-air presence of members of the four designated groups. See Public Notice CRTC 1997-34, and Public Notice CRTC 1995-98, 'Amendment to Reporting Requirements for Employment Equity in On-Air Positions.'

Service to the Hearing and Visually Impaired

Closed captioning translates the audio portion of a television program into subtitles. These subtitles, also called captions, allow hearing-impaired viewers to read what they cannot hear. Captions usually appear at the bottom of a television screen as white letters on a black background. To view closed captioning, the viewer's receiver must decode the part of the broadcast signal commonly known as 'line 21' by means of a caption decoder chip or an external decoder attached to the television set.

The CRTC's policy on closed captioning is set out in Broadcasting Public Notice 2007-54, 'A New Policy with Respect to Closed Captioning.' According to this policy, English- and French-language broadcasters will be required to caption 100 per cent of their programs over the broadcast day, with the exception of advertising and promotion. This requirement, which is being introduced at licence renewal time for existing licensees, allows for equipment or technical malfunctions and human errors that are beyond the broadcaster's control, or where captioning is not available. Furthermore, considering the challenge associated with the captioning of programming, the Commission is prepared to consider requests to delay the 100 per cent requirement. In such cases, the onus will be on broadcasters to demonstrate that it is impossible to meet the 100 per cent captioning requirement in the near future.

Described or descriptive audio refers to a vocal description of textual or graphic information, such as weather reports and sports, displayed on a television screen. Described video consists of a vocal description of a television program's main visual elements and permits the visually impaired to form a mental picture of what is broadcast. Descriptions are usually delivered over a secondary audio programming (SAP) service. The SAP channel is carried alongside a television signal as an alternative to the standard audio channel that accompanies the video portion of a television program. Listeners can obtain this secondary audio signal either by means of a television or stereo VCR equipped to receive the SAP signal or through a special decoder.

In Public Notice CRTC 1999-97, 'Building on Success: A Policy Framework for Canadian Television,' the CRTC encouraged television broadcasters to include audio description in their programming and stated that, at licence renewal time, it would explore the progress of individual broadcasters in implementing described video. In Broadcasting Public Notice CRTC 2004-2, 'Introduction to Broadcasting Decisions CRTC 2004-6 to 2004-27 Renewing the Licences of 22 Specialty Services,' the Commission established the required amount of described video programming for specialty services at two hours per week, increasing as of September 2008 to three hours per week.

Notes

1 According to Broadcasting Public Notice CRTC 2008-100, 'the Commission considers that it would be appropriate to retain access rights, in the digital environment, for Canadian analogue and Category 1 pay and specialty services. In the amended BDU Regulations, services with access rights will be referred to as Category A services. The existing Category 2 services and any new services that the Commission may choose to license without access rights will be referred to as Category B services.' See chap. 11 for definitions of Category 1 and Category 2 digital specialty services.

2 See Broadcasting Notice of Public Hearing CRTC 2008-12, 'Review of English- and French-Language Broadcasting Services.'

3 See CRTC, *Report to the Governor in Council. on English- and French-Language Broadcasting Services in English and French Linguistic Minority Communities in Canada*, 30 March 2009, http://www.crtc.gc.ca/eng/BACKGRND/language/ol0903-lo0903.htm.

4 As of December 2004, there were four ethnic over-the-air television stations and seventeen radio stations, all of which devoted a significant

portion of their schedules to third-language programming. There were also five general-interest third-language specialty services approved under the analogue licensing framework and twenty-one Category 2 ethnic specialty services for digital distribution, and several specialty audio services in operation. See Broadcasting Public Notice CRTC 2004-96, 'Improving the Diversity of Third-Language Television Services.'

5 In Public Notice 1999-117, 'Ethnic Broadcasting Policy,' the Commission reaffirmed the basic framework of its 1985 over-the-air ethnic broadcasting policy and announced several changes intended to provide more flexibility to ethnic broadcasters and to streamline regulatory requirements.

6 Hence, many U.S services, such as HBO, Showtime, ESPN, and Nickelodeon, have not been available in Canada until recently.

7 Public Notice CRTC 2005-24, 'Commission's Response to the Report of the Task Force for Cultural Diversity on Television.'

8 Referred to in para. 6 of Broadcasting Public Notice CRTC 2008-23 but otherwise apparently unavailable.

9 See Broadcasting Public Notice CRTC 2007-122, 'Canadian Association of Broadcasters' Best Practices for Diversity in Private Radio: Reporting Requirements on Cultural Diversity for Commercial Radio Operators.'

10 In 2006–7, the CBSC handled 1,426 complaints, of which 795 were referred by the CRTC. In 2007, the ASC handled 1,445 complaints. CRTC, *Communications Monitoring Report 2008*, tables 2.3.3 and 2.3.4, 21.

11 Although the law applies to all media, television is the only medium that is directly affected.

12 In August 2006, French-language children's specialty service, VRAK-TV, obtained permission from the CRTC to widen its target audience to include those fifteen to seventeen years of age, thereby enabling it to target adolescent audiences and to side-step the restrictions of the Quebec Consumer Protection Act in regard to any programming directed to adolescent audiences aged thirteen to seventeen.

13 Most pay television licensees, and public television broadcasters such as the CBC, are not members of the Canadian Broadcast Standards Council.

14 See von Finckenstein, 'Speech.'

15 The purpose of the Employment Equity Act is to achieve equality in the workplace, 'so that no person shall be denied employment opportunities or benefits for reasons unrelated to ability and, in the fulfilment of that goal, to correct the conditions of disadvantage in employment experienced by women, aboriginal peoples, persons with disabilities and members of visible minorities by giving effect to the principle that employment equity

means more than treating persons in the same way but also requires special measures and the accommodation of differences.'

16 The policy is set out in Public Notice CRTC 1994-69, 'Consultations
regarding On-Air Job Categories to Be Included in the Employment Equity
Plans of Broadcasters,' as amended by Public Notice CRTC 1995-98,
'Amendment to Reporting Requirements for Employment Equity in On-
Air Positions.'

10 Broadcasting Distribution

The conversion from analogue to digital formats is the basic technological change that is transforming the broadcasting industry at all levels.
This transformation is affecting audio-visual conception and development, production, distribution, exhibition, and the nature of social
engagement through media. Digital technologies offer the opportunity
for improved spectrum management and the possibility of fulfilling
the demand for specialized and personalized niche programming that
responds to individual needs. The transition to digital formats is creating new exhibition platforms that are reshaping the broadcasting environment and fragmenting audiences.

Growth in consumer demand for new digital media has accelerated
the spread of mobile devices and the Internet, the adoption of digital
technology by more traditional broadcast distribution undertakings
(BDUs) using over-the-air broadcast and coaxial cable transmission,
and the convergence of all digital media. This chapter outlines the
nature of broadcasting services distribution by over-the-air transmission, cable, multipoint distribution, satellite, and digital subscriber line
(DSL), as well as the impact of the digital transformation of audio-visual media on Canadian broadcasting policy.

Over-the-Air Transmission

Until the late 1970s, a majority of Canadians received their radio and
television signals via radio waves broadcast over-the-air. Television signal reception required a small set-top antenna (sometimes called rabbit
ears) or a rooftop antenna. Toward the end of the 1970s, analogue cable
distribution became the predominant means of receiving television signals for a majority of Canadian households, but significant numbers

of Canadians continued to receive their radio and television signals by direct transmission over-the-air.[1]

With a view to improving spectrum allocation and management, and in collaboration with Industry Canada, the CRTC published a transitional digital radio policy in October 1995 involving a two-stage approach for the transition from analogue to digital over-the-air radio services. The first stage involved establishing a licensing process for digital radio under which transitional digital radio licences would be issued for a term of three years. The second stage was intended to lead to the establishment of a permanent licensing regime for digital radio undertakings. By December 2006, the Commission had licensed seventy-six transitional digital radio undertakings in Toronto, Windsor, Montreal, Vancouver, Victoria, and Ottawa, but the transition to over-the-air digital radio was stalled. The apparent failure of Canadian over-the-air digital radio to attract listeners is attributable to a number of factors including technical and pricing issues, competition from satellite radio, and new media broadcasting via the Internet and podcasting to personal digital devices.[2]

With regard to the transition from analogue to digital over-the-air (OTA) television services, the CRTC established a policy framework for the licensing of digital services in 2002 based on a voluntary, market-driven model that did not set any specific date for the termination of analogue broadcasting.[3] Five years later, the Commission announced that television licensees would be required to transmit exclusively digital television signals over-the-air after 31 August 2011, although exceptions might be made for northern and remote communities where analogue transmissions would not cause signal interference.[4]

This means that most Canadians who receive their television signals off-air will be required to possess digital television receivers by that time. What is more, there is likely to be a reduction in the number of over-the-air transmitters in the years leading up to the termination of analogue transmission as broadcasters rationalize their over-the-air transmission infrastructure in response to the declining volume of over-the-air television reception by households (see figure 10.1).

According to figure 10.1, fewer than 10 per cent of Canadian households relied on off-air reception to receive television signals (i.e., did not subscribe to either cable or satellite delivery) in 2007–8.[5]

Broadcast Cable Distribution

Cable distribution delivers broadcast signals to large numbers of sub-

FIGURE 10.1 Distribution of broadcast signals to Canadian households, 2007–8 (%)*

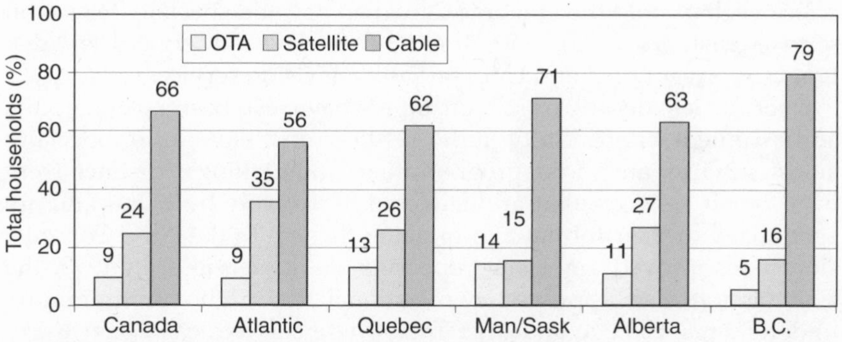

Sources: CBC/Radio Canada, *Comments*; Broadcasting Notice of Public Hearing CRTC 2008–12, 'Review of English- and French-Language Broadcasting Services,' 28
*Ontario was omitted in the original document because the proceeding concerned minority-language broadcasting.

scribers by a single headend. Instead of each individual household possessing a rooftop antenna, as was the case of many homes in the 1950s and 1960s, the cable system deploys one large master antenna or control centre in a given area, collects all local and distant broadcast signals in the area at the cable headend, and relays these signals by land-based fibre or coaxial cable to individual homes, apartment blocks, and businesses.

Cable systems, formerly known as master antenna television (MATV) or community antenna television (CATV) systems, developed originally as a means to deliver off-air television signals, especially U.S. signals, to Canadian homes in border areas. Since cable infrastructure is expensive to build, cable systems expanded first in those areas where there was the greatest concentration of population in close proximity to the United States – southern Ontario, southern Quebec, and southern British Columbia.[6] Those urban areas in southern Canada, such as Ottawa, that were at a distance from any major U.S. urban centre, initially relied on microwave relay infrastructure to receive U.S. signals at the cable headend that were then retransmitted by cable to the home. Cable systems were thus able to offer U.S. network television services to nearly all urban and semi-urban areas in southern Canada. Cable television expanded the range of broadcast services available and improved the quality of local signal reception.

In the 1980s, Canadian cable systems began to offer distant radio and television signals provided to them by satellite in addition to the local signals captured off-air. This significantly increased cable service offerings that could then include Canadian pay and specialty television services, distant Canadian off-air radio and television services, and distant U.S conventional and U.S. specialty television services.

Over the last decade or so, consumers have also been able to access audio content via specialty audio services and pay audio. Specialty audio services are radio programming undertakings, distinct from over-the-air services, that are delivered exclusively by BDUs and are specialized in their format and target audience. To date, the Commission has approved eight such specialty audio services. In 1995, the Commission also approved two national pay audio programming undertakings: Galaxie and Max Trax. These services each offer thirty channels of commercial-free music; subscriber revenue is their only source of revenue. Each channel is devoted to a specific category of music, such as classical, contemporary Christian, jazz, rap, and rock. Galaxie and Max Trax are distributed across Canada on a discretionary basis by the major cable distributors and by the satellite distributor, Shaw Direct. However, because they rely on BDU distribution for delivery of their programming, the pay audio services generally lack the portability and convenience of wireless services such as podcasting to mobile digital devices.

Satellite Radio

At a public hearing on 1 December 2004, the Commission examined three applications for licences to carry on multi-channel subscription or pay radio services, distributed by satellite or terrestrial transmitters for direct reception by subscribers:

- Canadian Satellite Radio Incorporated (CSR), in partnership with XM Satellite Radio Inc., for a broadcasting licence to carry on a national multi-channel subscription radio service, to be delivered by satellite and terrestrial transmitters, for direct reception by subscribers. CSR proposed to offer 101 channels, 4 of which would be produced in Canada by the applicant.[7]
- Canadian Broadcasting Corporation (CBC), in partnership with SIRIUS Satellite Radio and Standard Radio Inc., for a broadcasting licence to carry on a national multi-channel subscription radio service, to be delivered by satellite and terrestrial transmitters, for direct

reception by subscribers. The proposed service would initially offer 78 channels, 4 of which would be produced in Canada by the CBC.

- CHUM Limited, in partnership with Astral Media Radio, for a broadcasting licence to carry on a national multi-channel subscription radio service, to be delivered by terrestrial transmitters only, for direct reception by subscribers. The proposed service would initially offer 50 channels, all of which would be produced in Canada by the applicant.

Two of the applicants involved partnerships with existing U.S. satellite-delivered subscription radio services as well as the use of U.S. satellites (see below for a discussion of the use of foreign satellites to deliver Canadian signals).[8]

The CRTC decided to license all three services even though CHUM had said that if the Commission licensed the three services, it would not proceed.[9] Canadian Satellite Radio and Sirius Canada are currently operating but the CHUM terrestrial radio service (later acquired by CTVglobemedia) was never launched. Both Canadian services have incurred losses since their inception. Finding themselves in a similar financial situation, the Canadian satellite radio companies' U.S. partners merged to form Sirius XM Radio in July 2008 and, at the time of writing, exploration of the possibility of a merger in Canada was continuing.[10]

DTH Satellite Distribution

As discussed in chapter 3, the satellite distribution of Canadian broadcast signals commenced in the 1970s using very large dish-like receiving antennas. For the next two decades, satellite distribution was limited essentially to the transfer of programs and broadcast signals between programming services and distribution undertakings, which in turn relayed these services to Canadian households. The rise of direct-to-home (DTH) services in the 1990s permitted the delivery of broadcast signals from high-powered geostationary satellites directly to small dish antennas located adjacent to the household.[11] In this way, DTH services provided Canadians with an alternative source of television and radio programming distinct from land-based cable services.

To attain financial viability, cable services typically require a certain critical mass, that is, a minimum number of subscribers linked together by coaxial cable in a local geographic area. By contrast, the economic viability of DTH service depends on the number of subscribers for the service across an entire region or country (i.e., within the satellite's service area or 'footprint'). Since DTH services commenced in the 1990s, Canadians in rural Canada, where cable services were previously uneconomic and unavailable, have been able to access a diverse range of satellite-delivered broadcast services. DTH services also provide competition to the local monopolies formerly exercised by cable services in urban areas.

Until the introduction of reliable scrambling or 'encryption' technology, DTH satellite 'broadcasting' expanded slowly because the service providers could not offer their services on a selective (i.e., subscription) basis. The development of effective encryption technology and addressable set-top receivers permitted DTH companies to discriminate between paying and non-paying subscribers, allowing individual signals to be descrambled by a subscriber's receiver on payment of a subscription fee. Subscription fees help to pay for very expensive satellites (which typically cost over $300 million each) and for the hundreds of services containing television programming created by producers.

In Canada, there are two companies licensed by the CRTC to provide DTH services with coverage throughout most of Canada. Bell Express-Vu (now called Bell TV) received CRTC authorization in December 1995 and launched its DTH service across Canada in September 1997. In August 1996, the CRTC authorized Star Choice to operate a Canadian digital DTH satellite distribution system. Star Choice (now called Shaw Direct) launched its service in the spring of 1997 with the set-top box and sixty-one-centimetre dish. Since then, subscription and installation prices for consumers have declined as a result of economies of scale and the desire of the DTH services to compete directly with cable systems.

Who owns the satellites from which Bell TV and Shaw Direct provide their services? With thirty-five years of experience, Telesat is one of the early pioneers in satellite communications and systems management. Created initially as a government agency in 1969, Telesat made history with the launch of Anik A1 in 1972 – the world's first domestic communications satellite in geostationary orbit to be operated on a commercial basis. Based in Ottawa, today Telesat operates a fleet of satellites for the provision of broadcast distribution and telecommunications services.

In November 2000, Telesat launched Anik F1, its sixth series of satellites. Anik F1, equipped with forty-eight Ku-band transponders and thirty-six transponders in C-band, has a footprint covering all of North and South America. Anik F2 was successfully launched on 17 July 2004, the world's largest communications satellite at the time and the first to fully commercialize the Ka frequency band – a satellite communications technology for delivering cost-effective, two-way broadband services.

One of the legal and regulatory conundrums for the Canadian government and the CRTC has been to establish equitable rules of the game for the different broadcast distribution technologies. Generally speaking, the CRTC's objectives include encouraging technological innovation and change while, at the same time, ensuring a degree of equity (a so-called level playing field) among all of those involved. With regard to broadcast distribution policy, this involves adapting the policies developed for cable television systems in the 1970s and 1980s to the technical and commercial realities of satellite distribution. A controversial case arose with the treatment of DTH services in the 1990s.

Case Study of the Canadian Government's Direction to the CRTC on DTH

Ostensibly to simplify its regulatory framework, on 30 August 1994 the CRTC announced a decision to exempt DTH satellite distribution undertakings from licensing. This exemption order, pursuant to section 9(4) of the Broadcasting Act, set out the terms and conditions defining a new class of undertaking (DTH satellite distribution undertakings) that would not have to meet certain licensing and regulatory requirements normally imposed on other distribution undertakings. As it turns out, the Commission's terms and conditions were interpreted as favouring one potential satellite operator (which proposed to use Canadian satellites in keeping with Canadian policy up to that time) over another (which proposed using DirecTV U.S. satellite infrastructure to deliver certain signals to Canadian homes).

On 12 September 1994, the Government of Canada announced its intention to initiate a review of DTH satellite policies and, in November 1994, the government published a notice seeking public comment on certain issues and announced the creation of a three-member panel to undertake a DTH policy review. The *Report of the Policy Review Panel, Direct-to-Home Satellite Broadcasting*, released in April 1995, concluded that DTH broadcasting undertakings should be formally licensed, not exempted from licensing. To facilitate the implementation of its recommendations, the panel included a draft 'direction' that the Cabinet could issue to the CRTC pursuant to section 7 of the Broadcasting Act.

In a letter dated 14 June 1995, the Deputy Ministers of Industry Canada and Canadian Heritage sent a letter to the secretary general of the

CRTC clarifying the government's policy, which says in part,

> One of the policy objectives in section 7 of the *Telecommunications Act* is: 'to promote the use of Canadian transmission facilities for telecommunications within Canada and between Canada and points outside Canada.' A long-standing application of this policy is to ensure the use of Canadian satellite facilities for traffic originating in Canada and destined for Canadians.
>
> A policy objective of the *Broadcasting Act* is that: 'each broadcasting undertaking shall make certain maximum use, and in no case less than predominant use, of Canadian creative and other resources in the creation and use, and in no case less than predominant use, of Canadian creative and other resources in the creation and presentation of programming, unless the nature of the service provided by the undertakings, such as specialized content or format or the use of languages other than French and English, renders that use impracticable, in which case the undertaking shall make the greatest practicable use of those resources.'
>
> In this context, where a Canadian broadcasting undertaking wishes to use foreign satellite facilities, the Canadian policy concerning the use of satellite facilities should be interpreted as follows:
>
> - The undertaking should make use of Canadian satellite facilities to carry (i.e., receive and/or distribute to Canadians) all Canadian programming services but may use either Canadian or non-Canadian satellite facilities to carry foreign originated services that are intended primarily for foreign audiences and are authorized, in whole or in part, for distribution by the CRTC; and
> - Under no circumstances should an undertaking use exclusively foreign satellites for the distribution of its services to Canadians. However, in the case of emergencies leading to a lack of availability of Canadian or foreign satellite services, back-up agreements between the two countries would be utilized.

Thus, under the conditions specified above, the Canadian government opened the door to the use of non-Canadian satellites for the delivery of broadcast signals to Canadian households. Pursuant to the *Report of the Policy Review Panel*, on 6 July 1995, the Governor-in-Council issued two Orders in Council on policy for licensing DTH satellite distribution undertakings and DTH pay-per-view television programming undertakings.

In Order in Council 1995-1105, the Canadian government directed the

Commission to promote, through licensing, a dynamically competitive market for DTH distribution undertakings, and to ensure, by appropriate means, that, with respect to the operation of a licensed DTH distribution undertaking, substantially the same rules govern the selection of Canadian and foreign programming services that are offered by the undertaking to its subscribers that are in effect for other distribution undertakings.

In Order in Council P.C. 1995-1106, the Canadian government directed the Commission to establish a class of licences in respect of the carrying on of DTH pay-per-view television programming undertakings, to prohibit such undertakings from acquiring exclusive or other preferential rights to pay-per-view distribution of feature films and other programming within Canada, and to ensure that DTH pay-per-view television programming undertakings are subject to equitable regulatory obligations.

Following the government's policy directions, the CRTC called for DTH licence applications in July 1995, held public hearings in October 1995, and issued its decisions on 20 December 1995. The decisions approved the applications proposed by ExpressVu (a consortium led by BCE) and Power DirecTV (a consortium involving Power Corporation and DirecTV in the United States). Power DirecTV declined to accept its licence and never commenced operations.

After the issuance of the ExpressVu and Power DirecTV decisions on 20 December 1995, which licensed two new DTH satellite distribution undertakings, the Commission revoked its Exemption Order Respecting Canadian Direct-to-Home (DTH) Satellite Distribution Undertakings, effective in March 1996.

Signal Piracy

Encryption has not resolved all of satellite delivery's problems. Satellite signal piracy occurs when someone modifies a DTH receiver to defeat or bypass the encryption or 'scrambling' system in order to receive signals without paying for a subscription. In these circumstances, the satellite operator is not compensated for the service it delivers and the performers and producers of the broadcast programs are not compensated for the programs the pirate household views. Pirating is a form of theft and ultimately reduces employment and growth in the Canadian broadcasting industry.

The DTH 'black market' is the market for illegal devices that defeat or bypass the scrambling system in a DTH satellite receiver. In this context, the seller tries to entice consumers with the notion of 'free TV' or 'free-pay-per-view' when, in fact, the consumer is being asked to acquire television satellite services illegally. Consumers who purchase black market equipment are at risk of losing signal reception because DTH satellite service providers frequently send out electronic countermeasure signals to disable such equipment. DTH service providers may also implement upgrades to their encryption systems that can render black market devices useless. These devices have no warranty and any modifications made to satellite-receiving equipment in order to install a black market device will typically void the equipment manufacturer's warranty. However, this does not prevent some Canadians from acquiring equipment on the black market, avoiding subscription fees, and, if the signals they receive are directly from U.S. satellites, effectively bypassing the Canadian broadcasting system.

The DTH 'grey market' is the sale and marketing to Canadians of American DTH satellite receivers and subscriptions to American DTH satellite services. This may be done in Canada, or in the United States with the intention to receive the signals in Canada. In the grey market, the customer pays for the service using a U.S. postal address.[12] Although the grey market client pays subscription fees, the grey market poses problems very similar to that of the black market, and grey market adherents are effectively opting out of the Canadian broadcasting system.

Section 9(1)(c) of the Radiocommunication Act says, 'No person shall ... decode an encrypted subscription programming signal or encrypted network feed otherwise than under and in accordance with an authorization from the *lawful distributor of the signal or feed*' (emphasis added). This section of the Radiocommunication Act was the subject of court challenges involving retailers who sold U.S. DTH satellite receivers and services in Canada. For awhile this led to confusion over differing court decisions on the interpretation of the 'lawful distributor of the signal or feed.' In other words, is a U.S. satellite operator a lawful distributor of signals in Canada?

A Supreme Court of Canada decision on 26 April 2002, *Bell Express-Vu Limited Partnership v. Rex 2002 SCC 42*, confirmed that the above-mentioned provision in the Radiocommunication Act refers to Canadian distributors only and effectively outlawed the decoding of U.S. satellite television programming by Canadian households.

Multipoint Distribution Services

Multipoint distribution service (MDS) is a wireless distribution technology that relies on short-range microwave distribution technology to deliver television signals directly to the home. Introduced to Canada in the early 1980s, MDS signals are receivable by a standard television receiver equipped with a special antenna and converter. As with FM signals, the receiving antenna must be within the line of sight of the MDS transmitter. The spectrum assigned by the Department of Industry to each MDS transmitter is sufficient to deliver fifteen analogue television signals in any given service area, or alternatively between 75 and 120 low-definition digital television signals. These bandwidth limitations restrict the variety of service offerings and therefore the competitiveness of MDS with the other distribution technologies. Owing to the line-of-sight requirements (which complicate MDS distribution in urban areas with many buildings) and the limitations on capacity, MDS has not been successful in Canada. As a result, the CRTC has been more lenient with MDS operations in its application of certain of the requirements in the Broadcasting Distribution Regulations.[13]

DSL Distribution

In the last few years, a new form of BDU has arisen. Digital subscriber line (DSL) undertakings distribute programming to subscribers through a telephone line using Internet protocol (IP) technology. Digital modulation techniques permit the transmission of voice, high-speed data, and video on the same telephone line. If a distributor wants to distribute Canadian off-air broadcast signals, as does Manitoba's MTS Communications Inc. (MTS), then, for all practical purposes, it requires a BDU licence from the CRTC. Aliant Telecom Inc. (Aliant), Bell Canada (Bell), Saskatchewan Telecommunications (SaskTel), and Telus Communications Inc. (Telus) are also licensed by the CRTC as distribution undertakings to provide service using DSL technology.

At one time, it was believed that the telephone companies, which possess a huge telecommunications infrastructure, would be able to compete directly with cable systems in the terrestrial delivery of broadcast signals to Canadian households. However, until recently, this has not proved to be case. Essentially, the telecommunications terrestrial infrastructure lacks bandwidth sufficient to deliver a large array of broadcast signals, particularly high-quality video signals, directly into the consumer's home. This situation is gradually evolving as a result of the replacement of copper wire with fibre optic transmission lines, new digital compression techniques, and the adoption of DSL technology by telecommunications companies.

However, the provision of DSL television services by telecommunications companies continues to proceed relatively slowly.

Broadcasting and the Internet

Is it possible to distribute broadcast signals over the public Internet?
Clearly it is technically possible and several Canadian broadcasters
make their signals available in this way, including the Canadian Parliamentary Channel and the French-language educational service, Canal
Savoir.

Does the presentation of webpages, music, or moving pictures on the
Internet constitute 'broadcasting'? The answer to this question depends
on one's interpretation of the definition of broadcasting in the Broadcasting Act. Section 2 of the Broadcasting Act says that '"broadcasting"
("radiodiffusion") means any transmission of *programs*, whether or not
encrypted, by radio waves or other means of telecommunication for
reception by the public by means of broadcasting receiving apparatus,
but does not include any such transmission of programs that is made
solely for performance or display in a public place' (emphasis added).
In addition, it says that '"program" means sounds or visual images, or a
combination of sounds and visual images, that are intended to inform,
enlighten or entertain, but does not include visual images, whether or
not combined with sounds, that consist predominantly of alphanumeric text.'

By this very broad definition, it appears that the distribution of
much, though not all, Internet content would constitute broadcasting
according to the Broadcasting Act and could be regulated and supervised by the Commission. However, webpages and e-mail messages
consisting predominantly of alphanumeric text, as well as material that
is not intended 'for reception by the public' would appear to be exclud-
ed from the Commission's purview.

This said, in May 1999, the CRTC announced its intention to exempt
from regulation all new media activities on the Internet.[14]

Here are some of the reasons the Commission gave at the time:

- The majority of services on the Internet consist predominantly of
  alphanumeric text (i.e., e-mail) and therefore do not fall within the
  scope of the Broadcasting Act and are outside the Commission's
  jurisdiction.
- Also among the services that do not fall within the scope of the

definition of broadcasting are those where the potential for user customization is significant (i.e., services where end-users have an individual, or one-on-one, experience and where they create their own uniquely tailored content) since these types of services do not involve the transmission of programs for reception by the public and therefore are not broadcasting.

• For those undertakings that offer new media services that do fall under the definition of broadcasting (i.e., digital audio services and audio-visual signals), the Commission concluded that regulation is not necessary to achieve the objectives of the Broadcasting Act.

How does the CRTC fulfil its commitment not to regulate the Internet? As was discussed in chapter 5, the Commission may exempt licensees from any or all of the requirements of certain parts of the Broadcasting Act or the Commission's own regulations, as long as it is satisfied that such an exemption will not inhibit the implementation of the broadcasting policy set out in subsection 3(1) of the Act. In December 1999, the CRTC issued Public Notice CRTC 1999-197, 'Exemption Order for New Media Broadcasting Undertakings,' to give effect to its announced intention.

In Broadcasting Public Notice 2007-13, 'Exemption Order for Mobile Television Broadcasting Undertakings,' the Commission also exempted mobile television broadcasting undertakings that use point-to-point technology to provide mobile television services to mobile devices. This exemption order applied to undertakings providing television broadcasting services that are received by mobile devices, including cellular telephones and personal digital assistants, and that have obtained prior consent of a broadcaster for the retransmission of its signal.

In 2008, the Commission initiated a proceeding to examine whether these two exemption orders continue to be appropriate and to what extent, if any, they need to be revised.[15] Essentially, the Commission wanted to determine if the new media broadcasting environment was contributing sufficiently to the achievement of the broadcasting policy objectives of the Broadcasting Act. Here are the reasons offered by the Commission in Broadcasting Public Notice CRTC 2008-44, 'Call for Comments on the Scope of a Future Proceeding on Canadian Broadcasting in New Media,' to explain its review:

• Recent data published by the Commission indicate that high-speed residential Internet access is available to 93 per cent of households across the country and has been adopted by more than 60 per cent of Canadian households.

• Internet television, mobisodes, and podcasts now share mainstream awareness in Canadian society.
• The pace at which professionally produced broadcasting content is being made available online is accelerating, but Canadian participation is lagging with respect to the amount of high-value, professionally produced new media broadcasting content and the level of early stage investment in the new media broadcasting environment.
• Canadian Internet users are spending more time online, while traditional broadcasting consumption is experiencing little growth overall and a demonstrated decline among younger demographics.
• New advertising revenue business models are emerging in the new media broadcasting environment, with growing participation by advertisers indicating support for these new media broadcasting marketing strategies.
• Broadcasters are making content available online, new media broadcasting alternatives and business models are evolving on a continual basis, and creators, aggregators and content providers are increasingly distributing content directly to Canadians via fixed and mobile new media platforms.

In Broadcasting Regulatory Policy CRTC 2009-329, 'Review of Broadcasting in New Media,' the Commission announced that it will maintain its approach for broadcasting content distributed over the Internet and through mobile devices, which includes exempting new media broadcasting services from regulation. In addition, the CRTC claimed that it had not been presented with convincing evidence that additional financial support was needed to create and present Canadian broadcasting content in new media. This said, considering the dynamic nature of the new media environment, the Commission announced its intention to review its regulatory approach within five years and to introduce a reporting requirement for new media broadcasting services to ensure the best information is available for future proceedings. The Commission also announced it decision to initiate a reference to the Federal Court of Appeal to clarify the status of Internet service providers (ISPs). The Federal Court will be asked to determine whether the Broadcasting Act should apply to ISPs when they provide access to broadcasting content. The CRTC also endorsed the call by the National Film Board of Canada for a Canadian digital strategy.

Finally, in Broadcasting Order CRTC 2009-660, the Commission amended the exemption order for new media broadcasting undertakings to include mobile devices and revoked the exemption order for mobile television broadcasting undertakings.

Because the issue of the distribution of broadcast signals via the Internet is also closely related to copyright issues, a discussion of two attempts to distribute broadcast signals over the Internet is provided in chapter 12, following a brief review of copyright law.

Notes

1 As of 21 November 2006, there were 1,248 over-the-air radio stations and 171 television stations in Canada. Canadian Radio-television and Telecommunications Commission, 'Future Environment Facing the Canadian Broadcasting System,' 10, 16.
2 See Broadcasting Public Notice CRTC 2006-160, 'Digital Radio Policy,' which sets out a revised policy for digital radio broadcasting in Canada.
3 See Broadcasting Public Notice CRTC 2002-31, 'A Licensing Policy to Oversee the Transition from Analog to Digital, Over-the-Air Television Broadcasting.'
4 See Broadcasting Public Notice CRTC 2007-53, 'Determinations regarding Certain Aspects of the Regulatory Framework for Over-the-Air Television.'
5 Figure 10.1 does not indicate the number of households relying on over-the-air delivery for their secondary broadcast receivers. The number of subscribers to alternate delivery methods, such as MDS and DSL services, described later in this chapter, is relatively insignificant at the time of writing.
6 In fact, some U.S. network broadcasters (dubbed 'border' broadcasters) located specifically to take advantage of neighbouring Canadian urban markets, such as those in Plattsburg, NY, and Bellingham, WA.
7 CSR was offering 130 channels at the beginning of 2008. See Robertson, 'CSR Sees Hope.'
8 Pursuant to the *Bell ExpressVu Limited Partnership v. Rex 2002* Supreme Court decision, the U.S. services could not themselves service the Canadian market.
9 The rationale for the Commission's decisions is contained in Broadcasting Public Notice CRTC 2005-61, 'Introduction to Broadcasting Decisions.'
10 See Karim Bardeesy, 'Satellite Radio Firms Feel Static from Auto Woes, *Globe and Mail*, 3 July 2009.

11 A geosynchronous satellite is a satellite whose orbital speed equals the Earth's rotational speed. If such a satellite's orbit lies over the equator, it is called a geostationary satellite. The orbits are known as geosynchronous orbit and geostationary orbit. Geostationary satellites appear to hover over one spot above the equator. The 'magic' altitude is at 35,786 km at which a satellite's orbital speed exactly matches the rate at which the earth rotates: once every sidereal day (twenty-three hours, fifty-six minutes).

12 Usually, a Canadian grey-market dealer will provide the necessary equipment to receive and decode United States programming, and will make the payment on behalf of its customers through the United States post office box. United States DTH services have said they will not knowingly provide service to anyone in Canada because they are not allowed to broadcast in Canada and do not hold the programming distribution rights for Canada.

13 See Broadcasting Public Notice CRTC 2004-63, 'Licence Renewal for Various Multipoint Distribution System Undertakings,' for a statement of the Commission's policy regarding MDS systems.

14 See Broadcasting Public Notice CRTC 1999-84, 'New Media.'

15 That is, the exemption orders contained in Public Notice CRTC 1999-197, 'Exemption Order for New Media Broadcasting Undertakings,' and in Broadcasting Public Notice CRTC 2007-13, 'Exemption Order.'

11 Distribution Carriage Arrangements

Until the early 1980s, cable systems, the only broadcasting distribution undertakings (BDUs) in operation at the time, retransmitted off-air signals only. Every subscriber to a given cable system received the same bundle of Canadian services and U.S. services (if U.S. services were available). There were no optional or discretionary services offered in addition to the basic cable service, which consisted of relayed, general interest, off-air signals. As indicated in chapter 3, the CRTC authorized the first Canadian pay television services in 1982 and the first specialty television services in 1984. During its initial proceeding on Canadian specialty services, the Commission announced it would also allow the carriage of selected non-Canadian specialty television services by cable distributors, provided such services contributed, without adverse effects, to the development of the Canadian broadcasting system.

The advent of digital distribution technology in the 1990s opened the way to greater flexibility in the provision of audio and video services to Canadian homes and obliged the CRTC to reconsider and modify the distribution rules created for the prevailing analogue broadcast environment.[1] The pressure to revise the existing rules came not only from technological change within the broadcasting industry but also from the competition of unregulated digital services, including the Internet, which seemed to possess the capacity to draw, Canadian consumers of audio-visual services away from regulated broadcast signals.

Today, it appears that the future of audio-visual media consumption will be linked to discretionary on-demand services. What is unclear is the extent to which Canadians will choose to receive their on-demand audio-visual services via a terrestrial cable or satellite distribution undertaking, or via a personal computer or mobile device linked to the broadband Internet. For the foreseeable future, the answer to this is question is probably both. This chapter examines the contemporary nature of digital television services, including pay-per-view and video-on-demand, the migration of program content to digital distribution media, and the evolution of the CRTC's carriage requirements for broadcasting distribution undertakings (BDUs) as those requirements appear at this time.

Basic Definitions

The CRTC initially defined *specialty* television services as services offered on a discretionary basis (i.e., at the option of the subscriber) and consisting of narrowcast television programming that was complementary to the programming of the general interest off-air and discretionary pay television services. With respect to advertising, the early specialty services agreed not to distribute any local advertising and, on average, not more than eight minutes per hour of national advertising. Today, the local advertising prohibition continues to apply, but most specialty services are permitted to carry up to twelve minutes of advertising per hour.[2] Unless exempted by a condition of licence, specialty television services are required to adhere to all of the Specialty Services Regulations.

Pay television was conceived initially as a discretionary service for which subscribers paid a specific fee over and above the basic cable fee in exchange for premium programming, often recent theatrical feature films, delivered continuously in a linear, scheduled format with no advertising. Today, pay television services continue to be prohibited from distributing any commercial message. Unless exempted by a condition of licence, pay television services are subject to all of the Pay Television Regulations.

A *pay-per-view* (PPV) service allows television viewers to purchase individual television programs of their choice. The programs available on pay-per-view are often feature films but may, in principle, include any category of program, including live events such as boxing and wrestling. A pay-per-view program is presented continuously at regular intervals in a fixed schedule on a scrambled channel. The variety of program offerings on a given BDU is limited by the number of channels assigned to such services. The viewer who opts to purchase a program must signal to the distribution undertaking's set-top decoder the desire to access a particular channel and program. The linear pay-per-view signal is then unscrambled temporarily and the viewer is billed accordingly. In accessing the program, the viewer must adapt his or her viewing or recording to the pay-per-view schedule. Unless exempted by a condition of licence, pay-per-view services are generally required to adhere to all of the Pay Television Regulations.

A *video-on-demand* (VOD) service also allows television viewers to purchase individual television programs of their choice but, unlike pay-per-view, a digital server plays a role, the process is more interactive, and only one BDU channel need be involved. The viewer who opts to purchase a program signals the desire to view the program to the BDU's set-top decoder but, in this case, the digitized program, usually a feature film or pre-recorded television program, is streamed or downloaded to the subscriber's digital set-top box. Because of limitations on the capacity of most VOD servers to handle a large volume of requests simultaneously, and delays involved if the program is downloaded, up to now a VOD service has not been considered appropriate for the delivery of live events. Aside from such traffic problems and minor delays, a VOD service can provide a very wide range of choice of programs and the viewer can access a given program at any time. Unless exempted by a condition of licence, VOD services are generally required to adhere to all of the Pay Television Regulations.

A *subscription video-on-demand* (S-VOD) service offers packages of television programming over a period of up to one week. The regulatory restriction of one week does not apply to packages that exclusively comprise events, provided the events programming is limited to the events themselves and does not include 'wrap-around' programming, since such programming might render the package similar to a specialty service and undermine the specialty service format. Indeed, the potential for BDUs to create such S-VOD services (which are loosely regulated) that compete directly with licensed specialty services (which are subject to more onerous regulation, including Canadian content regulation) continues to be a preoccupation of the licensed specialty services and the CRTC.[3]

Digital Television Programming Services

Specialty television services are divided into two broad categories: those initially licensed as analogue services and those licensed as digital services. The specialty services initially authorized between 1984 and 1999 (MuchMusic, TSN, MetéoMédia, RDI, etc.) were licensed as analogue services and generally benefit from mandatory carriage on BDUs. They are the beneficiaries of the former analogue licensing framework but are currently available on both analogue and digital distribution systems.

In 2000, the CRTC set out a digital specialty and pay licensing framework intended to take advantage of the new distribution technology. The new framework initiated the licensing of what are called Category 1 and Category 2 digital services. In this policy framework, new digital pay-per-view and VOD services are treated as Category 2 services for the purposes of carriage. The Commission's approach was intended to accomplish several objectives:

- Provide a diverse selection of attractive new Canadian program-ming services to be distributed to Canadian viewers with digital technology
- Facilitate the rollout of digital distribution technology
- Create a balance between the traditional licensing approach and a more open-entry, competitive environment made possible by the expansion of digital capacity
- Promote alliances between Canadian and foreign services

Category 1 digital specialty services (such as the Canadian Documentary Channel, Independent Film Channel, LCN Affaires) were licensed in a competitive scenario involving a public hearing in 2000 and benefit from certain CRTC carriage requirements. Category 2 digital specialty services (of which hundreds have been authorized but many have not been launched) are continuing to be licensed with few barriers to entry but no assurances of carriage. Each Category 2 service must negoti-ate its own carriage arrangements with each distribution undertaking. In 2007, there were forty-nine Canadian analogue specialty services, eighteen Category 1 digital specialty services, seventy-eight Category 2 digital specialty services, fourteen pay television services, thirteen pay-per-view services, and ten video-on-demand services.[4]

Following a recent regulatory policy review, in Broadcasting Pub-lic Notice CRTC 2008-100, 'Regulatory Frameworks for Broadcasting Distribution Undertakings and Discretionary Programming Services,' the CRTC announced that it will remove most of the rules governing competition among digital television services by 31 August 2011 and replace them with a few simplified rules. For example, among other things, the Commission announced its intention to:

- Allow direct competition between Canadian specialty services in mainstream sports and national news
- Maintain exclusivity across other genres while allowing for greater flexibility in the types of programming that pay and specialty services may broadcast
- Maintain access rights for the major Canadian pay and specialty services in a digital environment

Pay-per-View and VOD Programming Services

The CRTC first announced it would be prepared to accept pay-per-view proposals in 1988.[5] The Commission's announcement appears to have been in response to the growing competition to the pay television industry from video retail stores. Allarcom Pay Television subsequently developed one of the first licensed Canadian pay-per-view services. Issued on an 'experimental and temporary basis' by the Commission in February 1990, the licence permitted Allarcom to provide an English-language pay-per-view service to subscribers of its existing pay service, SuperChannel; in 1991 the Commission licensed the first regular pay-per-view service, Viewer's Choice, to serve Eastern Canada.[6] These two pay-per-view licensees were required to adhere to the Pay Television Regulations and specific conditions of licence. Similar requirements were imposed on the five DTH PPV undertakings approved by the Commission in 1995.

In 1994, the CRTC issued an exemption order for experimental VOD programming undertakings.[7] For the purpose of this order, the Commission defined a VOD service as a service that provides programs transmitted by telecommunications where individual consumers make specific selections to be received by a broadcasting receiving apparatus at any time of their choosing. This order is still in effect and exempts from licensing anyone carrying on a VOD broadcasting undertaking who is involved in a limited field trial or experiment to determine the technical feasibility of delivering such a service.

Compliance with the CRTC's exemption order provided the sole means of providing an authorized VOD broadcasting service in Canada until the Commission issued licences to five applicants in 1997. In the introductory statement to the licensing decisions of 1997, the CRTC outlined its first VOD licensing framework and announced that VOD would be considered a new class of licence – distinct from the existing class of pay and pay-per-view television programming undertakings.[8]

However, as with the pay and pay-per-view services, the Commission regulates VOD licensees pursuant to the Pay Television Regulations, which generally prohibit them from carrying advertising.[9]

The Commission set out its current VOD, S-VOD, and pay-per-view licensing framework in 2000.[10] At that time, none of the VOD services licensed in 1997 were affiliated with a BDU and none had been launched.

The regulatory framework for VOD established in Public Notice CRTC 2000-172, 'Introductory Statement to Decisions CRTC 2000-733 to 2000-738,' is very similar to that of 1997 and contains the following elements:

- VOD services are permitted to offer programming packages (several programs for a single price) if the total period during which the programming that may be viewed does not exceed one week
- The categories of programming that the VOD services may offer are unrestricted
- The Commission expects that, to the maximum extent possible, each VOD service will make its on-demand program offering available to customers in both official languages and that licensees will adhere to their commitments with respect to French-language programming
- A minimum of 5 per cent of English-language feature films and a minimum of 8 per cent of French-language feature films carried by each VOD service at any time should be Canadian, and the VOD services should make available all Canadian feature films suitable for VOD exhibition
- For all programming other than feature films, a minimum of 20 per cent of the titles available at any time must be Canadian
- Each licensee is to contribute a minimum of 5 per cent of the annual gross revenues earned by its VOD programming undertaking to the Canadian Television Fund or to an independent production fund, as defined in the Broadcasting Distribution Regulations
- In the case of a VOD service that is affiliated to, or integrated with, a distributor, for the purposes of calculating its financial support for independent production, the VOD service's gross annual revenues will be deemed to be 50 per cent of the total retail revenues received from customers.

Given that VOD services and pay-per-view services compete in the digital distribution environment, the Commission considered that the regulatory approach to general interest pay-per-view and VOD services should generally be 'consistent.' In fact, the regulatory framework for VOD and pay-per-view services is becoming more and more similar. There continue to be some differences between the two classes of licence but these differences are gradually disappearing as licences are renewed. For example, in a recent decision renewing Bell TV's DTH pay-per-view service, the Commission adopted an approach similar to that for the VOD licensees.[11] This decision is an example of the Commission's desire to remove the differences in licensing conditions applied to pay-per-view and VOD services. Even the restriction on the exhibition of fee-based live event programming, programming that is currently available on pay-per-view undertakings but not permitted on VOD undertakings, could change in the future.

Since VOD and PPV services deliver programming chosen by consumers, the meaning of Canadian content scheduling requirements for such programming is unclear. In Broadcasting Notice of Public Hearing CRTC 2007-10-3, 'Review of the Regulatory Frameworks for Broadcasting Distribution Undertakings and Discretionary Programming Services' (see below), the Commission raised the following issues with regard to VOD and PPV services:

> The Commission therefore seeks comment on how BDUs and programmers can take advantage of the increasingly important on-demand platform, while ensuring that VOD and PPV undertakings continue to make an appropriate contribution to the objectives of the Act ... How should the Commission balance providing flexibility for VOD and PPV undertakings to innovate and provide diverse, attractive program offerings, while not unduly affecting linear [i.e., conventional] programming services? How can the Commission ensure that Canadian programming services, especially those that are unaffiliated to existing VOD undertakings, have access to the on-demand platform? How can the Commission assist in ensuring that there is sufficient and appropriate programming available for on-demand platforms?

Following a public process, in Broadcasting Public Notice CRTC 2008-101, 'Call for Comments on a Proposed Regulatory Framework for Video-on-Demand Undertakings,' the Commission addressed such issues as the packaging of VOD services, access to VOD services, the acquisition of program rights, advertising on VOD services, the provision of and contribution to Canadian programming, the availability of programming in both official languages, a common licensing framework for PPV and VOD undertakings, and possible issues related to the introduction of network personal video recorders. The results of the process were pending at the time of writing this book.

Conversion to Digital Distribution

Although the Canadian analogue licensing and distribution framework has evolved, until recently it continued to reflect the needs of the cable television distribution technology existing at the time the specialty and pay services emerged in the 1980s. At that time, the prevalent analogue technology deployed by cable BDUs provided relatively limited channel capacity and a dependence on negative traps (installed manually outside each subscriber's home) to deliver packages or tiers of discretionary services.

Pursuant to the Broadcasting Act and, in particular, the broadcasting policy set out in section 3 of the Act, the CRTC has established Broadcasting Distribution Regulations that provide the basic regulatory framework for all distribution undertakings. As discussed in chapter 6, these regulations set out a standardized package of Canadian services, the basic service, which BDUs are generally required to provide in each service area. Furthermore, the Broadcasting Distribution Regulations establish priority rules regarding the basic service that include requirements for channel placement on clear, interference-free channels, beginning with channels 2 to 13 on the basic band.[12] There are also rules about the distribution of discretionary services such as specialty, pay, pay-per-view, and video on demand (VOD) services (i.e., services in addition to the basic service that are provided for an additional fee). According to the current regulations, and subject to capacity considerations, a BDU is required to distribute a large array of Canadian specialty and pay services.[13]

The CRTC's carriage requirements vary by class of BDU. For example, the Broadcasting Distribution Regulations provide that every Class 1 cable BDU must carry all specialty television services (except Category 1 and Category 2 services), all pay television services (with the exception of Category 2 pay television services) and at least one pay-per-view service, operating in the official language of the majority of the population within their licensed area, to the extent of available channels.[14] In addition, Class 1 and Class 2 BDUs that have a capacity of at least 750 MHz and make use of digital technology must distribute at least one pay television service in each official language. DTH BDUs must carry all pay and specialty television services (with the exception of Category 2 services and limited point-of-view religious services) to the extent of available channels.

In 2003, the CRTC set out its first regulatory framework for the distribution of analogue and digital over-the-air signals in the new digital environment.[15] Among other things, the Commission required distribution undertakings to carry the primary signal of Canadian over-the-air digital television signals as set out in the Broadcasting Distribution Regulations (unless otherwise provided by a condition of licence).

In 2006, the Commission announced its initial policy framework to guide the migration of the pay and specialty services approved as analogue services to the digital distribution environment.[16] Also in 2006, the CRTC announced its policy framework for licensing and distribution high definition (HD) digital pay and specialty services.[17] This announcement sets out the licensing regime for pay and specialty programming services with HD content, the obligations of broadcasting distribution undertakings that wish to distribute such services, and the applicable distribution and linkage rules. To encourage the transition to HD services, the Commission offers 'fast track' consideration to applications by existing pay and specialty services for licence amendments authorizing the provision of HD programming or for new broadcasting licences to carry on HD-transitional digital pay and specialty television undertakings, provided that the applications accord with the policy objectives, principles, and licensing conditions set out by the Commission. As a result, existing analogue and digital television services are being offered in a distinct HD format on a separate channel to HD subscribers.

In Broadcasting Notice of Public Hearing CRTC 2008-100, 'Regulatory Frameworks Broadcasting Distribution Undertakings and Discretionary Programming Services,' having declared its intention to adopt a regulatory approach designed to reduce regulation to the minimum essential to achieve the objectives of the Broadcasting Act by relying on market forces wherever possible, the Commission announced policy decisions to

- Exempt from its licensing requirements broadcasting distribution companies with fewer than 20,000 subscribers[18]
- Harmonize as much as possible the rules between satellite and terrestrial distribution companies

- Eliminate most rules governing how programming services are packaged
- Require broadcasting distribution companies to continue offering a basic service package after the transition to digital technology

Issue of Fee-for-Carriage for Conventional Television Stations

As explained in chapter 12, the compulsory licensing regime set out in the Copyright Act applies only to terrestrial or off-air distant signals that use the broadcast spectrum. It does not apply to programming services that are distributed exclusively by technologies such as coaxial cable, satellite, or digital subscriber lines (DSL). As a result, specialty and pay services are not covered by the compulsory licensing regime, and distribution undertakings are required to negotiate a licence fee for copyright with each individual specialty and pay service the distributor wishes to retransmit. In this way, specialty and pay services possess a margin of negotiating power with BDUs that conventional over-the-air services do not. This has meant that BDUs are compelled to negotiate with specialty and pay services, some of which the Broadcasting Distribution Regulations declare must be carried, and are compelled to pay fees (usually calculated on a monthly per subscriber basis) to such services. There are no such copyright issues or fees associated with the distribution of conventional over-the-air services because they are covered by the compulsory licensing regime set out in the Copyright Act.

For many years, conventional broadcasters have decried this situation and, as part of its review of the regulatory framework for over-the-air television initiated in 2006, the CRTC considered whether to permit a subscriber fee for the carriage of over-the-air television signals by BDUs. After examining extensively the issue at a public hearing in November 2006, the Commission announced its determination in May 2007:

> The Commission is not persuaded that there would be a net benefit to the broadcasting system, both in terms of increased expenditures on Canadian programming and the availability of Canadian programming services to viewers. Accordingly, the Commission is not convinced that the case has been made for the making of such a fundamental change to the revenue structure of the broadcasting system at this time, or that the proposal would ultimately further the objectives of the Act.[19]

However, less than six months later, the Commission resurrected the same issue and put it on the agenda of an existing public hearing in April 2008, saying,

> Given the importance of OTA television in the creation of Canadian programming and the impact that the introduction of such a fee [fee-for-carriage for conventional television stations] could have on BDUs, BDU subscribers, and pay and specialty services, the Commission is of the view that any further consideration of this issue should take place within a broad context, such as that afforded by the upcoming review initiated by Broadcasting Notice of Public Hearing 2007-10. Accordingly, the Commission finds it appropriate to expand the scope of this proceeding to include consideration of the fee-for-carriage issue.[20]

After once again reviewing the rules that affect conventional television broadcasters, the Commission decided to

- Deny the request for a subscriber fee for the carriage of local conventional television stations
- Allow conventional broadcasters to negotiate payments for the retransmission of their signals to other markets (known as 'distant signals')[21]

To compensate for its second refusal to impose fee-for-carriage of conventional broadcast services, the CRTC announced its intention to increase from 5 per cent to 6 per cent the contribution BDUs must make to Canadian programming and thereby generate the funding necessary for new or improved local programming by these services. The Commission said the additional 1 per cent contribution would be disbursed by a new Local Programming Improvement Fund (LPIF) to be overseen by the Canadian Association of Broadcasters.[22]

Under pressure from parliamentarians and off-air licensees, in July 2009 the CRTC announced:

- An increase in the contribution to the LPIF by BDUs to 1.5 per cent of their gross revenues for the year 2009–10
- Combined negotiations on the distribution of distant television signals with those related to the value of local conventional television signals as regards the appropriate compensation for the distribution of local signals by BDUs.[23]

In other words, without fully explaining why, the CRTC finally accepted the principle of a subscriber fee for the carriage of local conventional television stations but declined to establish a fee schedule, leaving this to negotiations by the parties directly involved. In seeking comments on what mechanism should be used for establishing a negotiated, fair value for conventional signals, the Commission also stated that, in the absence of negotiated agreements, it would provide resolution through binding arbitration.[24]

Notes

1 Section 3(1)(t) of the Broadcasting Act sets out specific policy objectives for distribution undertakings. See Appendix A.
2 In Broadcasting Public Notice CRTC 2007-53, 'Determinations regarding Certain Aspects of the Regulatory Framework for Over-the-Air Television,' the CRTC announced a phasing out of the ceiling on advertising by conventional (off-air) television broadcasters by 1 September 2009. See also the discussion of advertising to children in chap. 9.
3 As a result, the commission has proposed a new regulatory framework for VOD undertakings. See Broadcasting Public Notice CRTC 2008-101, 'Call for Comments on a Proposed Regulatory Framework for Video-on-Demand Undertaking.'
4 CRTC, *Communications Monitoring Report 2008*, 114–15.
5 See Public Notice CRTC 1988-173, 'Introduction to Decisions CRTC 88-772 to 88-777: The Renewal of the General Interest Pay Television Network Licences and Certain Specialty Service Network Licences.'
6 See Decisions CRTC 90-78 and 91-160 respectively.
7 See Public Notice CRTC 1994-118, 'Exemption Order.'
8 See Public Notice CRTC 1997-83, 'Licensing of New Video-on-Demand Programming Undertakings: Introduction to Decisions CRTC 97-283 to 97-287.'
9 Recently, the Commission has authorized PPV licensees, by conditions of licence, to distribute programming that contains commercial messages where those messages are already included in a program previously aired by a Canadian programming service and the program is subsequently offered on an on-demand basis at no charge to the subscriber.
10 See Public Notice CRTC 2000-172, 'Introductory Statement to Decisions CRTC 2000-733 to 2000-738: Licensing of New Video-on-Demand and Pay-per-View Services.'
11 Broadcasting Decision CRTC 2006-22.

12 Generally speaking, interference-free or unimpaired channels on analogue cable systems are those channels on which local television station is
broadcasting its signal. Thus in Montreal, since CFCF-TV broadcasts off-air
on channel 12, channel 12 on the local cable systems is considered to be an
'impaired' channel and no Canadian service identified in the priority rules
may be placed on channel 12 (although another service may be).

13 Category 2 digital specialty and pay services are generally exempted from
compulsory distribution because of the open entry nature of the licensing
regime that governs them.

14 A Class 1 BDU is essentially one with six thousand or more subscribers. A
Class 2 BDU is essentially one with two thousand to six thousand subscribers. A Class 3 BDU is essentially one with fewer than two thousand
subscribers. But where a new terrestrial BDU chooses to operate within
the service area of an incumbent and competes with that incumbent, the
Commission assigns the same class of licence to the new entrant as it has
to the incumbent, regardless of the number of subscribers the new entrant
actually serves.

15 See Broadcasting Public Notice CRTC 2003-61, 'The Regulatory Framework for the Distribution of Digital Television Signals.'

16 See Broadcasting Public Notice 2006-23, 'Digital Migration Framework.'

17 See Broadcasting Public Notice 2006-74, 'Regulatory Framework.'

18 This policy decision is subject to several conditions, including one whereby terrestrial BDUs that compete in a market with another BDU that serves
twenty-thousand or more subscribers will continue to have to be licensed.

19 Broadcasting Public Notice CRTC 2007-53, 'Determinations.'

20 Broadcasting Notice of Public Hearing CRTC 2007-10-3, 'Review of the
Regulatory Frameworks.'

21 See Broadcasting Public Notice CRTC 2008-100, 'Regulatory Frameworks.'

22 The Commission subsequently accepted the CAB's proposal that the fund
be administered by a third party: McCay Duff LLP.

23 See Broadcasting Regulatory Policy CRTC 2009-406, 'Policy Determinations resulting from the 27 April 2009 Public Hearing.'

24 See Broadcasting Notice of Consultation CRTC 2009-411, 'Policy Proceeding on a Group-Based Approach to the Licensing of Television Services
and on Certain Issues relating to Conventional Television.' Subsequently,
in reaction to a notice of appeal to the Federal Court of Appeal by Bell
Canada, the Commission announced its intention once again 'to consider'
the principle of a (negotiated) subscriber fee at a public hearing. See Broadcasting Notice of Consultation CRTC 2009-411-3.

12 Copyright, Broadcasting, and the Internet

The flexibility and portability of digital media favour the globalization of audio-visual production and distribution as well as greater consumer access to audio-visual content. As a result of the multiple choices available on the Internet, Canadians frequently resort to foreign, often U.S., websites because there are few domestic alternatives. In the absence of a national strategy, Canada risks falling behind other countries in the establishment of a domestic presence in the new media environment. In this new environment, the presence of Canadian voices is central to the maintenance of Canadian identity. What is more, the new digital services, including mobile video broadcasting services, have the potential to draw audiences and advertising revenues away from licensed Canadian broadcast services and high-quality Canadian programs. The presence, side-by-side, of a regulated broadcast sector and an unregulated new media sector poses a number of problems for Canadian broadcast policymakers.

This chapter examines the interface between broadcasting and the Internet, with particular attention to copyright law. Since, for the time being, the CRTC has chosen not to regulate the Internet, copyright law has acquired greater importance in determining what is permissible in cyberspace and focused greater attention on problems of copyright law interpretation, enforcement, and reform. This said, the application of copyright law is very different from the application of broadcasting law insofar as copyright law does not give any preference to Canadian content. Rather, copyright law applies to works reproduced within Canada, and indeed outside Canada where the Canadian government has implemented reciprocal agreements or treaties with foreign countries.

Copyright Law

The primary objective of copyright law is to give authors certain rights of exploitation for their work, provided the work is original, and to attribute appropriate credit to authors of such work.[1] 'Moral rights' are related to the treatment of works subject to copyright so as to protect the author's reputation. In Canadian law, 'neighbouring rights' are related to rights similar to copyright that are accorded to performers, record producers, and broadcasters. Neighbouring rights derive from the interpretation, recording, and broadcast transmission of material and do not concern authorship or the original production of a work.

Copyright law differs from country to country. However, since the late nineteenth century, the international community has developed treaties, agreements, and conventions that have attempted to standardize copyright law across participating nations. This said, if Canada adheres to an international convention, the Canadian government must still enact domestic legislation to implement any resulting changes before adherence to the convention will have effect. As a general rule, only Canadian law applies in Canada and only Swiss law in Switzerland.

Canadian copyright law is set out in the Copyright Act and applies to any original literary, dramatic, musical, or artistic work. A wide range of expression is included in each of these categories. Drama presented in audio-visual works is an example of the type of expression that is protected as dramatic work. Instrumental compositions and compositions consisting of lyrics and music are examples of musical works. Artistic works include drawings, paintings, photographs, sculptures, and architectural works.

Generally, the copyright owner has the sole right to produce or reproduce his or her work for distribution in another form or to authorize such use. Anyone who engages in such an activity without the permission of the copyright owner is violating that owner's copyright, and is said to be 'infringing' copyright. There are, however, exceptions to this general rule sometimes called users' rights, of which important examples are 'fair dealing' and 'retransmission.'[2]

The producer of a new work for radio or television must be concerned not only with copyright in the work in production, but also the use of pre-existing music, an extract from another audio-visual work, a photograph, or some other pre-existing element for which copyright law in Canada and abroad requires a permission for its use. The act of obtaining such permission is sometimes called 'licensing' or 'clearing' the rights for such use.

What Is Protected?

The Copyright Act declares that 'copyright shall subsist in Canada, for the term hereinafter mentioned, in *every original literary, dramatic, musical* and *artistic work*,' subject to certain conditions (emphasis added).

A *dramatic work* is defined to include

- Any piece for recitation, choreographic work or mime, the scenic arrangement or acting form of which is fixed in writing or otherwise
- Any cinematographic work
- Any compilation of dramatic works

A *cinematographic work* 'includes *any* work expressed by any process analogous to cinematography, whether or not accompanied by a soundtrack' (emphasis added). In other words, any category of television program (news, public affairs, sports, variety, etc.) is considered a cinematographic work in copyright law – whether or not the program has a 'dramatic' character.

A *musical work* is defined as 'any work of music or musical composition, with or without words, and includes any compilation thereof.' And a *compilation* is

- A work resulting from the selection or arrangement of literary, dramatic, musical or artistic works or of parts thereof
- A work resulting from the selection or arrangement of data

Sound recordings, performances, and radio broadcasts are non-traditional elements that lack an author in the traditional sense and do not qualify as 'works.' However, in Canada, they are protected by copyright.

According to the Copyright Act, *sound recording* means 'a recording, fixed in any material form, consisting of sounds, whether or not of a performance of a work, but excludes any soundtrack of a cinematographic work where it accompanies the cinematographic work.' A given item may be subject to more than one form of copyright protection: for example, a sound recording has its own separate copyright distinct from the copyright in the music, lyrics, or performance recorded.

Performance means 'any acoustic or visual representation of a work, performer's performance, sound recording or communication signal, including a representation made by means of any mechanical instrument, radio receiving set or television receiving set.' And *performer's performance* means any of the following when accomplished by a performer:

- A *performance* of an artistic work, dramatic work or musical work, whether or not the work was previously fixed in any material form, and whether or not the work's term of copyright protection under this Act has expired,
- A *recitation* or *reading* of a literary work, whether or not the work's term of copyright protection under this Act has expired, or
- An *improvisation* of a dramatic work, musical work or literary work, whether or not the improvised work is based on a pre-existing work.

A *broadcast* is not defined in the Act, but a *broadcaster* is 'a body that, in the course of operating a broadcasting undertaking, broadcasts a communication signal in accordance with the law of the country in which the broadcasting undertaking is carried on, but excludes a body whose primary activity in relation to communication signals is their retransmission.'

Authorship

Who owns the copyright of a work? The first owner of copyright is usually the author of the work. Employees are an example of an exception to this rule, but someone on a service contract owns the initial copyright to his or her work. The author also owns the moral rights to the work. This said, a transfer or assignment of ownership of copyright to a third party, as well as a waiver of moral rights, is possible.

Who is the author of a cinematographic work? The author of a cinematographic work is not explained anywhere in the Act, and the issue of who is the author of such a work has rarely been addressed by the courts in Canada. In principle, the author is the person responsible for creating the work, more specifically, the person responsible for creating the dramatic character of the work (if this is a defining characteristic of the work, as it is in most fiction.)

This said, some identify the director as the author of a cinematographic work.[3] It appears to the present author that this interpretation is too general, and wrong in particular cases. For television and film drama, there is a spectrum of shared authorship, ranging from the writer to the director across various dramatic forms: teleplay, téléroman or 'soap,' télésérie or high-budget television series, telefilm (sometimes called a 'feature film for television' or movie of the week (MOW)), theatrical feature film, etc. To assign the appellation of 'author' to the director of a teleplay, téléroman or 'soap,' who films the work in sequence as set out in the original screenplay, appears wrong. Such an assignation would also be inaccurate or incomplete in the case of many television series and telefilms, and even some theatrical feature films. This said, in practice, the producer of a work usually acquires all of the rights necessary to control its production and distribution so that an explicit identification of the 'author(s)' is avoided.

Duration of Copyright

Copyright usually lasts for the life of the author, the remainder of the calendar year in which the author dies, and for fifty years following the end of that calendar year. Therefore, protection will expire on 31 December of the fiftieth year following the author's death. After that, the work becomes part of the public domain and anyone can use it. This is the general rule to which certain exceptions apply.

In the case of a cinematographic work, the duration of copyright protection varies. If the cinematographic work qualifies as a work 'in which the arrangement or acting form or the combination of incidents represented give the work a dramatic character,' the general rule concerning the duration of copyright applies and the copyright term is the life of its author plus fifty years. For a cinematographic work that does not have a 'dramatic character,' the copyright expires at the end of the fiftieth year following its publication (or the date of its creation if it was unpublished). Stock footage, footage caught on a security camera, or the recording of a sports event would thus probably qualify as a cinematographic work lacking dramatic character and be protected for fifty years from publication.

One problem with a particular cinematographic work being qualified as a work with 'dramatic character' is that the duration of copyright is calculated on basis of the life of the author. However, as was pointed out above, Canadian copyright law does not define or identify the author of a cinematographic work (who might be the writer, the director, or some combination of 'creators'), and the duration of the life of the author is therefore uncertain.

Any cinematographic work of a Crown corporation or a government agency, such as the CBC or the National Film Board, whether or not it is dramatic in character, is protected for the same duration as a cinematographic work lacking dramatic character. Copyright in the work belongs to the institution. Thus, any work, cinematographic or otherwise, prepared or published by, or under the control of the government is protected by copyright until the end of the fiftieth year following its publication, or the date of its creation if it was not published.

Retransmission of Broadcast Signals

As a result of the Free Trade Agreement between Canada and the United States that came into effect on 1 January 1989, Parliament amended the Copyright Act in Canada so that, beginning in 1990, distribution undertakings providing broadcast signals to Canadian subscribers are required to pay copyright holders for the transmission of their programs.

With respect to distant off-air signals, distribution undertakings are obliged to pay royalty fees to collectives that represent program rights holders at rates established by 'tariffs,' which are set by the Copyright Board of Canada. Such licensing arrangements are called 'compulsory licences' because all program rights users are obliged to acquire such rights use at the Copyright Board's tariff. Furthermore, all of the rights holders in a given class are required to accept payment of the Copyright Board's tariff as fair and complete payment for their rights. In other words, both rights holders and rights users are obliged to accept the rules of the Canadian copyright licensing regime. No negotiation between them is involved, although either may make representations to the Copyright Board regarding the appropriate tariff. The compulsory licence regime for the retransmission of broadcast signals constitutes an exception to authors' and other copyright owners' rights generally.

However, the compulsory licensing regime applies only to terrestrial or off-air distant signals that make use of the broadcast spectrum. It does not apply to signals that are distributed exclusively by other means, such as coaxial cable, satellite, or digital subscriber lines (DSL). Specialty and pay services are not covered by the compulsory licensing regime as long as their first transmission to the public is via a distribution undertaking and they are not retransmitted. Consequently, before commencing service, distribution undertakings are required to negotiate an affiliation agreement and licence fee with each individual specialty and pay service the distributor wishes to carry.

Why transmit more than a very few specialty or pay services, if any at all? As described in chapters 6 and 11, all licensed broadcasting distribution undertakings (BDUs) are required to distribute certain 'basic' Canadian services as set out in the Broadcasting Distribution Regulations. Under the current regulations, subject to capacity considerations, a BDU is required to distribute a large array of Canadian specialty and pay services. Thus, distributors who wish to distribute the specialty and pay services required by the regulations must negotiate with each specialty or pay service that the distributor wishes to carry in order to determine an appropriate payment for copyright that can be remitted to the rights holders of the program content. This negotiation process can be onerous.

The distribution of broadcast signals in Canada normally requires that the distributor possess a BDU licence from the CRTC. Since the publication of the CRTC's exemption order for new media, there have been two notable attempts to retransmit off-air broadcast signals over the Internet: one by iCraveTV and another by JumpTV. Neither of these two distributors possessed a BDU licence from the CRTC. In explaining their respective business plans, both iCraveTV and JumpTV claimed to be acting in accordance with the Commission's new media exemption order. However, a complicating factor relating to copyright frustrated their efforts to retransmit terrestrial broadcast signals over the Internet.

iCraveTV

The first notable attempt to retransmit broadcast signals over the Internet by a distributor that did not hold a BDU licence from the CRTC involved iCraveTV.com. From December 1999 to February of 2000, iCraveTV retransmitted sixteen off-air television signals from its headend in Richmond Hill, Ontario, using standard receive antennas and RealPlayer streaming technology. Streaming media on the Internet are best viewed with a high-speed connection that enables the viewer to receive images that are comparable to those obtained via conventional television reception. At the time, the screen resolution on a computer resulting from streaming was usually less than that on a television monitor, depending on Internet connection speed, computer speed and memory, monitor quality, and a variety of other factors.

All of iCraveTV's signals originated with television stations available off-air in the Toronto area. Six signals originated from the United States and ten from Canada. Users who reported a Canadian postal code and agreed to certain conditions obtained access to the site. A specific broadcast signal was streamed live in its entirety at no charge to the viewer once the viewer selected the signal. iCraveTV sold banner advertising on the opening TV guide page and below the television image in the streaming player to pay for its activities.

iCraveTV claimed that it was a new media broadcast undertaking as defined by the Commission's 'Exemption Order for New Media Broadcasting Undertakings' (see Public Notice CRTC 1999-197) and that its activities were therefore lawful under the Broadcasting Act. However, its retransmission of television broadcasting stations over the Internet met with heavy opposition from U.S. and Canadian program suppliers. The U.S. suppliers, primarily large Hollywood studios, claimed that iCraveTV made their programs available to U.S. Internet homes that accessed iCraveTV's website by using a Canadian postal code. The Motion Picture Producers Association of America and other U.S. program suppliers apparently contacted Canadian broadcasters to enlist them in the opposition to iCraveTV's operations.

iCraveTV said it had budgeted to pay the appropriate copyright fees as a percentage of revenues to program rights holders as required by the Copyright Board of Canada in accordance with the Copyright Act and that it expected to pay the applicable copyright fees as do cable and DTH satellite distribution undertakings. However, before commencing operations, iCraveTV did not apply to the Copyright Board for a tariff in regard to the retransmission of the off-air television services it was providing to the public.

iCraveTV claimed to have designed its service exclusively for Canada and to have acted in accordance with the technical and security capacities of the Internet at the time. But after an application to the courts by U.S. and Canadian program rights holders, iCraveTV ceased operations in exchange for an abandonment of the legal proceedings against it.

JumpTV

JumpTV is a Montreal-based company offering live online delivery of television services worldwide from a variety of broadcasters in various countries. JumpTV's services are available via streaming media to viewers with an Internet browser and Windows Media Player. Each of the channels offered on JumpTV is available by monthly subscription, at costs ranging from about US$5.95 monthly to about US$9.95 monthly for high-speed broadband access. Thematic packages of broadcast services are also available. JumpTV conducts its online streaming operations from facilities located in Canada and the United States and, from time to time, adds new television services to its existing channel line-up.

In 2001, before commencing the retransmission of any over-the-air television signals broadcast in Canada, JumpTV applied to the Copyright Board of Canada for a tariff to cover their retransmission. However, in this case, the Copyright Board declined to process JumpTV's application. Why?

Essentially, in the presence of opposition from Canadian and American rights holders and broadcasters to JumpTV's application to the Copyright Board, the Board stalled the application until the Government of Canada amended Canadian copyright law to prevent any Internet provider of broadcast signals from obtaining a compulsory licence.

Compulsory Licences and the Retransmission of Broadcast Signals

As a result of the opposition to JumpTV's application to the Copyright Board, on 12 June 2002, the Governor-General-in-Council issued Order in Council P.C. 2002-1043, directing the CRTC to seek public comment and report on

- The broadcasting regulatory framework for persons who retransmit the signals of over-the-air television or radio programming undertakings by the Internet
- The appropriateness of amending the New Media Exemption Order published in Appendix A to Public Notice CRTC 1999-197 regarding the retransmission by the Internet of signals from over-the-air television or radio programming undertakings
- Any other measures the Commission considers appropriate in order to meet the objectives of the broadcasting policy set out in the Broadcasting Act in this regard.

Before the CRTC reported back to the Cabinet on these issues, on 12 December 2002 the government enacted Bill C-11, an Act to Amend the Copyright Act. Bill C-11 amended section 31 of the Copyright Act and 'clarified' who is eligible to obtain a compulsory licence to retransmit broadcast signals by redefining the term *retransmitter* to exclude new media companies that retransmit such signals over the Internet and are exempt from CRTC regulation under the Broadcasting Act.

Bill C-11 ensured that cable and satellite retransmitters of broadcasting signals that benefit from the compulsory licence regime would continue to do so but that retransmitters who might wish to use the Internet, such as iCraveTV and JumpTV, would not be able to obtain a compulsory licence from the Copyright Board. As a result of this amendment, Internet retransmitters are required to negotiate copyright with each of the rights holders in order to obtain authorization to broadcast its works. However, many program rights holders, including most independent producers, refuse to cede Internet transmission rights because, once on the Internet, they fear that the digital versions of their programs will be widely copied. If they do cede Internet rights, they often do so at a prohibitive price.

On 17 January 2003, the CRTC announced its response to Order in Council P.C. 2002-1043 in Broadcasting Public Notice CRTC 2003-2, *Internet Retransmission: Report to the Governor General in Council Pursuant to Order in Council P.C. 2002-1043*. Essentially, the public notice says that it is not necessary or appropriate to require the licensing of Internet retransmitters. Instead, Internet retransmission undertakings would remain exempt from these and the requirements under Part II of the Broadcasting Act. Since the amendments to the Copyright Act addressed the main concern identified in the CRTC's proceeding, the Commission saw no need to amend the New Media Exemption Order at the time. Thus, Internet distributors, such as JumpTV, are deemed ineligible to obtain a compulsory licence to retransmit broadcast signals available in Canada and, by default, obliged to negotiate with each individual broadcast signal owner that it wishes to retransmit.

JumpTV continues to operate but it does not have a licence from the CRTC and does not distribute any Canadian or U.S. broadcast signals. JumpTV appears to distribute primarily channels from outside Canada, the United States, and Western Europe that broadcast programming produced exclusively by these channels. Very few of the channels distributed by JumpTV contain programming acquired by these channels from third parties, such as independent producers, and in this way JumpTV, and the channels themselves, avoids the copyright issues associated with acquiring independently produced programs.

With a few exceptions, Canadian broadcasters generally decline to transmit their signals or authorize their signals to be retransmitted in their entirety over the Internet for fear of infringing copyright. A few broadcaster distribute their own signals over the Internet, including CPAC (the Canadian Parliamentary Channel), which consists largely of House of Commons and parliamentary committee proceedings; Canal Savoir, a French-language educational service that broadcasts primarily university lectures and interviews; and the French-language news services RDI, LCN, and ARGENT. These services provide mostly live or live-to-tape programming, in low resolution, and very little independently produced programming. Individual independently produced programs made for television broadcast are often available on the Internet, either legally or illegally, but rarely as scheduled programming presented by a licensed broadcast undertaking.

Broadcasting on the Internet

There appear to be two possible ways to legally distribute Canadian broadcast signals over the Internet at the present time.

One way is to take advantage of the CRTC's new media exemption order (Public Notice CRTC 1999-197) and avoid the necessity of licensing by the CRTC. This route must be adopted if the distributor's signal is available on the public Internet (i.e., the Web). Furthermore, the distributor must then negotiate with each programming service to be carried (off-air services as well as specialty and pay services) and secure an agreement with each such service. Since Canadian broadcast services do not always acquire Internet rights for their acquired programs (the rights are either too expensive or not available), Canadian broadcast services, other than the exceptions noted above, generally refuse to negotiate with Internet-based broadcasting service providers.

The other approach is to obtain a BDU licence from the CRTC, in which case the licensed distributor falls automatically under the compulsory licence regime for off-air services established by the Copyright Act. However, because it has exempted the Internet from regulation, the CRTC declines to license any BDU that proposes to use the public Internet to distribute a Canadian broadcast service.

Other New Broadcast Media

There are several other operations currently involved in the distribution of television signals and programs.

TV on My PC

TV on My PC enables Aliant's high-speed Internet customers to view live broadcast television on their computers. TV on My PC functions like any other window-based application: it can be started, moved, minimized, maximized, and closed.[4] Once it is started, the subscriber can access broadcast television, change channels, view the electronic programming guide, and adjust volume.

In 2009, TV on My PC's channel line-up included

- TSN
- MuchMusic
- MuchMoreMusic
- Space
- TechTV
- Outdoor Life Network
- The Comedy Network
- STAR!
- CBC Newsworld
- CTV Newsnet

TV on My PC is a service available only to Aliant high-speed Internet service customers in New Brunswick and Nova Scotia. To obtain TV on My PC, the subscriber requires Aliant's high-speed Internet service, and must use the Aliant Connection Manager software to connect to the Internet. On 9 September 2009, Bell Aliant stopped selling TV on My PC.

Exemption Order for Mobile Television Broadcasting Undertakings

The CRTC has decided that mobile television broadcasting services, such as cellular telephones and personal digital assistants, are unlikely to compete significantly with traditional broadcasting services as a result of the limitations of the wireless technology employed, the battery life and screen size of the handset, the reduced image and audio quality, and the type and range of programming choices offered by the mobile broadcasters.

In Broadcasting Public Notice CRTC 2007-13, 'Exemption Order for Mobile Television Broadcasting Undertakings,' the Commission exempted from licensing requirements and associated regulations those mobile television broadcasting undertakings that provide mobile television services that are received by mobile devices and that meet the other criteria set out in the exemption order appended to the notice.

The four criteria set out in the exemption order are:

- The Commission would not be prohibited from licensing the undertaking by virtue of any Act of Parliament or any direction to the Commission by the Governor-in-Council.
- The undertaking provides television broadcasting services that are received by mobile devices, including cellular telephones and personal digital assistants.
- The undertaking uses point-to-point technology to deliver the service; that is, the undertaking transmits a separate stream of broadcast video and audio to each end-user.
- The undertaking has obtained the prior consent of a broadcaster for the retransmission of its signal.

Broadcasting Notice of Public Hearing CRTC 2008-11, 'Canadian Broadcasting in New Media,' initiated a public proceeding, including a public hearing in early 2009, to consider issues pertaining to Canadian broadcasting in new media, including whether the approaches the Commission adopted in 1999 and 2007 on the new media exemption orders were still appropriate. In Broadcasting Regulatory Policy CRTC 2009-329, 'Review of Broadcasting in New Media,' the Commission announced its decision to maintain the current approach for broadcasting content distributed over the Internet and through mobile devices, including the exemptions of new media broadcasting services, for at least another five years. (See chapter 10.)

Notes

1 Intellectual property law is a broader concept that embraces copyright, patents, trademarks, and other schemes to protect inventions, original designs, trade secrets, and other business interests.
2 'Fair dealing' is similar to the U.S. concept of 'fair use.' See section 29 of the Copyright Act.
3 Vaver, *Copyright Law*, 82.
4 At the time of writing, TV on my PC would not function with Microsoft Windows Vista.

13 Canadian Ownership and Competition Policy

Broadcasting is considered by many to constitute a unique cultural activity that requires special measures to ensure that Canada's cultural sovereignty is protected. Among other measures, this has led to limitations on the non-Canadian ownership of Canadian broadcasting undertakings. A second and distinct ownership policy issue concerns competition policy in broadcasting and addresses the potential losses in social, economic, political, and cultural welfare that can result from the common ownership of broadcasting undertakings. Industrial concentration can result in excessive market power and losses in consumer welfare in any industry, including broadcasting. While market failure due to limited spectrum access may be reduced by the advent of digital distribution technologies, digital technology raises new issues related to economies of scale and scope as well as new access issues for delivery platforms. This chapter addresses two aspects of ownership policy: policy related to the foreign ownership of Canadian broadcasting undertakings and policy related to the common ownership of multiple Canadian broadcasting undertakings by a single owner, which forms a part of 'competition policy.'

Foreign Ownership Policy in Broadcasting

Canadian ownership constitutes a fundamental element in the Government of Canada's broadcasting policy. Section 3(1)(a) of the Broadcasting Act says that 'the Canadian broadcasting system shall be effectively owned and controlled by Canadians.' This requirement is general and does not require that each and every broadcasting undertaking be owned and controlled by Canadians but only that the Canadian broadcasting system as a whole be effectively owned and controlled by Canadians.

However, Parliament's instructions to the CRTC extend further than this. As we have seen, section 26 of the Broadcasting Act permits the Cabinet to issue specific orders to the CRTC. More specifically, section 26(1)(c) gives the Cabinet the power to proscribe, or delimit by negation, certain classes of applicants for licences. The Commission has received several such orders, and one of these concerns the Canadian ownership of broadcasting undertakings.

The direction to the CRTC from the Cabinet on the 'Ineligibility of non-Canadians' narrows the scope of the requirements of Canadian ownership and control contained in the Broadcasting Act by stating clearly that 'no broadcasting licence may be issued, and no amendments or renewals thereof may be granted, to an applicant that is a non-Canadian.'[1]

What is a Canadian or a non-Canadian in this context? Essentially, to be considered Canadian for the purpose of the directive, a corporate licensee must satisfy certain criteria, including the criterion that 'Canadians beneficially own and control, directly or indirectly, in the aggregate and otherwise than by way of security only, not less than 80 per cent of all the issued and outstanding *voting shares* of the corporation and not less than 80 per cent of the votes.' Furthermore, any separately incorporated entity or holding company of such a licensee must fulfil the requirement that 'Canadians beneficially own and control, directly or indirectly, in the aggregate and otherwise than by way of security only, not less than 66 2/3 per cent of all of the issued and outstanding *voting shares* of the parent corporation and not less than 66 2/3 per cent of the votes' (emphasis added).

In other words, the rules are a little less restrictive for a holding company that controls a licence-holder than for the actual licence-holder itself, but they still constitute a meaningful limitation. However, these rules apply only to the voting shares of the company in question; they do not apply to non-voting shares or to debt.[2]

This said, even if a potential owner fulfils the first criterion related to share ownership, the direction to the CRTC gives the CRTC the authority to reject the application if the Commission 'determines that an applicant is controlled by a non-Canadian, whether on the basis of personal, financial, contractual or business relations or any other considerations relevant to determining control.' In other words, independent of the issue of who controls the voting shares, the CRTC may determine that a potential foreign owner controls the broadcasting undertaking on the basis of such considerations as the composition of its board of directors, provisions in the shareholders agreement relating to control, or the conditions on which the financing of the acquisition is accomplished. On any one of these issues, the Commission may deny the applicant's proposal to acquire the undertaking in question. Because it reaches beyond the simple criterion of voting share control, the Commission's application of this part of the directive (section 3) is sometimes referred to as the 'control in fact' test.

Why does the government maintain Canadian ownership rules? There are several reasons. In the past, particularly during wartime, there have been national security concerns that have led Canadian governments to treat broadcasting as a vital element in Canadian military defence strategy. Today, to the extent that national cultural sovereignty is an objective of government policy, Canadian ownership of broadcasting and other media is an important contributing element to the cultural defence of the nation as well. Many believe that, compared to non-Canadian owners, Canadian owners are more sensitive to the Canadian government's broadcasting objectives and more likely to conduct themselves in accordance with those objectives. And should the Canadian government, or one of its agencies, wish to correct the behaviour of a licensee, its potential leverage over a Canadian citizen or enterprise is much greater than that over a non-Canadian company, particularly a non-resident.

Do foreign firms really behave much differently from domestic firms in sectors of the economy where there are no restrictions? In other words, does the nationality of ownership matter in regard to (a) respecting Canadian law and (b) exercising good Canadian corporate citizenship? Respecting Canadian law means conforming to the letter of the law, whereas 'exercising good Canadian corporate citizenship' refers to striving to fulfil the objectives and spirit of the Broadcasting Act, not merely complying with the letter of the law. There is a concern that foreign-owned firms, including U.S. firms, might not understand the nuances of Canadian broadcasting policy and might underestimate the role of Canadian broadcasting undertakings in furthering the objectives of the Broadcasting Act. More importantly, they might be more willing to challenge Canadian law and call on their home government to back up their position.

Role of the Investment Canada Act

Outside of the broadcasting sector, the Investment Canada Act provides the legal framework that generally enables the Government of Canada to review foreign investment in Canada. According to this Act and its associated regulations and guidelines, proposed new investments that could result in ownership and control of Canadian cultural businesses by foreign investors are the responsibility of the Department of Canadian Heritage. Cultural businesses include those involved in the production, distribution, sale, or exhibition of film or video products and audio or video music recordings. The Investment Canada Act requires that foreign investments in the production, distribution, and exhibition sector of the film and video industries be compatible with national cultural policies. To this end, Canadian Heritage maintains a list of strategic objectives to which, where possible, foreign investments that are compatible with national cultural policies should contribute.

With regard to broadcasting, however, Industry Canada remains responsible for foreign investments because the authority to review broadcasting ownership transfers was not transferred to Canadian Heritage in 1999 along with the authority to review other cultural investments.[3] What is more, Industry Canada's Investment Review Branch has never reviewed a foreign investment involving a broadcasting undertaking. Instead, it is the Canadian Government's Direction to the CRTC (Ineligibility of Non-Canadians) SOR/97-192 that limits foreign investment in companies holding Canadian broadcasting licences. The direction presumably limits foreign investment in companies holding Canadian broadcasting licences to such an extent that, in practice, foreign investment in the broadcasting sector has never been reviewable under the Investment Canada Act.

Canadian Ownership Concentration

Competition policy is concerned with the degree or extent of competition in a market. According to conventional economic theory, the extent of competition in a given market is determined by the degree to which competition approximates an ideal type: 'perfect' competition. In a perfectly competitive market, the average return or profit to firms operating in the market approximates the average return in competitive financial markets. That is, the going interest rate (plus a return to risk-bearing, if the market involves some risk). One characteristic of perfect competition is that entry to the market is unrestricted or 'free.' In other words, there are no barriers to entry, and anybody, or almost anybody, can enter the market.[4]

In practical terms, an indication of the degree of competition in a giv-
en market is the number of different owners of the firms operating in
the market. An industry is said to be 'concentrated' if a few ownership
groups dominate most of the sales, and 'competitive' if there are many
diverse owners. Three different forms of industrial concentration are

• *Horizontal integration*: a horizontally integrated firm owns several
  broadcasting outlets in the same market. For example, Rogers
  Broadcasting owns two FM radio stations in the Winnipeg market,
  CITI-FM and CKY-FM.
• *Vertical integration*: a vertically integrated firm participates in more than
  one successive stage of the production, scheduling, or distribution of a
  service. For example, Groupe TVA produces television programs
  through its subsidiary TVA Production inc., and broadcasts those programs on its own TVA stations, whose signals are then distributed on
  cable by Vidéotron. All three of these companies (Groupe TVA, TVA
  Production inc., and Vidéotron) are owned by Quebecor Media.
• *Cross-media ownership*: constitutes ownership of more than one mass
  communications medium in the same market. For example, CTV-
  globemedia owns the conventional station CFTO-TV Toronto, the
  specialty services TSN and MuchMusic (among others), and Toronto's *Globe and Mail* daily newspaper.

These different forms of broadcasting industry concentration raise
issues of public policy, including the diversity of expression available
to the Canadian public.
Why does concentration arise? If there are no barriers to entry to an
industry, so that firms can freely enter and exit the industry, then the
industry is usually competitive. In this situation, as soon as profit levels
rise above the average profit level for all Canadian industries then, in
principle, new players enter to drive the average rate of profit down to
the norm. Why does this fail to happen in the real world? Many economists believe that barriers to entry may produce concentrated industries and 'imperfect' competition.
Barriers to the entry of new players can include

• High start-up costs (such as those for a daily newspaper or television station)
• Economies of scale (such as those available to radio and television
  networks)

- Concentration in the financial sector, which makes borrowing difficult for some parties
- Patents that restrict products or procedures to a few
- International trade barriers (such as foreign ownership restrictions)
- Natural monopolies involving natural resources (such as waterways)
- Government licensing procedures (such as those of the CRTC)

By issuing licences, a regulatory authority, whether in broadcasting, telecommunications, postal services, or electricity supply, restricts market entry to those who hold a licence or are prepared to accept price or 'tariff' rate regulation. Government licensing and regulation may therefore reinforce other pre-existing tendencies toward industrial concentration. To the extent this is true, 'deregulation' may favour competition. However, in the event that a market is already dominated by a small number of players, deregulation may actually lead to more concentration if the large players enjoy such a head start in the sector that many or all newcomers fail, or are swallowed up before establishing themselves.

International Context

Industrial concentration is certainly not unique to Canada. The digitization of media, the lowering of international trade barriers, and the partial deregulation of the audio-visual sector have encouraged the convergence of certain audio-visual technologies, products, and services, the consolidation of companies engaged in similar audio-visual activities (horizontal integration and cross-media ownership), and the vertical integration of creation, production, distribution, and marketing activities in the United States and Europe as well as in Canada.

While there are various explanations for the consolidation and convergence of the last few years, vertical integration usually confers advantages on those involved and is mostly the result of profit-seeking behaviour by private sector firms. When a major broadcast network, movie studio, or record label controls the production of the content it is distributing, it enjoys several benefits:

- Early involvement with the development of content to attract the desired demographic and build the corporate brand
- Ability to negotiate better terms with a related producer than with a third party, with the corporate parent as the ultimate beneficiary

- Leverage in negotiations with other production companies (in those cases where it is necessary to go outside the corporate family)
- Ability to repurpose content on alternative platforms (such as conventional, specialty, and pay television networks) and to distribute the content online at a lower incremental cost to the owner
- Ongoing participation in the profits from the sales of successful product (rather than simply a one-time fee for services)

Consolidation and vertical integration in the United States have made it more difficult for Canadian audio-visual producers, and those from other countries, to penetrate the huge U.S. broadcasting market. With a few major ownership groups controlling most broadcasting activity, it is not easy for independent production companies to sell high-quality television programs in the U.S. market and increasingly rare for non-U.S. production companies, including Canadian companies, to make television sales in the U.S. market. The U.S. and European markets have changed fundamentally since the mid-1990s, when Canadian television production companies such as CINAR, Nelvana, and Telescene made many sales of Canadian programs to U.S. broadcasters. Today, any Canadian business or government strategy that places too much emphasis on the development of international markets, particularly those in the United States and Europe, to develop growth opportunities will encounter difficulties. In an increasingly integrated world, Canadian broadcasting cannot escape the negative effects of media concentration within its major trading partners.

Competition Policy and Canadian Broadcasting

The Competition Act sets out a competition policy for the entire Canadian economy, and the Act's overriding objective is stated in section 1.1: 'The purpose of this Act is to maintain and encourage competition in Canada in order to promote the efficiency and adaptability of the Canadian economy, in order to expand opportunities for Canadian participation in world markets while at the same time recognizing the role of foreign competition in Canada, in order to ensure that small and medium-sized enterprises have an equitable opportunity to participate in the Canadian economy and in order to provide consumers with competitive prices and product choices.'

In a broader sense, however, the competition policy set out in the Competition Act may be reinforced or supplemented in government-regulated industries and, in fact, the CRTC plays an important role in determining the extent of competition in the broadcasting industry. Following an extensive review, the CRTC has set out a comprehensive ownership policy in Broadcasting Public Notice CRTC 2008-4, 'Regulatory Policy: Diversity of Voices,' which sets out the framework for economic competition in broadcasting.

What is CRTC policy on broadcasting industry ownership concentration? Does the CRTC have a clear mandate to limit industry concentration or to foster competition in broadcasting?

To begin, common ownership, concentration of ownership, horizontal integration, vertical integration, cross-media ownership, and economic competition are not directly addressed in the Broadcasting Act, and the CRTC has no explicit mandate in regard to competition issues. Attention by the Commission to industrial concentration and other competition issues is a by-product of the pursuit of objectives in the Act related to the 'diversity of voices.'

The Broadcasting Act addresses issues related to the diversity of voices as follows:

> 3. (1) It is hereby declared as the broadcasting policy for Canada that ...
>> (i) the programming provided by the Canadian broadcasting system should
>>> (i)   be *varied* and *comprehensive,* providing a balance of information, enlightenment and entertainment for men, women and children of all ages, interests and tastes, ...
>>> (iv) *provide a reasonable opportunity for the public to be exposed to the expression of differing views on matters of public concern,* and
>>> (v)   *include a significant contribution from the Canadian independent production sector.* [Emphasis added.]

Thus, although there is no explicit reference to competition issues in the Act, there are indirect references insofar as the programming provided by the Canadian broadcasting system should be 'varied and comprehensive,' the public should be exposed to 'differing views,' and programming should include a significant contribution from the 'independent' production sector.

How has the CRTC responded to these requirements in regard to competition policy? Essentially, the CRTC has acceded to market forces while trying to place some restrictions or fetters on the major players in order to fulfil the diversity of voices requirements of the Broadcasting

Act. In this context, the Commission has developed general policies on the common ownership of radio and television undertakings that are summarized in Public Notice 2008-4.

Radio

Until about ten years ago, the CRTC applied a relatively restrictive ownership policy in order to ensure there was a diversity of voices in each community across Canada.[5] Under the old policy, the Commission generally restricted a single owner to a maximum of one AM station and one FM station operating in the same language and in the same market.

With the publication of its Commercial Radio Policy 1998, this policy changed to include the following:

- In markets with fewer than eight commercial stations operating in a single language, an owner is permitted to own or control as many as three stations operating in that language, with a maximum of two stations in any one frequency band (AM or FM).
- In markets with eight commercial stations or more operating in a given language, an owner is permitted to own or control as many as two AM and two FM stations in that language.[6]

Why did the Commission make this change? Its stated objectives were

- A desire to achieve a new, but 'reasonable' balance between the concerns for preserving a diversity of news voices and the benefits to be obtained by common owners from economies of scale (bearing in mind, among other things, the financial losses occurring in AM radio)
- The belief that common ownership and consolidation can increase the diversity of formats in some markets, since competition may lead players to seek to occupy the same commercial territory (the common ground in the middle) and to offer a very similar format, whereas common ownership allows for the diversity and complementarity of formats

Furthermore, in its Commercial Radio Policy 1998, the CRTC said that it would consider issues regarding competition and the diversity of news voices in regard to media cross-ownership (radio, television, distribution undertakings, print, etc.) when assessing an application for a new licence to transfer the ownership or effective control of a radio station.

Thus, for example, in Broadcasting Decision CRTC 2003-205, the CRTC denied the applications by Groupe TVA (60 per cent) and Radio Nord (40 per cent) to acquire the assets of Quebec radio stations held indirectly by Astral Media, including eight AM stations, two digital stations, three radio networks, and an FM station. According to the Commission, the applications raised concerns about concentration of ownership and cross-media ownership. Groupe TVA and Radio Nord did not satisfy the Commission that their recovery strategy for AM radio in Quebec and the proposed benefits would significantly outweigh the concerns about concentration of ownership and cross-media ownership. Among other issues, the CRTC noted that the majority shareholder of TVA, Quebecor Media, is a major player in Quebec's newspaper and magazine sector, with such daily newspapers as *Le Journal de Montréal* and *Le Journal de Québec*, and magazines such as *Le Lundi, 7 jours*, and *Dernière heure*. In addition to its activities involving publishing houses and an Internet portal, Quebecor Media controls the largest cable undertaking in Quebec, Vidéotron ltée, as well as a major book and music retailer, Archambault Group Inc.

However, in Broadcasting Decision CRTC 2005-15, the Commission approved the applications by Astral Media Radio and a subsidiary of Corus Entertainment for authority to acquire several radio undertakings in Quebec as part of an exchange of assets that included the flagship French-language station CKAC-AM Montreal. At the time of the decision, Astral was the licensee of thirty AM and FM radio stations in Quebec, including six digital stations. Astral also operates several radio stations in Atlantic Canada and is a major presence in the French-language specialty and pay TV sector and in the outdoor advertising sector. Corus is one of the largest broadcasting groups in Canada, with a significant presence in all provinces except the Atlantic provinces. At the time of Decision CRTC 2005-15, Corus owned fifty-eight radio stations in Canada, including seven digital stations. Two AM and ten FM stations were located in Quebec, six of which were located in the greater Montreal area and six elsewhere in Quebec. Corus also operates numerous specialty television services. The Commission was of the view that the concerns identified in this decision would be offset by the benefits of an approval subject to the terms and conditions set out therein.

The CRTC's annual policy monitoring reports have provided some

TABLE 13.1 Audiences for the largest English-language commercial radio operators*

	Audiences (thousands of hours)			Share of audiences (%)		
	2005	2006	2007	2005	2006	2007
Corus Entertainment Inc.	67,880	64,498	61,834	17	17	16
Standard Broadcasting Corporation Limited (acquired by Astral Media in 2007)	65,643	61,653	60,604	17	16	16
Rogers Communications Inc.	48,243	46,772	47,380	12	12	12
CHUM Limited (acquired by CTVglobemedia in 2007)	36,116	34,004	35,008	9	9	6
Newcap Inc.	21,224	21,724	21,724	5	6	6
Total of the 5 largest ownership groups	239,106	228,651	226,550	61	59	59
Total Canadian English-language radio**	391,468	390,148	385,116	100	100	100

* Refer to 'Notes to tables 4.2.6, 4.2.7 and 4.2.9' following table 4.2.9 in the original source
** Listening hours include tuning to public and private Canadian English-language stations
Source: CRTC Communications Monitoring Report 2008, 95

information on concentration in English-language radio in recent years, such as that presented in table 13.1.

Tuning to the largest French-language commercial radio operations in Canada is even more concentrated than that for English-language radio. In 2007, for example, 63 per cent of all such tuning was attributable to three radio ownership groups: Astral Media, Corus Entertainment, and Cogeco.[7]

Industry concentration has certainly increased since the adoption of the CRTC's *Commercial Radio Policy 1998*, particularly in French-language radio.[8] Nonetheless, the Commission's recent commercial radio policy review that culminated in Broadcasting Public Notice CRTC 2006-158, 'Commercial Radio Policy,' did not address ownership concentration and left the pre-existing ownership policy in place, as did Broadcasting Public Notice CRTC 2008-4, 'Regulatory Policy: Diversity of Voices.'

Television

Part of the CRTC's current policy for television was set out in the Commission's 1999 policy statement, 'Building on Success: A Policy Frame-

work for Canadian Television.'⁹ Here is how the Commission presented
its policies on horizontal and vertical integration at that time:

- With regard to *horizontal integration*, the CRTC will generally permit
  ownership of no more than one over-the-air television station in
  one language in a given market. According to the Commission, this
  policy 'ensures the diversity of voices in the market, and helps to
  maintain competition in each market.'
- With regard to *vertical integration*, where an independent producer
  applies to participate in the ownership of a broadcasting undertaking, the Commission will expect the applicant to address the issues
  arising from the resulting vertical integration and propose appropriate safeguards. Where a broadcaster participates in the ownership
  of a production company, the Commission will expect the licensee
  to address the issues arising from vertical integration at the time of
  licensing or licence renewal.

Apart from the policy of limiting common ownership to no more
than one over-the-air television station in one language in a given market (a policy that has been set aside on several occasions), the CRTC
basically proceeded case by case until 2008. This case-by-case approach
also applied to cross-media ownership.

What follows are a few common ownership decisions that illustrate
the Commission's case-by-case approach to ownership up to the publication of Broadcasting Public Notice CRTC 2008-4, 'Regulatory Policy:
Diversity of Voices':

- In Decision CRTC 2000-747, the Commission approved the trans-
  fer of effective control of CTV Inc. to BCE Inc. (which owned Bell
  Telephone, Sympatico, and Bell ExpressVu at the time). In Decision
  CRTC 2001-457 renewing CTV's licence, the Commission addressed
  concentration issues as follows:
  - The Commission expects CTV to ensure that at least 75 per cent of
    all Canadian priority programming broadcast over the broadcast
    year is produced by independent production companies. For the
    purpose of this expectation, an independent production company
    is defined as a production company in which CTV, and any com-
    pany related to CTV, owns or controls less than 30 per cent of the
    equity (vertical integration).
  - The Commission considers that CTV must, as a minimum, main-

tain news management for its television stations that is separate from news management for the newspapers controlled by Bell Globemedia (including the *Globe and Mail*). In the decision, the Commission set out a Statement of Principles and Practices as a condition of licence for CTV.[10] The Commission also required CTV, by condition of licence, to establish a monitoring committee. CTV must establish an impartial, neutral committee to receive and handle all complaints concerning CTV's compliance with the Statement of Principles and Practices (cross-media ownership concentration).

- In Broadcasting Decision CRTC 2004-503, the CRTC approved applications filed by Groupe TVA and Sun Media Corporation (owner of the *Toronto Sun*), both subsidiaries of Quebecor Media, to transfer effective control of Toronto One to TVA and Sun Media. The Commission considered the applicants' position concerning the limited role that traditional news coverage and newscasts would play in the programming of Toronto One (now called 'Sun TV'). However, to preserve the editorial independence between the *Toronto Sun* and Toronto One, the Commission set out a Statement of Principles and Practices for Toronto One, as a condition of licence in the decision (cross-media ownership concentration).
- In Broadcasting Decision CRTC 2007-165, 'CTVglobemedia Inc. (formerly Bell Globemedia Inc.) on Behalf of CHUM Limited,' the Commission approved an application by CTVglobemedia to acquire effective control of CHUM, subject to the condition that CTVglobemedia divest itself of CHUM's five Citytv stations in Vancouver, Calgary, Edmonton, Portage La Prairie, and Toronto. In the decision, the Commission essentially reaffirmed its common ownership policy, which generally permits no more than one conventional television stations in one language in one market so as to ensure a diversity of voices in the market. CTVglobemedia was therefore obliged to reorganize its initial purchase and resale agreements by selling the Citytv stations (to Rogers Communications) and retaining seven A-Channel television stations in smaller cities that it had not previously contemplated owning (horizontal integration).

The CRTC's annual *Communications Monitoring Report* provides information on concentration in Canadian television, such as that in table 13.2 related to conventional over-the-air television.

However, the conventional television services also compete with spe-

TABLE 13.2 Revenues of the largest English-language conventional television ownership groups

Financial year ending 31 August	Total revenues (millions $)			Share of revenues (%)		
	2004	2005	2006	2004	2005	2006
CanWest Global	622	623	594	32	33	30
CTVglobemedia	684	761	776	36	40	39
CHUM[11]	191	223	227	10	12	11
Total of the 3 largest ownership groups	1,497	1,607	1,597	78	85	81
CBC (advertising revenues only)	223	133	224	12	7	11
Total of the 4 largest operators	1,720	1,740	1,821	90	92	92
Total Canadian English-language conventional television (incl. CBC ads)	1,916	1,897	1,980	100	100	100

Source: CRTC *Broadcasting Policy Monitoring Report 2007*, 71[12]

cialty and pay television services (many of which are owned by the four operators identified in table 13.2). Consequently, table 13.2 does not provide a complete perspective on concentration in the television sector. In 2006, for example, specialty and pay television services earned an additional $2,499 million in total revenues, including both advertising and subscriber revenues.

In Broadcasting Public Notice CRTC 2008-4, 'Regulatory Policy: Diversity of Voices,' the CRTC announced its intention to restrict cross-media ownership in order to ensure that Canadians benefit from a range of perspectives in their local news coverage. According to the Commission's new policy, one owner may control only two of the following types of media that serve the same market: a local radio station, a local television station, or a local newspaper. However, since the Commission defined the *Globe and Mail* and the *National Post* as national newspapers, its new policy did not affect CTVglobemedia and CanWest with regard to the ownership of radio stations, television stations, and local newspapers.

In Broadcasting Public Notice 2008-4, the CRTC also decided to impose limits on the horizontal ownership concentration of television broadcasting services. As a result, the Commission announced it would not approve a transaction that would result in one party controlling more than 45 per cent of the total television audience to conventional, specialty, and pay television services. This said, an ownership group can increase its audience share beyond 45 per cent by operating and growing its existing assets without infringing the Commission's policy.

Transactions that would result in one party controlling 35 per cent to

45 per cent of the total audience share will be carefully examined, and transactions that would result in one party controlling less than 35 per cent of the total audience share will be expeditiously approved, assuming there are no other concerns.

Broadcasting distribution undertakings (BDUs) also play an important role in providing a diversity of voices in the broadcasting system. In Broadcasting Public Notice 2008-4, the Commission announced that it would not approve a transaction that would result in one entity effectively controlling the delivery of programming services in a single market. In other words, the Commission is not prepared to allow a single entity to control all the BDUs in any given market.

The Competition Bureau

The Competition Bureau is responsible for the administration and enforcement of the Competition Act, and three labelling statutes.[13] The Competition Bureau's role is to promote and maintain fair competition so that Canadians can benefit from lower prices, product choice, and quality services. Under the Competition Act, the commissioner of competition can launch inquiries, intervene as a competition advocate before federal and provincial bodies, challenge civil and merger matters before the Competition Tribunal, and make recommendations on criminal matters to the attorney general of Canada.

Matters that may be reviewed by the Competition Tribunal (see Part VIII of the Competition Act) include mergers, and jurisdiction over competition in broadcasting is therefore shared between the two agencies. However, in the Competition Act, there is no reference to any cultural or social objectives such as those found in the Broadcasting Act. The Competition Bureau's role is to promote and maintain competition so that Canadians can benefit from competitive prices and product choices. Not only is the Competition Bureau's mandate limited to the promotion and maintenance of competition in the interests of competitive prices, but the Competition Bureau restricts its analysis largely to the consideration of advertising markets and is less concerned with manifestations of market power that are not reflected in consumer prices.

To reduce any potential conflict between the two agencies, in 1999 the Competition Bureau and the CRTC agreed on an 'interface' document that describes the authority of the CRTC under the Broadcasting and Telecommunications Acts and that of the Bureau regarding telecommunications and broadcasting. Among other things, the interface document says,

Under the *Broadcasting Act*, prior approval of the Commission is required for changes of control or ownership of licensed undertakings. Whereas the Bureau's examination of mergers relates exclusively to competitive effects, the Commission's consideration involves a broader set of objectives under the *Act*. This may encompass consideration of competition issues in order to further the objectives of the *Act*. *The Bureau's concern in radio and television broadcast markets relates primarily to the impact on advertising markets and, with respect to broadcast distribution undertakings, to the choices and prices available to consumers.* The Commission's concerns include those of the Bureau except that its consideration of advertising markets relates to the broadcasters' ability to fulfill the objectives of the *Act*.[14] [Emphasis added.]

However, this agreement has not resulted in complete harmony between the two agencies. For example, on 21 December 2001, the commissioner of competition filed an application with the Competition Tribunal, pursuant to the Competition Act, opposing the proposed acquisition by Astral Radio of eight French-language radio stations located in Quebec belonging to Télémédia and of Télémedia's 50 per cent ownership interest in Radiomédia.[15]

In Broadcasting Decision CRTC 2002-90, the Commission approved the applications for authority to transfer effective control of the broadcasting undertakings held by Télémédia in Quebec, New Brunswick, and Nova Scotia to Astral Radio, a subsidiary of Astral Media. Following Decision 2002-90, the commissioner of competition expressed concerns about the potential impact of this transaction on competition in the French-language radio industry in Quebec. Subsequently, Astral Media, Télémédia, and the commissioner of competition entered into a consent agreement dated 7 August 2002 requiring Astral Media to sell certain of its French-language AM radio stations in Quebec. The consent agreement was registered with the Competition Tribunal on 3 September 2002, and terminated the application filed by the commissioner of competition with the Competition Tribunal.

At the Communications Law and Policy Conference of the Upper Canada Law Society in April 2004, the commissioner of competition at the time, Sheridan Scott, a former legal counsel to the CRTC, expressed her view that the Competition Act and the Broadcasting Act should be amended to give the CRTC exclusive jurisdiction over competition in the realm of broadcasting. In January 2007, the former commissioner of competition and head of the Competition Bureau of Canada (1997–2003), Konrad von Finckenstein, was named chairman of the CRTC.

And in January 2008, the CRTC recommended that a merger review process for communications entities be implemented 'in which the roles of the Competition Bureau and the Commission are clearly defined, in which decisions are made openly and transparently, and in which the Commission, in the public interest, will have the ultimate responsibility for approval.'[16]

Notes

1 *Direction to the CRTC (Ineligibility of Non-Canadians)*, P.C. 1997-486, 8 April 1997, as amended by P.C. 1998-1268, 15 July 1998.

2 In Broadcasting Decision CRTC 2007-429, 'Transfer of Effective Control of Alliance Atlantis,' the CRTC approved an application by CanWest Media-Works Inc. to acquire effective control of Alliance Atlantis's broadcasting companies. Consequently, the holding company of Alliance Atlantis's broadcasting companies is now controlled by CanWest, the owner of 66.6 per cent of the holding company's voting shares. A private equity affiliate of the U.S. firm Goldman, Sachs & Co. is the owner of the remaining 33.3 per cent of the voting shares. Nonetheless, in terms of both voting and non-voting shares, CanWest holds a 36 per cent equity interest in the holding company, with Goldman, Sachs holding the remaining 64 per cent. Considering both equity and debt financing, Canadians provided less than 20 per cent of the approximately $1.5 billion purchase price for Alliance Atlantis's broadcasting assets.

3 In other words, broadcasting is not included in Schedule IV of the Regulations along with other cultural activities.

4 Normative economic analysis of the provision of broadcasting by competitive firms has focused on the type of programming produced and the viewer/listener benefits it generates. This literature concludes that a competitive market may provide programming sub-optimally: popular program types will be excessively duplicated, and speciality types of programming will tend not to be provided. See, for example, Owen and Wildman, *Video Economics*, chaps. 3, 4.

5 See Public Notice CRTC 1998-41, 'Commercial Radio Policy.'

6 See ibid.

7 CRTC, *Communications Monitoring Report 2008*, 95.

8 See figure 4.16. (The data in this figure do not distinguish between English- and French-language broadcasting.)

9 See Public Notice CRTC 1999-97, 'Building on Success.'

10 In essence, the Statement of Principles and Practices requires the licensee to maintain separate and independent news management and presentation structures for CTV television operations that are distinct from those of any CTV affiliated newspapers. It thus requires separation of news management functions, but not newsgathering activities. Cross promotion and cooperation between CTV's television stations and Bell Globemedia's (now CTVglobemedia's) newspapers in newsgathering are permissible.

11 In 2007, the CRTC approved the sale of CHUM's conventional television assets to CTVglobemedia and Rogers Communications. See Broadcasting Decisions CRTC 2007-165 and 2007-360.

12 Unfortunately, the CRTC declined to publish this information in its *Communications Monitoring Report 2008.*

13 The Consumer Packaging and Labelling Act, the Textile Labelling Act, and the Precious Metals Marking Act.

14 Competition Bureau Canada, CRTC/Competition Bureau Interface.

15 Télémédia was a former Canadian media company based in Montreal with holdings in radio, television, and magazine publishing whose broadcast holdings have now been dispersed among Astral, Rogers, and Newcap. Radiomédia was a joint undertaking of Télémédia and Astral.

16 CRTC, 'A Competitive Balance,' 11.

14 Broadcasting and International Trade Agreements

As a result of the globalization of economic activity, national governments can no longer design domestic cultural policy generally, and broadcasting policy in particular, without some reference to what is happening in other countries. This chapter examines the ways in which Canada's international relations, particularly its international trade agreements with other countries, influence the Canadian government's ability to implement its domestic broadcasting policy. The discussion will proceed partly in terms of the 'cultural' industries and 'cultural' policy because broadcasting, film, video recordings, music recordings, books, magazines, periodicals, and newspapers are often grouped together as cultural industries in regard to international trade issues.

Globalization and the Business Cycle

The lowering of barriers to international trade, capital flows, and information exchange since the Second World War has resulted in increased trade, a greater mobility of capital and human resources, and greater economic integration among nations. With the globalization of economic activity has come a more sharply defined world business cycle with increasingly synchronous economic fluctuations across all nations. Cross-border linkages in trade, capital, and information bind together nations and regions as never before and increase the importance of the economic cycles in determining the growth rate of the world's gross domestic product (GDP). Global trade – which increased to an unprecedented 25 per cent of world GDP in 2000 – now plays a greater role than ever before in transmitting economic fluctuations rapidly around the world. The globalization of economic activity has arguably increased

FIGURE 14.1 Population of G8 countries, 2007 (millions)

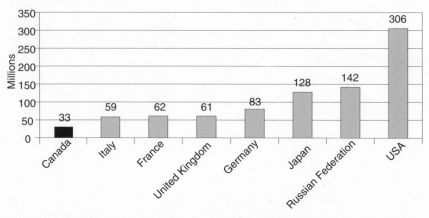

Source: United Nations, Department of Economic and Social Affairs, Population Division

aggregate economic welfare but, among other things, it has also result-ed in a certain loss of national economic independence and cultural sovereignty.

The impact of the U.S. business cycle, in particular, is uneven around the world and the United States' North American neighbours – Canada and Mexico – are among the most affected. In 2004, for example, Cana-dian exports to the United States accounted for 27 per cent of Canada's GDP. When the trade cycle enters into decline, Canadian GDP is usu-ally quick to follow and the cultural industries, including broadcasting, are directly influenced.

Not only does the high proportion of total exports in Canada's GDP (36 per cent in 2006) render the Canadian economy vulnerable to inter-national economic fluctuations, but the Canadian audio-visual sector is more vulnerable than the other G8 countries because Canada has a much smaller population[1] (see figure 14.1).

Canada's Two Distinct Broadcasting Environments

Canada possesses a relatively small population and yet Canada's domestic market supports an audio-visual community in each of two official languages – English and French – compared to unilingual systems in most other countries. In other words, the small Canadian population must finance the total costs of audio-visual products and services in two official languages (as well as ethnic services and services in indigenous languages) that, even when taken together, are much smaller than those of any of the other G8 countries. Since the total costs of producing a given quality of audio-visual product do not vary substantially from country to country in the industrialized world, production costs per capita are much higher in Canada (and potential returns much lower) than in other countries with substantially larger domestic markets. At a given level of quality, the proportion of the typical audio-visual budget that can be financed by Canada's private sector, in either of the two official languages, is relatively small. This helps to explain the active role of governments in the broadcasting sector and in other cultural industries.

Canada's Proximity to the United States

Canada borders on the United States, whose entertainment industry constitutes a special case not found in any other country. The U.S. entertainment industry produces an enormous quantity of music, television programs, theatrical feature films, and Internet content, whose costs are largely amortized in the huge U.S. domestic market that serves more than 300 million people. These products and services, whose basic costs have been covered in the U.S. market, can then be exported to other nations, including Canada, at low prices that cannot be matched by producers in these countries.

Consequently, governments and government agencies in Canada and the other industrialized countries have played a much more important role in cultural policy than in the United States. In the United States, there is no equivalent to the CBC, the National Film Board, or Telefilm Canada. Nor is there any equivalent to Canadian content rules. In fact, there is no Ministry of Heritage or Culture because, in the United States, the cultural industries are usually considered not different from any other industry, and specific policy support measures are believed unnecessary. In Canada and other industrialized countries, government subsidies and other measures are necessary to ensure that domestic cultural products are available in the home country.

Given the U.S. entertainment industry's pervasiveness and Canada's comparatively small population, open borders, close geographical proximity to the United States, and, for English Canadians, common language, government support is an essential element in Canadian cultural policy to ensure the availability of high-quality Canadian content. Canadian cultural policy, including broadcasting policy, is intended to safeguard, enrich, and strengthen Canadian identity and cultural diversity, and maintain a standard of quality comparable to that of the United States and the other industrialized countries.

This evaluation coincides with the view of a former Canadian ambassador for trade negotiations who was closely involved in the negotiations leading to the Canada-U.S. Free Trade Agreement (FTA) of 1987 and who writes, 'In its starkest terms, the Canadian cultural producer is forced to choose: sell to the American mass market by completely de-Canadianizing the work, or try to speak to a Canadian reality – and go broke in the process. This was not and is not a choice any self-respecting country should impose upon its creative talents. This has nothing to do with "elitism" versus consumer choice, as the chief propagandist for the movie cartel, Jack Valenti, would have you believe. It has everything to do with the intrinsic inability of the market to produce results compatible with fundamental national interests.'[2]

Canadian Trade and Investment Policy

The trend toward international trade liberalization and globalization is believed by many to enhance economic growth and consumer welfare. At the same time, trade liberalization tends to reduce national identities and create pressures to eliminate government policies that protect or strengthen domestic cultures and cultural diversity.

Consequently, domestic government policies that support the domestic audio-visual sector, such as those that favour Canadian content in broadcasting, may be at risk from the lowering of barriers to international trade and increased international economic integration. Some countries, such as the United States, would like to see an end to all 'discriminatory' policies against imported goods and services, including cultural products.[3] However, from the Canadian point of view, Canada's market for cultural goods and services is one of the most open in the world and pressures for greater openness must be balanced against the desire to retain some space (sometimes referred to as 'shelf space') available for Canadian cultural products and services that Canadians may choose if they so wish.[4]

Canada's obligations under international trade agreements provide the framework in which the lowering of international trade barriers occurs. These trade agreements, both bilateral and multilateral, are essentially treaties among nations and therefore constitute a part of international law. This said, the treaties themselves are not enforced in the courts of Canada, or other countries, and obligations under such agreements are instead subject to domestic laws and dispute settlement mechanisms together with public and political pressure. Once a trade agreement is concluded, there are usually consequential amendments to domestic laws ('enabling legislation') to ensure the relevant treaty obligations are respected in such domains as countervail, anti-dumping, and safeguard rules as well as other areas covered by the agreement. But as can be seen in the long saga concerning softwood lumber, the enforcement of international treaties is sometimes problematic.

Generally speaking, there are two types of trade agreements: bilateral agreements (between two countries) and multilateral agreements (among many countries). In its bilateral and regional trade agreements, such as the trilateral North American Free Trade Agreement among Canada, the United States, and Mexico, Canada has retained a 'cultural exemption' that is intended to provide a reasonable degree of protection for Canada's cultural industries.

North American Free Trade Agreement

The North American Free Trade Agreement (NAFTA) of 1994 is an outgrowth of the Canada-U.S. FTA of 1987 and is considered to be Canada's most far-reaching international trade agreement to date.[5] NAFTA provides for the application of a cultural exemption previously contained in the Canada-U.S. FTA. See Appendix F. This exemption, contained in Article 2005 of the FTA declares that cultural industries are exempt from the provisions of the agreement, with four exceptions.[6]

There is, however, an important qualifier attached to the cultural exemption in the Canada-United States FTA that carries over to NAFTA. This qualifier says, 'Notwithstanding any other provision of this Agreement, a Party may take measures of equivalent commercial effect in response to actions that would have been inconsistent with this Agreement but for paragraph 1 [the exemption itself].' Although the United States is not entitled to retaliate in regard to broadcast matters, the power of retaliation in other sectors could have a dampening effect on the introduction of significant new cultural policy measures by the Canadian government. The cultural exemption, accompanied by a right of retaliation outside the audio-visual sector, may not provide adequate protection against a foreign-owned firm that wishes to challenge Canadian broadcasting law or policy and pressure its home government to seek redress from Canada.

NAFTA is not presently the subject of formal disputes related to the cultural sector, but there are several potential trade irritants that could affect Canada-U.S. relations in the future. For example, the campaign of the American Federation of Television and Radio Artists against 'runaway' productions is based on claims that federal and provincial tax credits constitute 'unfair' subsidies to U.S. productions that choose to shoot in Canada. This issue, like the U.S. Screen Actors Guild's decision to enforce Global Rule One, concerns the shooting of U.S. productions in Canada rather than measures of government support for Canadian program production.[7] Even so, to the extent that runaway production focuses the U.S. government's attention on the cultural exemption in NAFTA, it constitutes a potential trade irritant with the United States.

In other bilateral trade agreements, such as the trade agreements with Chile, Costa Rica, and Israel, Canada has negotiated an absolute cultural exemption, with no right of retaliation. This is the objective in negotiations concerning a Free Trade Area of the Americas, a more focused trade agreement with Central America, and a new trade agreement with Singapore. Canadian objectives also provide for the inclusion of a preamble in support of cultural diversity and the New International Instrument on Cultural Diversity (see below).

World Trade Organization

The World Trade Organization (WTO) Agreement provides for a single institutional framework for multilateral trade among many countries and involved some 150 countries in 2007. The WTO began its life on 1 January 1995 but its antecedents go back some sixty years. Following the Second World War, the General Agreement on Tariffs and Trade (GATT) established a general framework for international trade that later came under the auspices of the WTO.

Membership in the WTO requires accepting the entire framework of rules for international trade, which includes agreements potentially affecting the audio-visual sector, including

- A revised General GATT with respect to the trade in products
- The General Agreement on Trade in Services (GATS)
- The Agreement on Trade-Related Investment Measures, which is quite limited
- The Agreement on Subsidies and Countervailing Measures
- The Agreement on Trade-Related Aspects of Intellectual Property Rights

Unlike the trilateral agreement, NAFTA, there is no general exemption for cultural industries under the WTO agreements. Even so, the application of WTO obligations has hereto remained largely outside the audio-visual sector. Article IV of the GATT allows participating countries to reserve screen time 'for films of national origin.' And, at the time of writing, the GATT contained no international obligations in respect of trade in services, of which broadcasting forms a part.

With regard to the GATS, some members (Brazil, Japan, Norway, Switzerland, and the United States) have tabled proposals related to audio-visual services. However, the 'bottom-up' structure of the GATS allows Canada, or any other country, to choose those sectors it wishes to open to foreign competition and to what extent. During the development of the Convention on the Protection of Cultural Diversity, Canada did not make any commitments that would restrict its ability to achieve the Canadian government's cultural policy objectives.

Given the pressure on Canada and other countries, including France, to open their cultural sectors to freer trade and reduce or eliminate policies favouring domestic products and services, such as broadcast content requirements, the Canadian government has developed a diplomatic strategy to institutionalize the cultural policy exemption found in Canada's bilateral trade agreements.

Convention on the Protection of Cultural Diversity

With regard to cultural diversity, the Government of Canada has supported the establishment of a New International Instrument on Cultural Diversity (NIICD) that sets clear ground rules for the maintenance of policies promoting culture while respecting the rules of the international trading system and ensuring markets for cultural exports, as recommended by the *Cultural Industries Sectoral Advisory Group on International Trade Report* of February 1999. The movement toward a NIICD underlined the importance of cultural diversity to international social and economic development and aimed to develop a common vision through an inclusive conceptual framework for cultural diversity as well as building domestic and international support for such a framework.

While the U.S. government has not lent its support to the movement to ensure cultural diversity, there is growing awareness among some parties within the United States of the importance of cultural diversity as a result of increased audio-visual industry concentration resulting from mega-mergers in the United States.

On the basis of the recommendation of its Executive Board, the General Conference of the United Nations Educational, Scientific and Cultural Organization (UNESCO) requested that its director-general submit a preliminary report accompanied by a preliminary draft of a convention on the protection of cultural diversity at UNESCO's session in October 2005. At that session, the overwhelming majority of UNESCO's member states adopted the Convention on the Protection and Promotion of the Diversity of Cultural Expressions.

Among other things, the convention recognizes that television programs, feature films, music, and other cultural goods and services convey identity and values, and should not be considered solely in regard to their commercial value. The convention reaffirms the right of governments to take specific measures to foster diverse cultural expressions and commits signatories to work together to promote the convention's objectives and principles in other international arenas.

UNESCO's convention required ratification by thirty countries before entering into force. In November 2005, Canada became the first country to ratify the convention and, following its ratification by the requisite number of countries, the convention came into force on 18 March 2007. In December 2007, Canada hosted the inaugural meeting of the UNESCO convention's Intergovernmental Committee.

Canada has been a leader in developing and promoting the UNESCO convention because its core provisions form an integral part of Canadian cultural policy. The principles and objectives of the convention are reflected in Canadian statutes, regulations, and policies related to the cultural industries. For example, section 3 of the Broadcasting Act (Broadcasting Policy for Canada) establishes that the Canadian broadcasting system should 'serve to safeguard, enrich and strengthen the cultural, political, social and economic fabric of Canada.' In other words, the objectives of Canadian broadcasting policy are multiple, and economic prospects are one consideration among several.

This said, the UNESCO declarations issued so far have been declarations of faith rather than international trading rules enforceable by law or international tribunals. And since the United States has not agreed to it, the Convention on the Protection of Cultural Diversity does not directly affect any current international trade obligations between its signatories and the U.S. government.

Certainly, the convention heightens awareness of international cultural diversity and dissuades nations from further liberalizing the cultural sector. But will the convention have any real impact on the WTO's framework of rules? Furthermore, even if it were to be enforceable in a concrete way, can the reconciliation of cultural and commercial objectives occur under the auspices of the WTO as long as the United States government refuses to collaborate meaningfully in such a resolution?

Notes

1 The first G8 Summit was held in 1975 in France to address economic problems. Since then, the annual G8 Summit has evolved from a forum dealing essentially with macroeconomic issues to an annual meeting with a broad-based agenda that addresses a wide range of international economic, political, and social issues.
2 Ritchie, *Wrestling with the Elephant*, 218.
3 Domestic policies that favour domestic products and services, such as Canadian content requirements, are sometimes referred to as 'non-tariff barriers,' to distinguish them from customs and excise taxes that constitute 'tariff barriers.'
4 81.8 per cent of retail sales from sound recordings, 54 per cent of all programs available on English-language Canadian television (61 per cent in the peak viewing hours), and 90.2 per cent of Canadian box office revenue were attributable to non-Canadian or foreign products and services in 2001.
5 In Canada, the FTA was implemented via the Canada-United States Free Trade Agreement Implementation Act (1988, c. 65).
6 The four exceptions concern tariff elimination, divestiture of a business in Canada in a cultural industry acquired indirectly, retransmission rights, and income tax deductions related to the printing in Canada of newspapers and periodicals.
7 'No member shall work as a performer or make an agreement to work as a performer for any producer who has not executed a basic minimum agreement with the Guild which is in full force and effect.' In other words, the SAG wants to enforce its collective agreements with U.S. companies shooting film material all around the world, including those operating in Canada.

15 Conclusion

In this work, the discussion has been conducted with particular attention to government broadcasting policy development and, while issues of political power have been addressed occasionally, power relationships have not been the primary focus. In this concluding chapter, questions are raised about the nature of nominations to the CRTC and the CBC, the role of political power, including partisan political influence in regulatory decision-making, and the possibility of interest groups unduly influencing the regulatory process. Furthermore, up to now, Canadian broadcasting has been examined in the context of the existing legislative framework, with particular attention to the Broadcasting Act. But over time, legislation can be amended by Parliament. This chapter moves beyond the confines of current legislation to consider legislative reform as a meaningful avenue for improving the institutional arrangements affecting broadcasting. Finally, the future direction of broadcasting policy is considered in light of the rise of the Internet and wireless personal digital communications.

CRTC and CBC Board Nomination Process

As we saw in chapters 1, 5, and 7, the CRTC and the CBC are subject to the political process in various ways that, at times, raise questions about their political neutrality. One source of political influence lies in appointments to the Commission and the CBC by the federal government.

The problems raised by the current nomination process to the CRTC and the CBC, indeed to the governing boards of all the agencies responsible for media policy, are part of a larger issue related to appointments in all sectors of government administration. How should appointments to government agencies be made? Is it appropriate for governments to favour appointments of people who are sympathetic to the government's agenda, even if they have little experience or competence in the domain of the appointment? Given the unique role of broadcasting in the political process, should appointments to agencies such as the CRTC and the CBC be treated differently from appointments to other government agencies? What of other media-related agencies such as Telefilm Canada and the National Film Board? Should the CRTC be treated separately from these other agencies because it is an administrative tribunal and appointees to the Commission exercise their function on a fulltime basis?

Here is an example of several recent appointments to the Board of Directors of the CBC. On 22 February 2008, the Minister of Canadian Heritage, appointed by the Conservative government led by Stephen Harper, announced the appointments of Linda Black, Mary McNeil, and Brian Mitchell to the CBC Board:

- Prior to her appointment, Linda Black worked in senior executive government roles and served as the founding general counsel at the University of Calgary. She is currently a member of the Alberta Secretariat for Action on Homelessness, a member of the Law Enforcement Review Board of Alberta, and governor for the Board of Governors of Mount Royal College.
- Mary McNeil is a fundraiser and charity executive by profession. Prior to her appointment to the Board of the CBC, she was chosen by Prime Minister Stephen Harper to compete for the nomination in a Vancouver riding but lost the bid.[1]
- Brian Mitchell is a former member of the Conservative National Council who once ran unsuccessfully for the leadership of the Progressive Conservative party and for the leadership of the Conservative Party. Until the CBC appointment, he served on the Conservative Party's national council.

None of these appointments proceeded via the Public Appointments Commission, whose mandate is described in the Federal Accountability Act of 2006.

As the current government conceded in the period leading up to the enactment of the Federal Accountability Act, 'Legislative provisions that govern the appointment of Agents and Officers of Parliament are uneven and do not fully respect Parliament in the process. The appointment process for agencies, commissions, and boards is not as transparent or as merit-based as it could be.'[2] The Public Appointments Commission Secretariat was created by Order in Council on 21 April 2006 to prepare the ground for the establishment of the Public Appointments Commission. However, in the early summer of 2009, the Public Appointments Commission was still inoperative. Critics claimed that the government was delaying the launch of the Commission's responsibilities until outstanding agency, commission, and board nominations had been filled by government sympathizers and that the government might never establish the commission at all.[3]

Finding qualified candidates to govern public agencies is an arduous task. The relative importance of experience (which may be accompanied by a vested interest) and arm's-length objectivity (which may be accompanied by a lack of qualifications) is very difficult to balance.

Political Power

The intention of the Canadian Radio-television and Telecommunications Commission Act, and of the Broadcasting Act, was to establish an independent agency to implement Canada's broadcasting policy. As an administrative tribunal with quasi-judicial powers, the CRTC holds public hearings and renders decisions based on the evidence presented to it. It should not search for evidence on licensing matters outside the public hearing process or initiate proceedings without due cause. However, on occasion, the CRTC, like other government agencies, appears to be swayed by the political power exercised by its licensees. What follows is an example of a Commission proceeding that is difficult to explain in the absence of the exercise of political power.

The CRTC's Broadcasting Distribution Regulations require Class 1 and Class 2 cable distribution licensees, broadcast satellite, and multipoint distribution system (MDS) licensees to contribute to the financing of Canadian programming no less than 5 per cent of their annual gross revenues from broadcast operations. The regulations stipulate that at least 80 per cent of the 5 per cent contribution must be provided to the Canadian Television Fund (CTF).

In a letter sent to the CTF on 20 December 2006, Jim Shaw, the CEO of Shaw Communications Inc., announced that the company was ceasing its contributions to the CTF. Shaw claimed that the CTF was financing unpopular television programs and, among other things, subsidizing the public broadcaster, the CBC. He insisted on a major revision of the CTF's mandate and governance structure. On 23 January 2007, Quebecor Media adopted the same position and, in a press release, informed the chair of the Board of the CTF that its subsidiary Videotron was 'suspending its monthly payments to the CTF and asking the Hon. Bev Oda, Minister of Canadian Heritage at the time, to launch a thorough review of the Fund's management and membership structures.'[4]

In fact, the CRTC circular that sets out the modalities of contributions by broadcasting distribution undertakings (BDUs), including a requirement for monthly payments, is not incorporated into the BDU regulations.[5] The regulations require a payment but, at the time, BDUs could withhold their contributions to the end of the broadcast reporting year without infringing the regulations themselves. Since the principal photography of most Canadian television production occurs in the spring and summer months, withholding production financing until the end of the broadcast reporting year (31 August) would have a very damaging impact on Canadian program production.

Following a public and political outcry, Shaw and Quebecor agreed to resume monthly payments to the CTF. On 25 January 2007 Konrad von Finckenstein was appointed chairman of the CRTC by the government of prime minister Stephen Harper, and on 20 February the CRTC established an internal task force headed by its vice-chair of broadcasting 'to develop a consensus to resolve the concerns raised by stakeholders or, failing that, to set out possible options to resolve any remaining issues.'[6] To many observers, there was no reason to establish such a task force because no particular issue had been raised by Shaw and Quebecor that had not already been raised many times before. All of the matters raised by the two dissidents had been addressed by the CTF – though not necessarily resolved in favour of the two giant cable operators.

On 29 June 2007, the CRTC released the *Report of the CRTC Task Force on the Canadian Television Fund*, which, among other things, proposed that the CTF establish a market-oriented private-sector funding stream consistent with the draft objectives set out by the task force, reduce the requirements of qualifying Canadian programs to a minimum of eight out of ten points (instead of ten out of ten) using the CAVCO scale, and ensure that audience success be the primary criterion for CTF funding. While not entirely endorsing Shaw and Videotron's vision, the recommendations of the task force offered concessions to all their principal concerns. On 29 June 2007, the CRTC endorsed the recommendations of the *Report of the CRTC Task Force* and requested public comments 'to help ensure that the procedural and substantive steps needed to implement the recommendations are as effective as possible.'[7]

Among other things, the Commission's rush to judgement involved a number of procedural errors and emissions. For example,

- Recommendations of the *Report of the CRTC Task Force* were based on private meetings with selected parties and conducted on a confidential basis.
- There was no public record of the content of these meetings.
- On the basis of these confidential meetings, the task force admitted that it was unable 'to develop any form of consensus on the major issues.'
- The *Report of the CRTC Task Force* did not expose the committee's rationale underlying the recommendations of the report and, in the absence of a public hearing, there would have been no further opportunity for interested parties to comment on such a rationale, even if it had been provided.
- The contribution agreement between Canadian Heritage and the CTF, a central element in evaluating the overall effectiveness of the CTF's objectives, was not placed on the CRTC's public file and was not a public document.

With respect to the content of the report, it was unclear which objectives in section 3 of the Broadcasting Act would have been directly served by implementing the recommendation of the *Report of the CRTC Task Force* to establish a funding stream within the CTF separate from BDU funding. What is more, the implementation of the report's recommendations appeared to advocate a return to the status quo ante that had precipitated many of the CTF's governance and administration problems of the past. If such a return were implemented, many of the CTF's former governance and administrative problems would probably have reappeared.

In summary, the CRTC rushed to judgement on issues raised by the bullying tactics of Shaw and Videotron, both of which maintain close ties with the federal Conservative Party in power at the time. The recommendations of the *Report of the CRTC Task Force* were ill-considered, the public process proposed in Broadcasting Public Notice CRTC 2007-70 was flawed, and the Commission's actions in this dossier tended to discredit its reputation of impartiality and political non-partisanship.

After reviewing the public comments received, most of which were opposed to the CRTC's proposals, the Commission revised its initial implementation schedule to include an oral hearing to consider the issues.[8]

After the Commission's public hearing, but prior to the announcement of the Commission's decision, in February 2008, the Minister of Canadian Heritage announced the government had asked the CRTC to report and make recommendations on the Canadian Television Fund (CTF). The minister also announced the government would 'build on the work begun by the CRTC and focus on functional and sustainable solutions that reward excellence.'[9] In effect, the minority government placed the CTF file on hold until it had decided on its own priorities in the sector – following a pending federal election (that eventually occurred in October of the same year).

In its 5 June 2008 report to the Minister of Canadian Heritage, the CRTC backed off from its June 2007 *Report of the CRTC Task Force*. While retaining its recommendation to create two distinct funding streams – a public sector stream and a private sector stream each managed by its own board of directors – the Commission retreated to the following rather modest initiatives:

• Amend the Broadcasting Distribution Regulations to require that BDUs make their contributions to the CTF on a monthly basis, once the DCH has addressed the major issues identified in this report
• Conduct ongoing regular reviews to ensure that the CTF implements a private sector funding stream
• Begin a process to amend its benefits policy, so that tangible benefits can be used to support the CTF
• Begin a process to review its certified independent production funds policy with a view to providing greater support for new media projects[10]

Having set out on what appears to have been an essentially political agenda, in this case, the Commission backtracked once the prevailing political winds realigned themselves.

Finally, in March 2009, the Department of Canadian Heritage decided to reassert its authority in the domain of production funding and to repossess the CTF dossier by announcing the creation of a new fund, the Canada Media Fund, to supplant the CTF and Telefilm's Canada New Media Fund (see chapter 8). Following public consultations to deter-

mine its policies and procedures, the launch of the CMF is planned for
1 April 2010.

According to the government's news release, the following principles will eventually guide the CMF:[11]

- A smaller fully independent board made up of nominees of the
  funders (the Canadian government and BDUs) will be created.
- The fund will favour projects produced in high definition and those
  that have the most potential to achieve success in terms of audience
  and return on investment.
- Applicants will be required to make their projects available across a
  minimum of two distribution platforms, including television.
- The fund will put particular emphasis on drama, comedy, and children's programs.
- The fund will also finance documentaries, variety, and performing
  arts programs if they demonstrate that the market alone would not
  support their production.
- Broadcaster in-house production will be phased in gradually.
- Broadcasters will be put on a level playing field, including provincial educational broadcasters and the CBC/Radio-Canada, whose
  guaranteed envelope will be removed.[12]

Regulatory Capture

According to conventional economic theory, consumer welfare is usually maximized in an environment of freely functioning markets. However, this general principle does not apply in the presence of market
failures, such as the presence of 'public goods.'[13] The limited availability of scarce resources, including the radio frequency spectrum, also
makes such resources susceptible to being monopolized by private
interests to the detriment of the public interest and consumer welfare.
Such monopolies are called 'natural' monopolies.

In the pursuit of the public interest, governments intervene to regulate and supervise natural monopolies and other market failures to
guide profit-seeking firms toward socially beneficial outcomes. In conventional economic thought, there are two broad approaches to such
government intervention: one suggests that government intervention is
usually successful, and indeed necessary, to correct market failures and
advance the public interest; the other suggests that government intervention is usually unsuccessful, partly because the intervening agency

is 'captured' by private sector interests and its policies shaped to further their particular objectives rather than the public interest.

The 'public interest' approach emphasizes the government's role in correcting market imperfections and market failures. While regulatory agencies may not always achieve their goals, they are viewed as being in benevolent pursuit of the public interest and social welfare. Almost all of the economic theory on the regulation of natural monopolies and industry concentration, for example, adopts this approach.

The 'regulatory capture' approach suggests that the regulatory process can be captured by firms operating in the regulated industry.[14] Indeed, regulation is supplied in response to the demands of competing interest groups to maximize the incomes of their members. For a given issue, the smaller and more homogeneous the interest group, the greater the per capita benefit and therefore the greater the incentive for the group's members to coalesce and seek particular regulatory results. Cohesive interest groups have more incentive to organize a particular outcome than a large, dispersed public for which each individual has a low personal stake.

The authors of one media economics textbook suggest that 'a case can be made that for a number of years the CRTC, the Canadian broadcast regulator, was captured by the cable TV industry. CRTC regulation in Canada certainly served to delay competition from satellite.'[15] Although the authors provide no analysis to support their contention, there is no doubt the CRTC considers broadcasting programming and distribution undertaking licensees as its primary clients. It is therefore more sympathetic to their needs than it is to those representing labour: creators' guilds, journalists' associations, and technicians' unions, which are not viewed as 'clients' of the Commission.

Legislative Consolidation

As we have seen in the preceding chapters, new digital devices and services are transforming the Canadian broadcasting landscape. The flexibility and universality of digital technology is accelerating the convergence of audio-visual media predicted more than fifteen years ago. Whereas off-air broadcasters were first licensed to serve Canadians with local radio and television services (see chapter 2) and master antenna (MATV) cable systems initially provided broadcast services to local communities (see chapter 3), the lines between programming services and signal distribution activities are gradually dissolving.

The new digital environment raises difficult issues for broadcasting policymakers. As unregulated media increasingly compete with the regulated broadcast sector, the Canadian regulatory framework is increasingly being questioned. This questioning is not new but its intensity has increased in the last few years. In partial response, the CRTC has proposed that a single Act should govern broadcasting, telecommunications, and radiocommunications.

> Efficiency requires that the Commission be given the flexibility to respond to a changing broadcasting environment to minimize disruption for enterprises in the space. Treatment of communications companies as single entities avoids treating individual components of their businesses – wireless, telecommunications, broadcasting, television distribution and Internet access – as discrete elements with overlapping and potentially conflicting regulatory treatment.
>
> Breaking down the regulatory silos between the *Acts* must be a priority for the Government as the separate objectives of multiple legislative frameworks result in conflicts between various bodies. These administrative conflicts, for example with respect to the issue of spectrum licensing for broadcasting, have been considered by some to hinder the innovation and experimentation that are the cornerstone of Canadian communications companies' future competitiveness.[16]

While there are no doubt administrative conflicts in administering the Broadcasting Act, the Telecommunications Act, and the Radiocommunication Act, there are also considerable differences in their objectives. For example, the Telecommunications Act and the Radiocommunication Act do not contain cultural and political objectives such as those related to Canadian content or the opportunity for the public to be exposed to the expression of differing views on matters of public concern. For its part, the Broadcasting Act does not contain objectives related to enhancing the efficiency and competitiveness of the regulated industry.

In the presence of both media convergence and industry concentration, there is increased political pressure exerted by large corporations on governments and government agencies to consolidate and deregulate government licensing and surveillance. The convergence of audio-visual media tends to undermine the rationale for regulating and supervising some media while others are left alone. Thus there is pressure to treat all media equally by deregulating the broadcast sector.

As we have suggested, this pressure also raises important issues about the regulatory process itself and the extent to which the CRTC is able to withstand external political influences.

Section 5(2)(g) of the Broadcasting Act says that the Canadian broadcasting system should be regulated and supervised in a flexible manner that 'is sensitive to the administrative burden that, as a consequence of such regulation and supervision, may be imposed on persons carrying on broadcasting undertakings.' This is the sole policy objective in the current Broadcasting Act that can be interpreted as encouraging a deregulatory agenda. Moreover, this subsection is subordinate to the pursuit of the objectives contained in subsection 3(1) of the Act. Even so, there are a variety of objectives in subsection 3(1), and their relative importance is open to interpretation by the Commission.

The Commission, and in particular its current chairman, Konrad von Finckenstein, has said that ensuring a strong Canadian presence in the broadcasting system in the form of distinct and diverse Canadian programming and services continues to be a primary objective. However, the importance of Canadian content objectives relative to the other objectives is, in practice, continuously being re-evaluated. In consolidating the three Acts, there is a potential danger that certain economic objectives of the Telecommunications Act, such as enhancing efficiency and competitiveness or fostering an increased reliance on market forces, would be transferred inappropriately to broadcasting.

This said, the consolidation of broadcasting-related legislation into one act would certainly be desirable. When a radio applicant wants to launch a new station or change a broadcasting frequency, it must receive approval from both the CRTC and Industry Canada. When a broadcast applicant wants to acquire the ownership of broadcasting assets from a licensee, in certain circumstances, it must seek approval from the Competition Bureau as well as the CRTC.[17] These kinds of overlapping jurisdiction often create delays in licensing, additional expense for applicants, and the duplication of activities. There are undoubtedly activities such as these for which the Government of Canada might integrate the processes of the CRTC, Industry Canada, and the Competition Bureau through legislative reform.

Broadcasting Policy in the Future

The rise of the Internet has shaken the foundations of the broadcasting industry and poses an immense challenge to broadcasting policymaking and the CRTC, as we know them today. The distribution of audio-visual content on the Internet is drawing listeners and viewers away from licensed broadcasting undertakings and thereby undermining the revenue base on which advertising-supported broadcasting undertakings have depended up to now. This decline in revenues has led broadcasters to reduce their expenditures on lesser performing activities, including the programming of television programs in the underrepresented or 'priority' categories. Faced with declining revenues, commercial broadcasters are favouring low-cost news, talk, variety and reality-based programs, as well as live events involving professional sports, Olympic sports, or awards programs, such as the Academy Awards, which are used to attract mass audiences, even though they seldom generate significant net returns.[18]

Not all forms of audio-visual content on the Internet are affecting the broadcasting industry in the same way. According to one account, the Internet is distributing audio-visual content of at least three kinds: user-generated content; relatively inexpensive commercial content; and high-quality, relatively expensive programming such as drama and documentary.[19] To date, the Internet is recycling high-cost, high-quality audio-visual programming without participating in its development and financing. Thus while new media are drawing viewers and revenues away from licensed broadcast media, in part by recycling such programs, they are undermining the financial model that has permitted their creation, particularly high-quality drama, documentaries, and children's programs.

Given the challenge provided by unregulated new media to the regulated broadcasting environment, there is pressure to harmonize the regulatory environment for all broadcasting distribution technologies. Some parties are proposing that the CRTC reduce or eliminate its regulation of the Canadian broadcasting system in favour of little or no supervision. By one approach, the rules for commercial broadcasting regulation would be aligned with those applied to the unregulated theatrical feature film industry, although individual productions would continue to receive government financing.[20] Others are proposing to harmonize the regulatory environment for broadcast distribution by urging the CRTC to extend its regulation of the broadcasting system to include the provision of Internet and wireless digital distribution services.[21] By this approach, the CRTC would exercise its powers under the Broadcasting Act and license Internet services providers and wireless mobile service providers just as they license BDUs.

An intermediate position adopted by many television producers, creators, and technicians, as well as a few public broadcasters, such as the CBC and TFO, favours the imposition of a levy on new media distribution activities that would be similar to the levy currently placed on broadcasting distribution undertakings to help finance the activities of the Canada New Media Fund. This would involve revising the new media exemption order (see chapter 10) to require a contribution by exempted undertakings to Canadian program production financing as a condition for exemption. In Broadcasting Regulatory Policy CRTC 2009-329, 'Review of Broadcasting in New Media,' the CRTC rejected the argument that additional financial support was needed for the creation and presentation of Canadian broadcasting content in new media.

New media distribution contributes to the recycling of high-cost programming produced for initial release by licensed broadcasters and movie theatres. However, new media distribution is not generating sufficient revenues to maintain such programming, which is in decline. New media benefit from the advertising and promotion of programs broadcast by traditional media but no new financial model has developed, involving the new media, that would permit the continued financing of high-cost television programs, and none appears to be in sight. In a sense, the new media are slowly strangling the goose that lays the golden eggs. Unless a solution to this structural problem is developed, the continued availability of high-quality Canadian television in the CRTC's 'priority' categories of drama, documentaries, and children's programs, which are so essential to Canadian identity, appears to be highly problematic.

Notes

1 Mary McNeil stepped down from the Board of Directors before attending her first Board meeting apparently to run for provincial office.
2 http://www.faa-lfi.gc.ca/docs/ap-pa/ap-pa07-eng.asp.
3 See, for example, http://www.canada.com/topics/news/politics/story. html?id=d03e0480–78c9–45ca-add1-df42c821399e&k=61038.
4 Quebecor, 'Videotron Suspends Contributions to Canadian Television Fund.'
5 CRTC, Circular 426, 'To the Licensees of Broadcasting Distribution Undertakings.'
6 CRTC, 'CRTC Creates a Task Force on the Canadian Television Fund.'

7 CRTC, 'Task Force Releases Its Report on the Canadian Television Fund,' and Broadcasting Public Notice CRTC 2007-70, 'Call for Comments.'
8 Broadcasting Notice of Public Hearing CRTC 2007-15, 'Proceeding on the Canadian Television Fund'
9 Verner, 'Speaking Notes.'
10 *CRTC Report to the Minister of Canadian Heritage*.
11 Canadian Heritage, 'Minister Moore Announces Canada Media Fund.'
12 Until a few years ago, BDUs were not permitted to own television programming undertakings. Since Quebecor Media acquired the TVA network (and Videotron) in 2001 and Rogers Communications acquired CHUM's CITY-TV television stations in 2007, BDUs have developed more and more antipathy to the rule (enshrined in the government's contribution agreement) that the CBC's television networks receive 49 per cent of the CTF's total financing.
13 'Public goods' are commodities or services whose cost of production is unrelated to the number of consumers of the good and for which one person's consumption does not diminish the consumption of that good by another consumer. The 'public good' characteristics of radio frequency spectrum use sometimes provide an explanation of the need for the regulation of broadcasting. See chap. 1.
14 This approach was first formalized in George J. Stigler in 'Theory of Economic Regulation.'
15 Hoskins, McFadyen, and Finn, *Media Economics*, 307.
16 CRTC, 'A Competitive Balance for the Communications Industry,' 7.
17 Approval is required from the Competition Bureau if the assets or annual gross revenue of the target company amount to $50 million or more and the assets or gross annual revenue of the purchaser and target company, including affiliated companies, are $400 million or more.
18 The live events are being used to attract mass audiences even though they seldom generate significant net returns. And this phenomenon is not, of course, limited to Canada. See, for example, Arango, 'Broadcast TV Faces Struggle to Stay Viable.'
19 See CRTC, *Report on the Future Environment*, para. 352.
20 See, for example, Noam, 'TV or Not TV.'
21 See, for example, Communications, Energy, and Paperworkers Union of Canada, 'Old Questions, New Media.'

Appendices

APPENDIX A: SECTION 3 OF THE BROADCASTING ACT, 1991

Broadcasting Policy for Canada

3. (1) It is hereby declared as the broadcasting policy for Canada that
   (a) the Canadian broadcasting system shall be effectively owned and controlled by Canadians;
   (b) the Canadian broadcasting system, operating primarily in the English and French languages and comprising public, private and community elements, makes use of radio frequencies that are public property and provides, through its programming, a public service essential to the maintenance and enhancement of national identity and cultural sovereignty;
   (c) English and French language broadcasting, while sharing common aspects, operate under different conditions and may have different requirements;
   (d) the Canadian broadcasting system should
      (i) serve to safeguard, enrich and strengthen the cultural, political, social and economic fabric of Canada,
      (ii) encourage the development of Canadian expression by providing a wide range of programming that reflects Canadian attitudes, opinions, ideas, values and artistic creativity, by displaying Canadian talent in entertainment programming and by offering information and analysis concerning Canada and other countries from a Canadian point of view,
      (iii) through its programming and the employment opportunities arising out of its operations, serve the needs and interests, and reflect the circumstances and aspirations, of Canadian men, women and children, including equal rights, the linguistic duality and multicultural and multiracial nature of Canadian society and the special place of aboriginal peoples within that society, and
      (iv) be readily adaptable to scientific and technological change;
   (e) each element of the Canadian broadcasting system shall contribute in an appropriate manner to the creation and presentation of Canadian programming;
   (f) each broadcasting undertaking shall make maximum use, and in no case less than predominant use, of Canadian creative and other resources in the creation and presentation of programming, unless the nature of the service provided by the undertaking,

such as specialized content or format or the use of languages other than French and English, renders that use impracticable, in which case the undertaking shall make the greatest practicable use of those resources;

(g) the programming originated by broadcasting undertakings should be of high standard;

(h) all persons who are licensed to carry on broadcasting undertakings have a responsibility for the programs they broadcast;

(i) the programming provided by the Canadian broadcasting system should

    (i)   be varied and comprehensive, providing a balance of information, enlightenment and entertainment for men, women and children of all ages, interests and tastes,

    (ii)   be drawn from local, regional, national and international sources,

    (iii) include educational and community programs,

    (iv) provide a reasonable opportunity for the public to be exposed to the expression of differing views on matters of public concern, and

    (v)   include a significant contribution from the Canadian independent production sector;

(j) educational programming, particularly where provided through the facilities of an independent educational authority, is an integral part of the Canadian broadcasting system;

(k) a range of broadcasting services in English and in French shall be extended to all Canadians as resources become available;

(l) the Canadian Broadcasting Corporation, as the national public broadcaster, should provide radio and television services incorporating a wide range of programming that informs, enlightens and entertains;

(m) the programming provided by the Corporation should

    (i)   be predominantly and distinctively Canadian,

    (ii)   reflect Canada and its regions to national and regional audiences, while serving the special needs of those regions,

    (iii) actively contribute to the flow and exchange of cultural expression,

    (iv) be in English and in French, reflecting the different needs and circumstances of each official language community, including the particular needs and circumstances of English and French linguistic minorities,

(v)   strive to be of equivalent quality in English and in French,

(vi)   contribute to shared national consciousness and identity,

(vii)   be made available throughout Canada by the most appropriate and efficient means and as resources become available for the purpose, and

(viii) reflect the multicultural and multiracial nature of Canada;

(n) where any conflict arises between the objectives of the Corporation set out in paragraphs (l) and (m) and the interests of any other broadcasting undertaking of the Canadian broadcasting system, it shall be resolved in the public interest, and where the public interest would be equally served by resolving the conflict in favour of either, it shall be resolved in favour of the objectives set out in paragraphs (l) and (m);

(o) programming that reflects the aboriginal cultures of Canada should be provided within the Canadian broadcasting system as resources become available for the purpose;

(p) programming accessible by disabled persons should be provided within the Canadian broadcasting system as resources become available for the purpose;

(q) without limiting any obligation of a broadcasting undertaking to provide the programming contemplated by paragraph (i), alternative television programming services in English and in French should be provided where necessary to ensure that the full range of programming contemplated by that paragraph is made available through the Canadian broadcasting system;

(r) the programming provided by alternative television programming services should

(i)   be innovative and be complementary to the programming provided for mass audiences,

(ii)   cater to tastes and interests not adequately provided for by the programming provided for mass audiences, and include programming devoted to culture and the arts,

(iii)   reflect Canada's regions and multicultural nature,

(iv)   as far as possible, be acquired rather than produced by those services, and

(v)   be made available throughout Canada by the most cost-efficient means;

(s) private networks and programming undertakings should, to an extent consistent with the financial and other resources available to them, .

     (i)   contribute significantly to the creation and presentation of Canadian programming, and

    (ii) be responsive to the evolving demands of the public; and

(t) distribution undertakings

     (i)   should give priority to the carriage of Canadian programming services and, in particular, to the carriage of local Canadian stations,

    (ii) should provide efficient delivery of programming at affordable rates, using the most effective technologies available at reasonable cost,

   (iii) should, where programming services are supplied to them by broadcasting undertakings pursuant to contractual arrangements, provide reasonable terms for the carriage, packaging and retailing of those programming services, and

   (iv) may, where the Commission considers it appropriate, originate programming, including local programming, on such terms as are conducive to the achievement of the objectives of the broadcasting policy set out in this subsection, and in particular provide access for underserved linguistic and cultural minority communities.

[Further declaration]

(2) It is further declared that the Canadian broadcasting system constitutes a single system and that the objectives of the broadcasting policy set out in subsection (1) can best be achieved by providing for the regulation and supervision of the Canadian broadcasting system by a single independent public authority.

APPENDIX B: SCHEMATIC OVERVIEW OF THE BROADCASTING POLICY FRAMEWORK

Canada Act, 1982

Constitution Act, 1867
- Establishes the powers of the federal and provincial governments (and can be amended only by a special process)

Constitution Act, 1982
- Charter of Rights and Freedoms
- Amending Formula for the Constitution
- Amendment to the Constitution Act, 1867

Federal government
- Canadian Parliament (House of Commons, Senate)
- Prime minister and Cabinet
- Ministries or departments (e.g., Canadian Heritage).
- CAVCO (office within Canadian Heritage)

Provincial governments
- Provincial legislatures
- Ministries or departments (e.g., Ministère de la Culture et des Communications du Québec, Ontario Ministry of Culture, BC Ministry of Tourism, Culture and the Arts)

Canadian laws
- Broadcasting Act
- Telefilm Canada Act
- Copyright Act
- Competition Act

Provincial laws
- Loi sur la société de télédiffusion du Québec (Télé-Québec), Ontario Educational Communications Authority Act, Knowledge Network Corporation Act (BC), etc.

Judiciary
- Interprets laws in light of the Constitution and the Charter
- Supreme Court of Canada is the final arbitrator of the law

Federal government agencies
- CRTC
- CBC/Radio-Canada
- Telefilm Canada
- National Film Board of Canada

Provincial government agencies
- Télé-Québec, TVOntario, TFO, Knowledge (British Columbia), etc.
- SODEC, OMDC, British Columbia Film, etc.

CRTC (a creation of the CRTC Act, administers the Broadcasting Act)
- Power to issue, amend, renew, and revoke broadcast licences
- Power to create regulations, conditions of licence, policies

Broadcasting industry
- Radio, television, and distribution undertakings and networks
- Licensees of the CRTC (e.g., companies such as CTVglobemedia, CanWest, Rogers, Quebecor, Corus, Astral)
- Industry partners (e.g., television and film producers, writers, directors, actors, technicians, advertisers, distributors, etc.)

APPENDIX C: OVERVIEW OF BROADCASTING LEGISLATION, 1932–1968

Canadian Radio Broadcasting Act, 1932	Canadian Radio Broadcasting Act, 1936	Broadcasting Act, 1958	Broadcasting Act, 1968
Canadian Radio Broadcasting Corporation (CRBC) • Regulates and controls broadcasting • Carries on (public) broadcasting	**Canadian Broadcasting Corporation (CBC)** • Makes regulations to control the establishment, operation, and programming of broadcasting • Carries on a national broadcasting service	**Board of Broadcast Governors (BBG)** • Regulates the establishment and operation of broadcasting	**Canadian Radio-television Commission (CRTC)** • Regulates and supervises all aspects of the Canadian broadcasting system • Issues, amends, renews, and suspends licences (subject to technical advice from the Minister of Transport)
Minister of Marine • Licenses broadcast stations	**Minister of Transport** • Issues, renews, or cancels broadcast licences	**Canadian Broadcasting Corporation (CBC)** • Operates a national broadcasting service	**Canadian Broadcasting Corporation (CBC)** • Provides the national broadcasting service contemplated by the Broadcasting Act
		Governor-in-Council • Approves the issue of licences • Minister of transport is responsible for broadcast licence amendments	**Minister of Transport*** • Regarding a licence issue, amendment, or renewal, certifies to the Commission that the applicant has satisfied the requirements of the Radio Act and regulations

* As of 1969, the Minister of Communications

Appendix D: Summary of Canadian Content and Expenditure Requirements

Across its regulations and decisions, the CRTC has established a range of Canadian content and expenditure requirements for English-language radio based on the nature of the broadcasting service and the programming distributed by each service.

Type of broadcasting service	Canadian content requirements	Canadian program expenditures / Canadian content development
Satellite subscription radio undertakings	85% average on a minimum of 8 Canadian channels; may carry up to 9 U.S. channels per Canadian channel	5% of revenues
Terrestrial subscription radio undertakings	Popular music: 35% Special interest: 10% Ethnic: 7%	2% of revenues
Commercial radio stations	Popular music: 35% Special interest: 10% Ethnic: 7%	Sliding scale ranging from $500 to $1,000 plus 0.5% of the previous year's total revenues over $1,250,000
Specialty audio services	Popular music: 35% Special interest: 10% Ethnic: 7%	No requirement
Pay audio services (Galaxie / Max Trax)	35% average on Canadian channels; may carry one U.S. channel for each Canadian channel	4% of revenues
Conventional TV stations	60% overall; 50% during evening hours for private stations and 60% for CBC stations	No general requirement, a few specific requirements related to ownership transfers
Analogue specialty services	Case-by-case requirements (30%–100%)	Case-by-case requirements (average 42% of revenues)
Digital specialty services	Category 1: Case-by-case (25%–85%) Category 2: 35% Category 2 Ethnic: 15%	Category 1: case-by-case (average 45% of revenues) Category 2: no requirements
Pay television services	30% in the evening 25% at other times	Case-by-case requirements (18%–32%, depending upon the number of subscribers)
Distribution undertakings (cable and direct-to-home satellite)	Priority to the presentation of Canadian channels	6.5% of revenues

Source: CRTC Information Bulletin, Subscription Radio Undertakings, 16 June 2005 as amended by subsequent public notices.

APPENDIX E: HISTORY OF THE CANADA MEDIA FUND

The Canada Media Fund (CTF) originated with the announcement of the creation of the Cable Production Fund in Public Notice CRTC 1993-74, 'Structural Public Hearing,' in which the CRTC asserted its authority to require each element of the broadcasting system to contribute to Canadian programming and said, 'Accordingly, the Commission, by majority vote, intends to make certain changes to its cable rate regulation mechanisms, the purpose of which is to provide significant financial support for Canadian programming. Specifically, the Commission intends to link contributions by cable licensees to a production fund to the capital expenditure (CAPEX) component of the cable fee structure.'

In other words, in the beginning, contributions by broadcasting distribution undertakings (BDUs) to the Cable Production Fund were voluntary and linked to cable companies' desire to continue benefiting from an existing capital expenditure allowance (which was about to lapse) that was intended to encourage investment in new technology by permitting participating cable companies to pass on a corresponding amount to subscribers.

Public Notice CRTC 1994-10, 'The Production Fund,' launched the Cable Production Fund and set out the basic rules of eligibility for financing from the fund. These rules included a definition of the eligible categories of programs, an emphasis on drama, and a requirement to attain eight CAVCO points for access to the fund.

In its convergence report, entitled 'Competition and Culture on Canada's Information Highway: Managing the Realities of Transition,' 19 May 1995, the Commission announced that all new licensed distribution undertakings should make a contribution to the development and production of Canadian programming. This general approach was given effect in Public Notice 1996-69, 'Call for Comments on a Proposed Approach for the Regulation of Broadcasting Distribution Undertakings,' wherein the Commission proposed regulations to make BDU contributions mandatory. To justify its regulatory approach, the CRTC said, 'Broadcasting distribution undertakings are important participants in the Canadian broadcasting system and play a crucial role in achieving the objectives of the Act. The Act stipulates in paragraph 3(1)(e) that "each element of the Canadian broadcasting system shall contribute in an appropriate manner to the creation and presentation of Canadian programming." The Commission has determined that all distributors should contribute a minimum of 5% of their gross annual revenues derived from broadcasting activities to achieve this funda-mental objective.'

In September 1996, the Minister of Canadian Heritage announced the creation of the Canada Television and Cable Production Fund (CTCPF) uniting Telefilm Canada's Broadcast Fund and the Cable Production Fund. Consequently, in Public Notice CRTC 1996-159, 'Transfer of Oversight of the Cable Production Fund (CPF),' the Commission announced its intention to transfer oversight of the Cable Production Fund to the Ministry of Canadian Heritage. Public Notice 1996-159 indicated that the new fund would receive supplementary government funding amounting to $250 million over a three-year period commencing in fiscal year 1996–7. The new government financing would be split between Telefilm Canada's Equity Investment Program (EIP) and the Licence Fee Program (LFP) previously administered by the Cable Production Fund.

In transferring its responsibility for oversight of the Cable Production Fund to Canadian Heritage in Public Notice 1996-159, the Commission referred to the following:

- The continued representation on the CTCPF Board of a wide range of cultural and financial interests in which 'a balance of views and a wide range of cultural interests and financial concerns will continue to be represented.'
- The absence of any need for a duplication of supervisory roles. 'Further, by having one supervisory body, it would be easier to ensure that one set of guidelines is established in respect of both sources of funding for the Licence Fee Program.'
- The need to ensure that the interests of the public and of cable subscribers continue to be represented. 'The Commission is satisfied that these interests will be safeguarded through the presence of the Department of Canadian Heritage on the Board of the CTCPF and through the Department's involvement with the Contribution Agreement.'

As set out in Public Notice 1997-150, 'Broadcasting Distribution Regulations,' the Commission's revised BDU Regulations required that all Class 1, Class 2, and DTH licensees make predetermined contributions to independent production funds for the development of Canadian programming as of 1 January 1998. The CTCPF was renamed the Canadian Television Fund (CTF) in 1998. According to the current Broadcasting

Distribution Regulations, at least 80 per cent of BDU contributions to Canadian programming must be directed to the CTF and up to 20 per cent may be directed to one or more approved independent production funds. (As noted in chapter 8, the CRTC has announced its intention to require BDUs to make an additional contribution to Canadian programming of 1.5 per cent of their annual gross revenues to finance the Local Programming Initiatives Fund.)

For 1999–2000, the Board of Directors of the CTF established new guidelines for access based on two principles: making requirements more Canadian and making decisions more market focused. Consequently, a ten-out-of-ten CAVCO point requirement was introduced to place greater emphasis on distinctively Canadian programs.

In the year 2006–7, Telefilm Canada acquired responsibility for the administration of all CTF disbursements (both licence fee top-ups and equity investments) under the direction of the Board of Directors of the CTF. For the year 2008–9, the CTF expected to receive $161 million from BDUs, and $120 million from Canadian Heritage, as well as an estimated $8 million in investment and interest revenues.

On 9 March 2009, the Government of Canada announced the amalgamation of the CTF and the Canada New Media Fund, administered by Telefilm Canada, to form the Canada Media Fund (CMF). Following public consultations to determine its policies and procedures, the launch of the CMF is planned for 1 April 2010.

APPENDIX F: EXCERPTS FROM THE NORTH AMERICAN FREE TRADE AGREEMENT (NAFTA)

Article 2106: Cultural Industries

Annex 2106 applies to the Parties specified in that Annex with respect to cultural industries. (See below.)

Article 2107: Definitions

For purposes of this Chapter:
cultural industries means persons engaged in any of the following activities:
  (a) the publication, distribution, or sale of books, magazines, periodicals or newspapers in print or machine readable form but not including the sole activity of printing or typesetting any of the foregoing;
  (b) the production, distribution, sale or exhibition of film or video recordings;
  (c) the production, distribution, sale or exhibition of audio or video music recordings;
  (d) the publication, distribution or sale of music in print or machine readable form; or
  (e) radiocommunications in which the transmissions are intended for direct reception by the general public, and all radio, television and cable broadcasting undertakings and all satellite programming and broadcast network services;

Annex 2106: Cultural Industries

Notwithstanding any other provision of this Agreement, as between Canada and the United States, any measure adopted or maintained with respect to cultural industries, except as specifically provided in Article 302 (Market Access – Tariff Elimination), and any measure of equivalent commercial effect taken in response, shall be governed under this Agreement exclusively in accordance with the provisions of the Canada–United States Free Trade Agreement. The rights and obligations between Canada and any other Party with respect to such measures shall be identical to those applying between Canada and the United States.

Glossary

analogue broadcast: picture or sound information encoded and transmitted as a variable signal that is continuous in time and amplitude. As analogue systems become more complex, effects such as non-linearity and noise eventually degrade analogue resolution, which does not occur with digital technology.

ASC: Advertising Standards Canada – an industry association that regroups advertisers, advertising agencies, media organizations, and suppliers to the advertising sector.

aspect ratio: in a television or computer screen image, the width of the image compared to its height (as in 4:3 or 16:9).

bandwidth: the channel capacity of a digital communications system.

basic service: an ensemble or tier of broadcasting programming services that must be provided by a BDU to all subscribers, as opposed to discretionary services, which are optional.

BBC: British Broadcasting Corporation – the public service broadcaster in the United Kingdom.

BBG: Board of Broadcast Governors – a creation of the Broadcasting Act of 1958 and a forerunner (1958–68) of the CRTC.

BDU: broadcasting distribution undertaking, an operation that retransmits broadcast services (see *distribution undertaking* for a formal definition).

BNA Act: British North America Act (now known as the Constitution Act, 1867) – legislation by which the British colonies of Upper and Lower Canada, Nova Scotia, and New Brunswick were united in a confederation called the Dominion of Canada.

broadcasting ('radiodiffusion'): according to the Broadcasting Act, 'any transmission of programs, whether or not encrypted, by radio waves or other means of telecommunication for reception by the public by means of broadcasting receiving apparatus, but does not include any such transmission of programs that is made solely for performance or display in a public place.'

CAB: Canadian Associations of Broadcasters, trade association and lobby group representing Canada's private sector broadcasters.

Canada New Media Fund (CNMF): fund under the umbrella of Telefilm Canada that encourages the creation and development of Canadian interactive digital content (see also CMF).

Canadian Charter of Rights and Freedoms: legislation protecting human rights that is 'enshrined' in the Canadian Constitution and therefore takes precedence over other legislation.

Canadian programs: programs that fulfil specific criteria and are recognized by the CRTC as Canadian for the purposes of fulfilling the CRTC's Canadian content requirements.

Category 1 service: Canadian digital specialty television service that must be carried by all digital cable and DTH satellite BDUs that have the capability to do so. This designation is scheduled to disappear as of 31 August 2011.

Category 2 service: Canadian digital specialty or pay television service that may be carried by digital cable and DTH satellite BDUs by agreement between the service and the BDU. This designation is scheduled to disappear as of 31 August 2011.

Category A services: Canadian analogue and Category 1 digital pay and specialty television services with access rights to BDUs as of 1 September 2011.

Category B services: Category 2 digital pay and specialty television services, and any existing or new services that the Commission may choose to license, without access rights to BDUs as of 1 September 2011.

CATV: community antenna television system – involves sharing one antenna among multiple television homes linked via coaxial cable.

CAVCO: Canadian Audio-visual Certification Office – an office of the Ministry of Canadian Heritage responsible for certifying Canadian audio-visual productions for federal tax credit purposes.

CBC: Canadian Broadcasting Corporation [Société Radio-Canada] – the national public broadcaster. Note that, in common parlance, CBC is used to designate the English-language services of the Corporation while Radio-Canada is used to designate its French-language services.

CBSC: Canadian Broadcast Standards Council – a non-governmental organization created by the Canadian Association of Broadcasters to administer program standards established by its members. See *self-regulation*.

CCD: Canadian content development, to which all licensees of private commercial radio stations are required by the CRTC to make an annual financial contribution.

Class 1 cable BDU: a cable system with more than 6,000 subscribers. (Note that where a new terrestrial BDU chooses to operate within the service area of an existing BDU, and therefore competes with it, the Commission grants the same class of licence to the new entrant as it has to the incumbent, regardless of the number of subscribers the new entrant actually serves.)

Class 2 cable BDU: a cable system with 2,000–6,000 subscribers.

Class 3 cable BDU: a cable system with fewer than 2,000 subscribers.

closed captioning: translates the audio portion of a television program into subtitles, also called captions, which allow hearing-impaired viewers to read what they cannot hear.

CMF: Canada Media Fund – an amalgamation of the CTF and the Canada New Media Fund to form the Canada Media Fund, scheduled to launch on 1 April 2010.

coaxial cable: a form of high-capacity shielded cable used for the terrestrial transmission of radiocommunication signals to households and firms.

compulsory licence: the obligation to pay a royalty fee, at a rate specified by a 'tariff' that is set by the Copyright Board of Canada, to a collective that represents rights holders who must accept this tariff as fair compensation for use of the copyright material in question.

conventional television service: a service providing a broad range of programming from many or all categories and traditionally associated with off-air broadcast.

copyright: the right to reproduce intellectual property as set out in the Copyright Act.

CPAC: Canadian Parliamentary Channel – a privately owned, commercial-free, not-for-profit, bilingual, licensed television service created in 1992 by a consortium of cable companies to provide a window on Parliament, politics, and public affairs in Canada.

CRBC: Canadian Radio Broadcasting Commission – a creation of the Canadian Radio Broadcasting Act of 1932 and the forerunner (1932–6) of the CBC.

cross-media ownership: the ownership of more than one mass communications medium in the same market.

CRTC: Canadian   Radio-television   and   Telecommunications Commission.

CTF: Canadian Television Fund – a private-public partnership that finances television programs and new media (see also CMF).

cultural diversity: in broadcasting, reference to how different social groups, such as ethno-cultural minorities, Aboriginal peoples, and persons with disabilities are represented in programming.

DBS: direct broadcast satellite.

described audio or video: described audio is a vocal description of textual or graphic information, such as weather reports and sports, displayed on a television screen, whereas described video consists of a vocal description of a television program's main visual elements and permits the visually impaired to form a mental picture of what is broadcast.

digital broadcast technology: the production, broadcast, or reception of moving images or sound using a quantized discrete-time signal. (A discrete-time signal is, in fact, a sampled analogue signal.)

discretionary service: a broadcasting programming service that a subscriber may choose to obtain from a BDU, for a fee, over and above the basic services provided by the BDU.

distribution undertaking: according to the Broadcasting Act, 'an undertaking for the reception of broadcasting and the retransmission thereof by radio waves or other means of telecommunication to more than one permanent or temporary residence or dwelling unit or to another such undertaking.'

DSL: digital subscriber line – an undertaking that distributes programming to subscribers through a telephone line using Internet Protocol (IP) technology.

DTH: direct-to-home satellite system such as that of Bell TV (formerly Bell ExpressVu) or Shaw Direct (formerly Star Choice).

DTH black market: the market for illegal devices that defeat or bypass the scrambling system in a DTH satellite receiver.

DTH grey market: the market for illegal services involving the decoding of U.S. satellite television programming by households in Canada.

electromagnetic spectrum: the range of electromagnetic waves that can be classified by their wavelengths and are divided into sections. The collection of these waves constitutes the electromagnetic spectrum and consists of gamma rays, X-rays, ultraviolet rays, visible light, infrared waves, and radio waves.

employment equity: the principle that no person be denied employment opportunities or benefits for reasons unrelated to ability.

encryption: according to the Broadcasting Act, a signal that is 'treated electronically or otherwise for the purpose of preventing intelligible reception,' also known as 'scrambling'

ethnic programs: programs, including cross-cultural programming, directed specifically to a culturally or racially distinct group other than one that is Aboriginal Canadian, or from France or the British Isles.

exemption: power granted to the CRTC by section 9(4) of the Broadcasting Act that allows the Commission to exempt persons who carry on broadcasting undertakings of any class from any or all of the requirements in Part II, or regulations pursuant to Part II, of the Act.

FACTOR: Foundation to Assist Canadian Talent on Records – a private non-profit organization that provides financial assistance for the growth and development of the English-language Canadian independent recording industry.

FCC: Federal Communications Commission – responsible for regulating and supervising broadcasting and telecommunications in the United States (the U.S. equivalent of the CRTC).

footprint: coverage area, often used in reference to the area covered by a satellite signal.

FTA: Free Trade Agreement of 1987 between Canada and the United States – entered into effect in January 1989.

GATT: General Agreement on Tariffs and Trade – following the Second World War, established a general framework for international trade that later came under the auspices of the WTO.

Governor-in-Council: the council of ministers or Cabinet that carries out the executive government of Canada and almost always consists of elected members of Parliament.

HD: high-definition television (HDTV) – a digital television system having approximately twice the vertical and horizontal picture resolution of analogue television and an aspect ratio of 16:9.

horizontal integration: a horizontally integrated firm owns several broadcasting outlets in the same market.

independent production: production that is not controlled by a broadcaster. The CRTC usually defines an independent production company as a production company in which a broadcasting licensee, or any company related to a broadcasting licensee, owns or controls less than 30 per cent of the equity of the production company.

in-house production: production by a broadcaster or an affiliated company.

ITU: International Telecommunications Union – an organization responsible for the allocation of radio frequencies among countries with a view to minimizing cross-border interference.

Knowledge: the public educational media network of the government of British Columbia.

licence: according to the Broadcasting Act, 'a licence to carry on a broadcasting undertaking issued by the Commission under this Act.'

MAPL: the MAPL system determines whether a song qualifies as Canadian by determining if its elements respect the CRTC's requirements for four elements: music, artist, production, and lyrics.

MATV: master antenna television – system that involves sharing an antenna among multiple television homes linked via coaxial cable.

MDS: multipoint distribution system – a wireless distribution technology that relies on short-range microwave distribution technology for delivery of television signals directly to the home.

MusicAction: a non-profit organization whose primary objective is to encourage the development of French-language music via the production and distribution of recorded works.

NAFTA: North American Free Trade Agreement of 1994 involving Canada, the United States, and Mexico.

network: according to the Broadcasting Act, 'includes any operation where control over all or any part of the programs or program schedules of one or more broadcasting undertakings is delegated to another undertaking or person.'

NFB: National Film Board of Canada.

original program: a program that, at the time of its broadcast by a licensee, has not been previously broadcast by the licensee or any other licensee.

pay television: initially conceived as a discretionary service for which subscribers paid a specific fee over and above the basic cable fee in exchange for premium programming delivered continuously in a linear, scheduled format with no advertising.

PBS: Public Broadcasting System – a non-governmental, non-profit organization that provides educational broadcast services to affiliated stations in the United States.

PPV: pay-per-view – a service that allows television viewers to purchase individual television programs of their choice. A pay-per-view program is presented continuously at regular intervals in a fixed schedule on a scrambled channel.

priority television programs: Canadian drama, music and dance, and variety programs, long-form documentary programs, certain regionally produced programs, and Canadian entertainment magazine programs.

program: according to the Broadcasting Act, 'sounds or visual images, or a combination of sounds and visual images, that are intended to inform, enlighten or entertain, but does not include visual images, whether or not combined with sounds, that consist predominantly of alphanumeric text.'

programming undertaking: according to the Broadcasting Act, 'an undertaking for the transmission of programs, either directly by radio waves or other means of telecommunication or indirectly through a distribution undertaking, for reception by the public by means of broadcasting receiving apparatus.'

radio frequency spectrum: a range of frequencies that permits the communication of information via radio waves.

radio waves: according to the Broadcasting Act, 'electromagnetic waves of frequencies lower than 3000 GHz that are propagated in space without artificial guide.'

Radio-Canada: the French-language designation of the 'Société Radio-Canada' ['Canadian Broadcasting Corporation'], the national public broadcaster. Note that, in common parlance, 'Radio-Canada' is used to designate the French-language services of the Corporation while 'CBC' is used to designate its English-language services.

regulation: a form of law that carries out the purposes of a general law or expands on it, but is limited in scope by the general law.

repeat program: a program that, at the time of its broadcast by a licensee, has been previously broadcast by the licensee or any other licensee.

SAP: secondary audio programming channel – a service carried alongside a television signal as an alternative to the standard audio channel that accompanies the video portion of a television program.

SD: standard definition television (SDTV) – a digital television system that may use either a 4:3 aspect ratio or a 16:9 aspect ratio. While SDTV generates a significantly better picture resolution than analogue television, it is inferior to HDTV.

self-regulation: adherence to the guidance provided by industry organizations that address social policy concerns raised by the Broadcasting Act, without the direct intervention of the CRTC.

simultaneous substitution: regulation that requires a Canadian BDU to substitute a local signal for a distant signal when the two are 'comparable.' Most often, this involves substituting a local Canadian signal for a U.S. signal.

specialty service: a service providing a narrow-cast range of programming usually relating to a limited number of program categories and, in the case of television, available only from BDUs

SRDU: satellite relay distribution undertaking – a satellite BDU essentially designed to provide broadcast signals to cable BDUs

streaming technology: digital information that is presented or played back to an end-user while it is being delivered by the streaming provider

S-VOD: subscription video-on-demand – service offering packages of television programming over a period of up to one week

Télé-Québec: the public educational service of the government of Quebec

TFO: l'Office des télécommunications éducatives de langue française de l'Ontario – the French-language educational service of the Government of Ontario

TVO: TVOntario, the English-language educational service of the Government of Ontario

UNESCO: United Nations Educational, Scientific, and Cultural Organization

vertical integration: a vertically integrated firm participates in more than one successive stage of the production, scheduling, or distribution of a service.

VOD: video-on-demand – service allowing television viewers to purchase individual television programs of their choice, whereby the digitized program is streamed or downloaded to the subscriber's digital set-top box. Unlike pay-per-view, a digital server is deployed and only one BDU channel need be involved.

WTO Agreement: World Trade Organization Agreement – provides for a single institutional framework for multilateral trade among many countries.

Selected Bibliography

Note: All of the decisions and notices contained in this book are available on the CRTC's web site at http://www.crtc.gc.ca.

An Act Respecting the Société de télédiffusion du Québec, R.S.Q, c. S-12.01. http://www.canlii.org/qc/laws/sta/s-12.01/index.html.

Advertising Standards Canada. http://www.adstandards.com/en/.

Arango, Tim. 'Broadcast TV Faces Struggle to Stay Viable.' *New York Times*, 28 February 2009.

Babe, Robert E. *Canadian Television Broadcasting Structure, Performance and Regulation*. Ottawa: Minister of Supply and Services Canada, 1979.

Bird, Roger, ed. *Documents of Canadian Broadcasting*. Ottawa: Carleton University Press, 1988.

Broadcasting Act (1991, c. 11). http://laws.justice.gc.ca/en/B-9.01/index.html.

Canada-U.S. Free Trade Agreement (1987). http://www.international.gc.ca/trade-agreements-accords-commerciaux/assets/pdfs/cusfta-e.pdf.

Canadian Association of Broadcasters. 'Reflecting Canadians: Best Practices for Cultural Diversity in Private Television.' July 2004. http://www.cab-acr.ca/english/social/diversity/taskforce/report/cdtf_report_jul04.pdf

Canadian Broadcast Standards Council. http://www.cbsc.ca/english/.

Canadian Broadcasting Corporation (CBC). http://cbc.radio-canada.ca/home.asp.

Canadian Broadcasting Corporation. *CBC/Radio-Canada Annual Report 2007–2008*, Vol. 2, *Management Discussion and Analysis and Financials*. http://www.cbc.radio-canada.ca/annualreports/2007-2008/pdf/vol2/CBCAR08EVol2.pdf.

Canadian Film and Television Production Association. *09 Profile: An Economic Report on the Canadian Film and Television Production Industry.* February 2009. http://www.cftpa.ca/news/pdf/profile/profile2009-en.pdf.

Canadian Radio-television and Telecommunications Act (R.S., 1985, c. C-22). http://laws.justice.gc.ca/en/C-22/.

Canadian Radio-television and Telecommunications Commission. http://www.crtc.gc.ca.

– *2008–2009 Estimates: Part III – Report on Plans and Priorities.* http://www.crtc.gc.ca/eng/publications/reports/rpps/2008_09.htm.

– *Broadcasting Policy Monitoring Report 2007.* http://www.crtc.gc.ca/eng/publications/reports/PolicyMonitoring/2007/bpmr2007.htm.

– Broadcasting Public Notice CRTC 1999-84. 'New Media.' 17 May 1999. http://www.crtc.gc.ca/eng/archive/1999/PB99-84.htm

– Broadcasting Public Notice CRTC 2003-2. *Internet Retransmission: Report to the Governor General in Council Pursuant to Order in Council P.C. 2002-1043.* 17 January 2003. http://www.crtc.gc.ca/eng/archive/2003/pb2003-2.htm.

– Broadcasting Public Notice CRTC 2006-158. 'Commercial Radio Policy.' 15 December 2006. http://www.crtc.gc.ca/eng/archive/2006/pb2006-158.htm.

– Broadcasting Public Notice CRTC 2007-70. 'Call for Comments on the Canadian Television Fund (CTF) Task Force Report.' 29 June 2007. http://www.crtc.gc.ca/eng/archive/2007/pb2007-70.htm.

– Broadcasting Public Notice CRTC 2008-4. 'Regulatory Policy: Diversity of Voices.' 15 January 2008. http://www.crtc.gc.ca/eng/archive/2008/pb2008-4.htm.

– Broadcasting Public Notice CRTC 2008-100. 'Regulatory Frameworks for Broadcasting Distribution Undertakings and Discretionary Programming Services.' 30 October 2008. http://www.crtc.gc.ca/eng/archive/2008/pb2008-100.htm.

– *Communications Monitoring Report 2008.* July 2008. http://www.crtc.gc.ca/eng/publications/reports/policymonitoring/2008/cmr2008.htm.

– 'A Competitive Balance for the Communications Industry: Submission of the Canadian Radio-television and Telecommunications Commission to the Competition Policy Review Panel.' 11 January 2008. http://www.crtc.gc.ca/eng/publications/reports/cprp.htm.

– 'The Future Environment Facing the Canadian Broadcasting System.' 14 December 2006. http://www.crtc.gc.ca/eng/publications/reports/broadcast/rep061214.htm

– *Perspectives on Canadian Broadcasting in New Media: A Compilation of Research and Stakeholder Views.* 15 May 2008. http://www.crtc.gc.ca/eng/media/rp080515.pdf.

- Public Notice CRTC 1999-97. 'Building on Success: A Policy Framework for Canadian Television.' 11 June 1999. http://www.crtc.gc.ca/eng/archive/1999/PB99-97.htm.
- Public Notice CRTC 2000-1. 'A Distinctive Voice for All Canadians: Renewal of the Canadian Broadcasting Corporation's Licences.' 6 January 2000. http://www.crtc.gc.ca/eng/archive/2000/PB2000-1.htm.
- *Report to the Governor in Council on English- and French-Language Broadcasting Services in English and French Linguistic Minority Communities in Canada.* 30 March 2009. http://www.crtc.gc.ca/eng/BACKGRND/language/ol0903-lo0903.htm.
- 'Statistical and Financial Summaries.' (Annual.) http://www.crtc.gc.ca/eng/stats.htm.
Canadian Television Fund. *Annual Report 2007–08.* http://www.ctf-fct.ca/assets/AR0708/en/AR_0708.html.
- *Broadcaster Performance Envelope Guidelines 2009–2010.* http://www.ctf-fct.ca/assets/producers/09-10/bpe.pdf.
Collins, Richard. *Culture, Communication & National Identity: The Case of Canadian Television.* Toronto: University of Toronto Press, 1990.
Communications, Energy, and Paperworkers Union of Canada. 'Old Questions, New Media.' 18 February 2009. http://support.crtc.gc.ca/applicant/docs.aspx?pn_ph_no=2008-11&call_id=74333&lang=E&defaultName=CEP&replyonly=&addtInfo=&addtCmmt=&fnlSub=.
Competition Bureau Canada. 'CRTC/Competition Bureau Interface.' 19 November 1999. http://www.cb-bc.gc.ca/eic/site/cb-bc.nsf/eng/00815.html.
Consumer Protection Act, R.S.Q. c. P-40.1. http://www.canlii.org/qc/laws/sta/p-40.1/.
Dalfen, Charles. 'The Future of Canadian Communications Policy and Regulation: Preserving the Essential.' Speech to the Sixth Annual Conference of the International Institute of Communications, Canadian Chapter, 5 December 2006. http://www.crtc.gc.ca/eng/NEWS/SPEECHES/2006/s061205.htm.
Department of Justice. *Constitution Acts 1867 to 1982.*
Dunbar, Laurence J.E., and Christian Leblanc. *Review of the Regulatory Framework for Broadcasting Services in Canada: Final Report.* Prepared for the CRTC. 31 August 2007.
Gasher, Mike. 'Invoking Public Support for Public Broadcasting: The Aird Commission Revisited.' *Canadian Journal of Communications* 23, no. 2 (1998). http://www.cjc-online.ca/index.php/journal/article/view/1032/93.
Geist, Michael. *Internet Law in Canada.* 3rd ed. Concord, ON: Captus, 2002.
Goldman, William. *Adventures in the Screen Trade: A Personal View of Hollywood and Screenwriting.* New York: Warner Books, 1983.

Government of Canada. *Report of the Task Force on Broadcasting Policy* (Caplin-Sauvageau Report). Ottawa: Ministry of Supply and Services, 1986.

Grant, Peter S. *Canadian Communications Law and Policy.* Vol. 1. Toronto: Upper Canada Law Society, 1988.

Grant, Peter S., and Grant Buchanan. *Regulatory Guide to Canadian Radio.* 2nd ed. Toronto: McCarthy Tétrault, 2008.

Grant, Peter S., Grant Buchanan, and Monique T. Lafontaine. *Regulatory Guide to Canadian Television.* 4th ed. Toronto: McCarthy Tétrault, 2008.

Grant, Peter S., Monique T. Lafontaine, and Grant Buchanan. *Canadian Broadcasting Regulatory Handbook 2008.* 9th ed. Toronto: McCarthy Tétrault, 2008.

Grant, Peter S., and Chris Wood. *Blockbusters and Trade Wars: Popular Culture in a Globalized World.* Vancouver: Douglas & McIntyre, 2004.

Hoskins, Colin, Stuart McFadyen, and Adam Finn. *Media Economics: Applying Economics to New and Traditional Media.* Thousand Oaks, CA: Sage, 2004.

Industry Canada. *Canadian Table of Frequency Allocations: 9 kHz to 275 GHz (2005 Edition).* May 2005. Ottawa: Industry Canada.

Kerr, Donald, and Deryck W. Holdsworth. *Historical Atlas of Canada*, Vol. 3, *Addressing the Twentieth Century.* Toronto: University of Toronto Press, 1990.

Knopf, Howard P. *Canadian Copyright Collectives and the Copyright Board: A Snap Shot in 2008.* Law Society of Upper Canada Continuing Legal Education Program of 28 February 2008. http://www.macerajarzyna.com/pages/publications/Knopf_Canadian_Copyright_Collectives_Copyright_Board_Feb2008.pdf.

Krauss, Clifford. 'Bad Mouth or Free Mouth, He Ruffles Genteel Airwaves.' *New York Times*, 23 September 2004.

Laffont, J.J., and J. Tirole. 'The Politics of Government Decision Making: A Theory of Regulatory Capture.' *Quarterly Journal of Economics* 106, no. 4 (1991): 1089–1127

Lee, Timothy B. 'Entangling the Web.' *New York Times.* 3 August 2006.

Levine, M.E., and J.L. Forrence. 'Regulatory Capture, Public Interest, and the Public Agenda: Toward a Synthesis.' *Journal of Law Economics & Organization* 6 (1990): 167–98.

McKeown, Larry, Anthony Noce, and Peter Czerny. 'Factors Associated with Internet Use: Does Rurality Matter?' *Rural and Small Town Canada Analysis Bulletin* 7, no. 3 (September 2007).Catalogue no. 21-006-XIE. Ottawa: Statistics Canada. http://dsp-psd.pwgsc.gc.ca/collection_2007/statcan/21-006-X/21-006-XIE2007003.pdf.

McKinsey & Company. *Public Service Broadcasters around the World.* McKinsey & Company, 1999.

McLean, Catherine, and Grant Robertson. 'Bell Postpones Launch of Land-line TV Service.' *Globe and Mail*, 26 October 2007.

Noam, Eli. 'TV or Not TV: Three Screens, One Regulation?' 11 July 2008.
  http://www.crtc.gc.ca/eng/media/noam2008.htm.
North American Free Trade Agreement (1994). http://www.international.
  gc.ca/nafta-alena/agree-en.asp.
Ontario Educational Communications Authority Act, R.S.O. 1990, c. O.12.
  http://www.canlii.org/on/laws/sta/o-12/20061120/whole.html.
Owen, Bruce W., and Steven S. Wildman. *Video Economics*. Cambridge, MA:
  Harvard University Press, 1992.
Peers, Frank W. *The Politics of Canadian Broadcasting 1920–1951*. Toronto: Uni-
  versity of Toronto Press, 1969.
– *The Public Eye: Television and the Politics of Canadian Broadcasting 1952–68*.
  Toronto: University of Toronto Press, 1979.
Raboy, Marc. *Missed Opportunities: The Story of Canada's Broadcasting Policy*.
  Montreal and Kingston: McGill-Queen's University Press, 1990.
Ritchie, Gordon, *Wrestling with the Elephant: The Inside Story of the Canada-U.S.
  Trade Wars*. Toronto: Macfarlane Walter & Ross, 1997.
Robertson, Grant. 'CSR Sees Hope after Two Years of Losses.' *Globe and Mail*,
  16 January 2008.
Roth, Lorna. *Something New in the Air: The Story of First Peoples Television Broadcasting in Canada*. Montreal and Kingston: McGill-Queen's University Press,
  2005.
Royal Commission on National Development in the Arts, Letters and Sciences
  1949–1951. *Report*. Ottawa: Royal Commission on National Development in
  the Arts, Letters and Sciences, 1951. http://www.collectionscanada.gc.ca/
  massey/h5-400-e.html#part1.
Rutherford, Paul. 'Researching Television History: Prime-Time Canada,
  1952–1967.' *Archivaria* 20 (Summer 1985): 79–93. http://journals.sfu.ca/
  archivar/index.php/archivaria/article/view/11178/12116.
– *When Television Was Young: Primetime Canada 1952–1967*. Toronto: University
  of Toronto Press, 1969.
Standage, Tom. *The Victorian Internet: The Remarkable Story of the Telegraph and
  the Nineteenth Century's On-line Pioneers*. New York: Berkley Books, 1999.
Standing Committee on Canadian Heritage. 'CBC/Radio-Canada: Defining
  Distinctiveness in the Changing Media Landscape.' February 2008. http://
  www2.parl.gc.ca/HousePublications/Publication.aspx?DocId=3297009&La
  nguage=E&Mode=1&Parl=39&Ses=2.
– *Our Cultural Sovereignty: The Second Century of Canadian Broadcasting*. June
  2003.http://cmte.parl.gc.ca/Content/HOC/committee/372/heri/reports/
  rp1032284/herirp02/herirp02-e.pdf.
Standing Senate Committee on Transport and Communications. *Final Report
  on the Canadian News Media*. Vol. 1 of 2. June 2006. http://www.parl.

gc.ca/39/1/parlbus/commbus/senate/Com-e/TRAN-E/rep-e/repfinjun-06vol1-e.htm.

Statistics Canada. *Daily*. http://www.statcan.ca/english/dai-quo/.

– *Historical Statistics of Canada*. Ottawa: Statistics Canada, 1983.

Stewart, Andrew, and William H.N. Hull. *Canadian Television Policy and the Board of Broadcast Governors, 1958–1968*. Edmonton: University of Alberta Press, 1994.

Stigler, George. 'The Theory of Economic Regulation.' *Bell Journal of Economic and Management Sciences* 2 (1971): 3–21.

Telefilm Canada. http://www.telefilm.gc.ca/accueil.asp?LANG=EN&.

United Nations Educational, Scientific and Cultural Organization. Convention on the Protection and Promotion of the Diversity of Cultural Expressions 2005. http://portal.unesco.org/en/ev.php-URL_ID=31038&URL_DO=DO_TOPIC&URL_SECTION=201.html.

U.S. Bureau of the Census. *Statistical Abstract of the United States: 1950*. Washington, DC, U.S. Bureau of the Census, 1950.

Vaver, David. *Copyright Law*. Toronto: Irwin Law, 2000.

Verner, Josée. 'Speaking Notes of the Minister at the CFTPA Prime Time in Ottawa Conference Opening Reception.' 20 February 2008. http://www.pch.gc.ca/pc-ch/minstr/arc_disc-spch/verner/2008/20080220-eng.cfm.

Vipond, Mary. 'The Beginnings of Public Broadcasting in Canada: The CRBC, 1932–1936.' *Canadian Journal of Communications* 19, no. 2 (1994). http://www.cjc-online.ca/index.php/journal/article/view/806/712.

– *Listening In: The First Decade of Canadian Broadcasting, 1922–1932*. Montreal and Kingston: McGill-Queen's University Press, 1992.

Von Finckenstein, Konrad. 'Speech: Notes for an Address by Konrad von Finckenstein ... to the Standing Committee on Canadian Heritage ... March 4, 2008.' http://www.crtc.gc.ca/eng/news/speeches/2008/s080304.htm.

Willis, Andrew. 'Satellite Rivals Tune In to Same Wavelength.' *Globe and Mail*, 20 January 2009.

Index

ABC (Australian Broadcasting Corporation), 112

Aboriginal broadcasting. *See* broadcasting, Aboriginal

Aboriginal peoples, 15, 136, 144, 159, 161n15, 247, 249. *See also* programming, Aboriginal

Aboriginal Peoples Television Network (APTN), 147–8

Advertising Standards Canada (ASC), 149, 151, 152, 154, 161n10

advertising, commercial, 8, 12, 29, 40n15, 45–6, 47, 48, 49, 54nn10–11, 67, 84, 97, 104, 106, 113, 121, 123, 123n1, 149, 150, 153, 154, 159, 180, 184, 185, 190n2, 199, 214, 219, 220, 243; local, 67, 180; revenues, 8, 14, 25, 31, 70, 72, 75n14, 110n7, 111n8, 115, 116, 121, 133, 146, 176, 192, 218, 242; to children, 16, 120, 149, 150–4

Aird Commission (Royal Commission on Radio Broadcasting), 24–7, 28

Alliance of Canadian Cinema, Television and Radio Artists (ACTRA), 86

Anik, A1 satellite, 44, 168; F1 satellite, 168; F2 satellite, 168

antenna, rooftop, 32, 38, 44, 163, 165

Applebaum-Hébert Committee (Federal Cultural Policy Review Committee), 46–7

Associations des producteurs de film et de télévision du Québec (APFTQ), 86

Astral Media, 75n12, 167, 214–15, 220, 222n15

barriers to market entry, 4, 182, 208, 209–10

BBC (British Broadcasting Corporation), 25, 30, 31, 39n7, 112, 113, 123n1

BBG (Board of Broadcast Governors), 35–7, 43, 113, 252

Bell TV (Bell ExpressVu), 168, 172, 178n9, 185, 216

Bill C-11, an Act to Amend the Copyright Act, 200–1

Bill C-58, 45

black market, 171–2

BNA (British North America) Act, 1867. *See* Constitution Act, 1867

British Columbia Film, 78, 138
Broadcast Code for Advertising to Children. *See* Code for Advertising to Children, Broadcast
Broadcasting Act
  1958, 35–8, 252
  1968, 20, 38, 41–4, 46, 47, 52, 53n1, 252
  1991, 3–18, 19n5, 41, 47, 52, 53, 53n1, 53–4n2, 54n4, 76–85, 87–8, 90, 94–5, 99, 103, 109, 113–18, 122, 124n4, 126, 130, 135, 143–5, 149, 158, 169–70, 174–5, 177, 186–7, 190n1, 199, 201, 205–7, 212, 219–20, 230, 232, 234, 236, 240–2, 247–50
  exemption, 87, 169–71, 175–7, 178n16, 183, 198–204, 227, 243
  regulations, 5, 11, 13, 15, 16, 36–7, 40n25, 43, 46, 51, 54n8, 83–5, 87, 89–91, 95, 97, 98, 103, 105, 109, 111n8, 111n15, 114, 122–3, 125, 135, 142n11, 149, 151–3, 158, 173, 175, 180–1, 183–4, 186–8, 198, 203, 234, 235, 237, 253
  section 3 (Broadcasting Policy for Canada), 12, 14, 15, 16, 78, 80–1, 83, 87, 88, 90, 94–5, 114, 117, 118, 122, 126, 130, 143–4, 175, 186, 205, 230, 236, 241, 247–50
  section 5 (Objects of the Commission), 79, 80–1, 241
broadcasting
  Aboriginal, 141, 143, 145, 146–8, 149, 159, 247
  commercial, 14, 23, 112, 242
  community, 14, 45, 96, 122–3, 125n20, 128, 142, 145, 146, 247, 248

complaints, 79, 85, 89, 149–50, 154–5, 156, 161n10, 217
condition of licence, 11, 15, 46, 51, 52, 55n18, 83, 87, 89, 90, 95, 104, 105, 106, 117, 128, 139, 147, 150, 151, 152, 155, 156, 157, 158, 180–1, 183, 187, 190n9, 217
conventional (over-the-air), 3, 7, 8, 18, 28, 43, 44–5, 51, 53, 54n10, 95, 146, 150, 160n4, 161n5, 163–4, 166, 177n1, 187, 188, 190n2, 200, 216, 217
definition of, 3–4, 8, 16, 42, 141n5, 54n4, 87, 174–5, 176
distribution undertaking. *See* undertaking, broadcasting distribution (BDU)
educational, 14, 24, 118–22
ethnic, 72, 74n10, 96, 97, 104, 145–7, 148, 156, 160n4, 160–1nn4–5, 224, 253
exhibition requirements, 99, 103–4, 107, 253
expenditure (spending) requirements, 51, 52, 55n18, 96, 99, 103–4, 188, 253
French-language, 30–2, 34, 37, 53n2, 54n10, 63–4, 65, 66, 68, 70, 72–3, 75n16, 89–92, 98, 105, 111n9, 116, 119, 122, 124n3, 130, 133, 136, 140, 141, 145, 146, 148, 154, 159, 161n12, 174, 184, 202, 214, 215, 220
Internet, 11, 15–16, 56, 59, 60, 87, 164, 174–7, 179–80, 192, 198–203, 204, 225, 232, 240, 241–2. *See also* Internet
licence, 11, 13, 22, 23, 30, 35–7, 43, 46, 50–2, 54n4, 54n7, 55n18, 63, 70, 79, 82–3, 85–8, 89–92,

95–6, 104–6, 114, 117–18, 120–1, 125n20, 127–8, 137, 139, 147, 157, 158, 159–60, 164, 166, 167, 171, 173, 183, 185, 187, 191n14, 198, 201, 202, 206, 208, 210, 214, 216, 252

over-the-air. *See* broadcasting, conventional

pay television. *See* pay television services

private sector (commercial), 14, 23, 25–37, 42, 43, 47, 52, 54n10, 70, 72–4, 75n13, 103, 105–7, 116, 117, 118, 120, 124n7, 130

public, 12, 14, 23–4, 26, 27, 28–38, 112–25

public access to, 3, 10, 45, 86, 94, 97, 120, 122, 123, 124n14, 144–5, 168, 192, 249, 250

religious, 25

signal retransmission, 45, 53, 55n19, 175, 189, 193, 195, 197–201, 204, 231n6

social issues, 15, 16, 143–62

specialty television. *See* specialty television services

business cycle, 223–4

CAB (Canadian Association of Broadcasters), 27, 148, 149, 151, 152, 154, 155

Cabinet (Governor-in-Council), 6, 7, 12, 13, 14, 27, 30, 36, 43, 79, 80, 82, 87, 88, 93n4, 115, 135, 169, 170, 200, 204, 206, 252; direction, Ineligibility of non-Canadians, 206, 208; directions, 32, 43, 53, 54n6, 77, 82, 169–71, 204, 206, 208

cable distribution, coaxial. *See* distribution, cable

call sign, 22

Canada Act, 1982, 6, 251

Canada Media Fund (CMF), 13, 15, 19n6, 77, 78, 126, 131–5, 137, 138, 237, 238, 254–6. *See also* Canadian Television Fund (CTF)

Canada Music Fund, 129, 141n3

Canada New Media Fund (CNMF), 19n6, 137, 138, 237, 243, 256

Canada-U.S. Free Trade Agreement (FTA), 13, 53, 226, 227, 231n5

Canadian Association of Broadcasters (CAB), 27, 148–9, 151, 152, 154, 155

Canadian Broadcast Development Fund (Broadcast Fund), 50, 51, 138, 255

Canadian Broadcast Standards Council (CBSC), 149, 154–8, 161n10, 161n13

Canadian Broadcasting Corporation (CBC), 10, 11–12, 13, 20, 28, 30–7, 42, 44, 47, 52, 55, 73, 74n10, 75n13, 77, 78, 96, 99, 103, 106, 109, 110, 112–13, 113–18, 119, 124n3, 124n7, 144, 145, 156, 157, 161n13, 166, 197, 203, 218, 225, 232–4, 235, 238, 243, 244n12, 252; advertising, 47, 113, 115, 152; and the CRTC, 117–18; board of directors, 35, 36, 115–16, 232–4; Guidelines on Sex-Role Portrayal, 156; mandate, 113–15; organization, 115–17

Canadian Coalition for Cultural Expression (CCCE), 136

Canadian Conference of the Arts (CCA), 86

Canadian content, 7, 8, 17, 18, 34, 36, 37, 43, 51, 56, 62–6, 76, 94–111, 126–42, 146–7, 181, 185, 192, 225,

226, 231n3, 240, 241; certification
of, 77, 100–3, 131–3, 140; requirements, radio, 36, 43, 44, 62–3,
96–9, 127–9, 241; requirements,
television, 36, 37, 43, 51, 63–6, 77,
99–106, 126, 131–3, 140, 146–7, 181,
185, 241. *See also* MAPL system
Canadian Content Development
(CCD), 127–9, 141n1
Canadian Film or Video Production
Tax Credit (CPTC), 101, 102, 131,
132–3, 139–40
Canadian Heritage, Department of,
6, 12, 13, 53, 76–8, 100, 102, 103,
110n3, 126, 129, 131, 134, 135, 136,
137, 141n3, 147, 169, 208, 236, 237,
255, 256
Canadian Heritage, Minister of, 78,
116, 117, 135, 233, 235, 237, 255
Canadian Radio Broadcasting Act,
1932, 28–9, 252; 1936, 29–30, 33,
252
Canadian Radio League, 27, 29, 30
Canadian Radio-television and
Telecommunications Commission
(CRTC), 1991– , 5, 10, 11–17, 63, 66,
69–70, 74n8, 75nn13–14, 75nn16–
17, 76–93, 94–111, 113, 114, 117–18,
120, 122, 123, 124n10, 126–28, 131–
32, 134–35, 139, 142n11, 143–162,
164–65, 167, 168, 169–171, 173–77,
179–191, 192, 198–204, 206, 208,
210, 212–221, 222nn11–12, 232–33,
234–37, 239, 240–43, 253, 254–256
Canadian Radio-television and
Telecommunications Commission
(CRTC), Act, 1976, 4, 46, 47, 78–9;
appeals, 13, 55n18, 87–8, 91–2,
93n4; appointments to, 77, 232–3;
Cabinet directions to, 12, 13, 14,

43, 53, 77, 80, 82, 145, 169–71,
200–1, 204, 206, 208; chairperson, 80; decisions, 86–7; objects
and powers, 12, 76, 78, 79, 80–3,
117–18; public hearings, 85, 89–90;
rules and procedures, 82, 92
Canadian Radio-television Commission, 1968–76, 5, 41–9, 51–3, 53n1,
54n4, 54n8, 55nn18–19, 252
Canadian Satellite Radio, 166–7
Canadian Table of Frequency Allocations, 9
Canadian Television Fund (CTF),
19n6, 120, 131, 132–3, 134–7, 138,
139, 140, 141, 142n8, 142n11,
142n16, 184, 234–8, 244n12, 254–6;
Broadcaster Performance Envelope Stream, 136, 142n16; contribution agreement, 134, 135, 236,
244n12, 255; licence fee top-up,
137, 256. *See also* Canada Media
Fund (CMF);
Canal Vox, 123
Canal Savoir, 119, 174, 202
CANCOM, 44, 55n19
CanWest Global Communications,
73, 105, 124, 218, 221n2
Caplan-Sauvageau Task Force (Task
Force on Broadcasting Policy,
1986), 52–3
CAVCO (Canadian Audio-Visual
Certification Office), 77, 100–2,
131–3, 136, 139–40, 235, 254, 256
CBC. *See* Canadian Broadcasting
Corporation
CBS, 25, 55n19
censorship, 32, 155
certification, Canadian content. *See*
Canadian content, certification of
CFDC (Canadian Film Development

Corporation), 51, 55n17, 137–8
CFTPA (Canadian Film and Television Production Association), 86
Charter of Rights and Freedoms, 47–8
CHOI-FM, 88, 89–92, 96, 156
CHUM Limited, 73, 75n12, 75n17, 129, 167, 215, 217, 218, 222n11, 244n12
Citytv, 124n7, 217
closed captioning, 159
Code: Equitable Portrayal, 149, 154, 155–6; for Advertising to Children, Broadcast, 120, 150–2, 153; of Advertising Standards, Advertising Standards Canada's, 151; for Broadcast Advertising of Alcoholic Beverages, 151, 152–3; of Ethics, 90, 91, 154, 157; regarding Violence in Television Programming, CAB, 154, 157–8; regarding violence, Pay Television and pay-per-view programming, 157; Sex-Role Portrayal, 89, 148, 155–6
codes, industry, 89, 90, 91, 120, 148–58
Commercial Radio Policy, 1998, 128, 213–14, 215; 2006, 66, 110n2, 127, 128, 141n1, 215
common ownership policy, radio, 79, 85, 213–15, 219–21; television, 33, 79, 85, 99, 106, 107, 111n11, 120, 215–20
Communications, Energy and Paperworkers Union of Canada (CEPUC), 86
community channel. See broadcasting, community
Competition Act, 78, 92n1, 211–12, 219–20

competition among firms, economic (market), 16–17, 25, 36, 76, 164, 168, 179, 182, 183, 208–10, 211, 212, 213, 216, 229, 239,
Competition Bureau, 78, 219–21, 241, 244n17
competition policy, 16, 205, 208–10, 211–21
Competition Tribunal, 219, 220
compilation, 194
complaints, 79, 85, 89, 149–50, 154–5, 156, 161n10, 217
compulsory licence, copyright. See copyright, compulsory licences
Constitution Act, 1867, 6, 7, 14, 21, 118
Consumer Protection Act, Quebec, 120, 153–4, 161n12
co-productions, official (treaty) international, 100, 136,
Copyright Act, 16, 53, 188, 193–7, 199, 200–1, 202, 204n2
Copyright Board, 78, 197, 199, 200, 201
copyright, authorship, 193, 195–6; compulsory licences, 197, 200–2; duration, 196–7; licensing, 194, 197; tariffs, 197. See also copyright, compulsory licences
Corus Entertainment, 75n12, 139, 214, 215
co-venture, (CRTC) international, 101, 102
CPAC (Canadian Parliamentary Channel), 202
CRBC (Canadian Radio Broadcasting Commission), 24, 28–9, 40n15, 40n25
cross-media ownership, 131, 209, 210, 212, 214, 216, 217, 218

CRTC. *See* Canadian Radio-television and Telecommunications Commission
CTF. *See* Canadian Television Fund
CTV network (CTVglobemedia), 12, 37, 54, 55n18, 73, 75n12, 75n17, 105, 124n7, 124n9, 167, 203, 209, 215, 216–17, 218, 222nn10–11
cultural diversity, 7, 17, 94, 112, 130, 148–9, 226, 228, 229–31
cultural objectives, 17, 31, 103, 132, 133–4

Department of Canadian Heritage. *See* Canadian Heritage, Department of
Department of Communications, 47, 52
Department of Industry (Industry Canada), 10, 11, 13, 18, 78, 151, 164, 169, 173, 208, 241
Department of Justice, 6,
Department of Transport, 29, 30, 31, 35, 36, 44, 54n8, 252
deregulation, 16, 81, 210
described (descriptive) video, 159–60
digital device, mobile, 56, 57, 60, 62, 83, 163, 166, 175, 176, 177, 179, 192, 203–4, 242
digital distribution, 16, 50, 161, 179, 180, 182, 184, 186–8, 205, 242
digital production, 16
digital radio. *See* radio, digital
digital specialty television services, Category 1, 104, 160n1, 182, 186, 253; Category 2, 104,160n1, 182, 186, 187, 253; Category A, 145, 160n1; Category B, 145, 160n1
digital subscriber line (DSL), 15, 163, 173–4, 177n6, 188, 197

digital technology, 7, 8, 61, 163, 182, 186, 188, 205, 239
Directors Guild of Canada (DGC), 86
DirecTV, 169, 171
distant signals, 45, 111n8
distribution requirements, 109–10
distribution
    cable, 12, 14, 15, 18, 38, 43, 44–6, 48–50, 53, 54n10, 55n19, 59–60, 77, 79, 109–10, 110n7–8, 122, 123, 124n14, 134, 142n15, 145, 148, 154, 163, 164–6, 167–8, 169, 173, 179, 180, 186, 188, 191n12, 197, 199, 201, 209, 214, 234–5, 239, 253, 254–5, 257
    DTH (direct-to-home) satellite, 12, 18, 59–60, 74n2, 77, 79, 109, 110n7, 111n8, 122, 124n14, 142n15, 145, 148, 154, 164–5, 166, 167–72, 179, 187, 188, 197, 199, 201, 234, 239, 253
    satellite, 12, 14, 15, 18, 18n4, 44, 46, 53, 55n19, 58, 59–60, 74n2, 77, 79, 88, 109, 110n7, 111n8, 116, 122, 124n14, 142n15, 145, 148, 154, 163, 164–5, 166–72, 178n12, 179, 187, 188, 197, 199, 201, 234, 239, 253, 257
diversity of expression, 17, 209
documentary television programs, 8, 65, 66, 105, 108, 116, 130, 136, 139, 140, 182, 238, 242, 243
drama, television, 8, 40n15, 51, 55n12, 55n18, 65, 66, 68, 103, 104–5, 107, 109, 130, 136, 193–7, 238, 242–3, 254
DTH (direct-to-home). *See* distribution, DTH (direct-to-home) satellite
Duplessis, Maurice, 31–2

DVD (digital video disc), 60, 65, 66, 158

Edmonton Journal, 24
electromagnetic waves, 4, 8, 9, 39, 42
Employment Equity Act, 158, 161n15
encryption (scrambling), 4, 50, 54n3, 168, 171–2, 174
ethnic stations (services). *See* broadcasting, ethnic
exemption. *See* Broadcasting Act, exemption
expenditure requirements. *See* Canadian content requirements, television

FACTOR (Foundation to Assist Canadian Talent on Records), 77, 126, 127, 129
fair dealing, 193, 204n2
Federal Communications Commission (FCC), 10, 31
Federal Accountability Act, 2006, 233
Federal Court of Appeal, 13, 88, 91–2, 177, 191
Federal Cultural Policy Review Committee. *See* Applebaum-Hébert Committee
federal-provincial relations, 26, 27
Fédération nationale des communications (FNC), 86
Film or Video Production Services Tax Credit (PSTC), 133, 139–40
financing, production, 14, 15, 25, 51, 77, 78, 96, 105, 120, 126–42, 234–5, 242, 243, 244n12, 254–5
Fowler Commission (Royal Commission on Broadcasting), 34–5, 36
Fowler Committee, 37–8
France Télévisions, 112–13

Free-Trade Agreement (FTA), Canada-U.S., 53, 226, 227, 231n5
Friends of Canadian Broadcasting, 86, 124n7
funding, automatic, 133–4, 139
funding, discretionary, 133–4, 139

GATT (General Agreement on Tariffs and Trade), 228–9
Genex Communications inc., 89–92
genre protection policy, 49
Globe and Mail (Toronto), 209, 217, 218
grey market, 172, 178n13

horizontal integration of firms, 209, 210, 212, 216, 217
House of Commons, Standing Committee on Canadian Heritage, 115
household behaviour, 3, 31, 32, 38, 39n7, 44, 49, 56, 59, 60, 61, 124n14, 163, 164, 165, 167, 170–3, 175, 176, 177n6

iCraveTV , 198–9, 201
Income Tax Act, 45
industry concentration, 17, 69–70, 73, 75n12, 75n18, 205, 208–21, 229, 239, 240
interest groups, 85–6, 232, 239
international trade. *See* trade, international
Internet, 11, 15–16, 17, 48, 56, 59, 60, 61–2, 87, 123, 163, 164, 173, 174–7, 179–80, 192, 198–203, 204, 214, 225, 232, 240, 241–2
Investment Canada Act, 207–8
IP (Internet protocol) technology, 173
iPod, 58, 62
ITU (International Telecommunications Union), 10, 18n4, 24

judiciary, 5, 7
JumpTV, 198, 199–201

Knowledge Network, 54n4, 78, 113, 118

La Presse (Montreal), 31
Leader-Post (Regina), 31
licences, compulsory, 16, 188, 197, 200–2
linkage rules, 109–10, 187
Local Programming Improvement Fund (LPIF), 125n18, 189, 191n22
location shooting, foreign, 70, 139–40
logger tapes, 89–90, 155

Manitoba Film and Sound Recording Development Corporation, 138
market entry, barriers to. *See* barriers to market entry
market failure, 7, 8, 112, 205, 238–9
Massey Commission (Royal Commission on National Development in the Arts, Letters and Sciences), 33–4, 46, 47
MDS (multipoint distribution service), 60, 74n2, 79, 172–3, 177n6, 178n14, 234
minorities, linguistic, 114, 144–5, 248, 250
MuchMusic, 110, 181, 203, 209
music, Canadian content requirements, 63, 97–8. *See also* Canadian content requirements, radio
music, definition of Canadian, 98–9, 101
music, French-language, 63, 70, 129
MAPL system, 98–9, 101
music, popular (Category 2), 97

MusicAction, 77, 126, 127, 129–30

NAFTA (North American Free Trade Agreement), 227–8, 229, 257; cultural exemption, 227–8, 229, 257
National Film Board of Canada (NFB), 13, 77, 100, 101, 177, 197, 225, 233
NBC, 25, 26, 55n19
network. *See* undertaking, network
New International Instrument on Cultural Diversity, 17, 228, 229
new media, 19n6, 61–2, 83, 87, 115, 137, 138, 145, 164, 174–7, 192, 198–9, 200–1, 202, 204, 237, 242–3, 256; exemption order, 83, 87, 174–7, 198–9, 200–1, 202, 204, 243
newspaper, 4, 23, 31, 91, 106, 209, 214, 217, 218, 222n10, 223, 231n6, 257
non-Canadian satellites, 88, 169–71
non-Canadian services, distribution of, 49, 63, 109, 147, 171, 179
Nova Scotia Film Development Corporation, 138

official languages, 130, 146, 184, 186, 224–5
On-Air Presence, CRTC Policy Respecting, 159
Ontario Media Development Corporation (OMDC), 78, 138
Ottawa Citizen, 26
ownership, Canadian, 16, 42, 43, 96, 136, 205–8; common, 49, 70, 73–4, 75n18, 85, 131, 208–10; foreign (non-Canadian), 16, 43, 205–8. *See also* common ownership policy

Parliament, 4, 5, 6, 7, 12, 13, 22, 29,

32, 34, 35, 36, 41, 42, 43, 47–8, 52,
    76, 78, 88, 99, 113, 115–16, 158, 189,
    197, 202, 204, 206, 232, 233–4
pay audio. *See* undertaking, pay
    audio programming
pay television services, 4, 43, 48–50,
    51, 55n13, 59, 73, 75n14, 84, 95,
    103, 105, 124n14, 157, 161n13,
    179–84, 186–7, 211, 218, 253
PBS (Public Broadcasting System),
    55n19, 112, 113, 121
peak viewing hours, 66, 106, 107,
    116–17, 150, 231n4
Peers, Frank, 31
perfect competition, 16, 208–9
podcasting, 164, 166
point system, Canadian content rec-
    ognition. *See* CAVCO (Canadian
    Audio-Visual Certification Office)
political power (influence) vis-à-vis
    broadcasting, 232, 234–8
principal-agent problem, 112
principle of minimum differentia-
    tion, 8
priority television programs, 65, 99,
    104–6, 107, 109, 111n11, 120, 121,
    130, 131, 131–2, 141n6, 216, 242, 243
production financing. *See* financing,
    production
production, funds, 15, 123, 126,
    131, 140, 141, 237, 255–6; French-
    language, 140–1; independent, 47,
    51, 65, 70, 100, 101, 127, 130–1, 140,
    141, 142n11, 184, 201, 211, 212, 216,
    237, 248, 255–6; in-house, 55n12,
    70, 100, 101–2, 130, 238
profitability, radio, 68–9, 110n6; tel-
    evision, 72–3, 104, 110nn6–7
program, development, 15, 30, 96,
    127–30, 136, 138–9, 141n1, 242,

253, 254, 255; distribution, 7, 15,
    16, 116, 129, 131, 136, 141, 163, 196,
    208, 257; production, 14, 15, 16, 33,
    47, 50–2, 55n12, 65–8, 70–1, 77, 86,
    96–7, 98, 99–105, 107–8, 116, 126,
    127, 129, 130–1, 132–3, 136, 163,
    192, 193, 196, 208, 211, 212, 216,
    225, 228, 235, 238, 248, 257. *See*
    Canadian content, certification of.
    See also financing, production
programming, Aboriginal, 15, 136,
    141n5, 144, 145–9, 159, 247, 249;
    standards, 16, 90, 130, 144, 149
programs, children's television, 51,
    104, 105, 108, 120, 121–2, 124n14,
    130, 136, 151–4, 157, 161n12, 238,
    242, 243; ethnic, 97, 141n5, 145–46,
    148, 253; U.S., 10, 26, 30, 31, 33,
    37, 44, 45, 48, 54n10, 66, 105,
    106–7, 111n8, 130, 199, 228. *See*
    documentary television programs;
    drama, television; production,
    independent
promotion of artists and programs,
    101, 106–7, 127, 138, 159, 176,
    222n10, 243
public goods, 18n1, 238, 244n13

Quebecor Media, 209, 214, 217, 235,
    244n12

radio, AM, 9–10, 44, 57, 67, 69, 79,
    213–14, 220; campus, 96, 146; CBC,
    28–32, 34, 96, 116; commercial,
    62–3, 66–7, 69, 70, 75n12, 92, 97–8,
    110n2, 127–8, 141n1, 213–14, 215,
    253; community, 14, 96, 128, 145,
    146; content categories, 96–7;
    digital, 58, 116, 164, 166–7, 177n2;
    ethnic, 97, 145–7; FM, 9–10, 57–8,

67, 79, 92, 151, 209, 214; format,
57; French-language, 30, 31–2, 63,
68–9, 70, 89–92, 98, 116, 129–30,
148, 214, 215, 220; listening, 56–8,
63, 67, 98, 215; satellite, 58, 116,
164, 166–7; transitional digital,
164; waves, 4, 8–9, 28, 54, 163,
174. *See also* broadcasting, ethnic;
spectrum, radio frequency
Radio Act, 37, 54n8, 252
Radio-Canada, 55, 113, 115, 117,
124n3, 154, 238. *See also* Canadian
Broadcasting Corporation (CBC)
Radio Nord. *See* RNC Media
Radio Regulations, 10, 89–90, 97, 98
Radiocommunication Act, 10, 18, 80,
172, 240
Radiotelegraph Act, 1913, 22–3, RAI,
112, 113
regulations. *See* Broadcasting Act,
regulations
regulatory capture, 18, 238–9
retransmission, broadcast signal,
45, 53, 55n19, 175, 189, 193, 195,
197–204, 231n6
revenues (fees), subscriber, 14, 72,
110n7, 154, 166, 218
revenues, advertising. *See* advertising, revenues
rights, assignment of, 195; moral,
193, 195; neighbouring, 193;
waiver of, 195
RNC Media (Radio Nord Communications), 92, 214
Rogers Communications, 75n12,
75n17, 105, 129, 139, 209, 215, 217,
222n11, 222n15, 244n12
Royal Commission on Broadcasting.
See Fowler Commission
Royal Commission on National

Development in the Arts, Letters and Sciences. *See* Massey
Commission

SAP (secondary audio programming), 160
satellite delivery. *See* distribution,
satellite
satellite signal piracy, 171–2
satellite, geostationary, 167, 168,
178n12
scale, economies of, 25, 33, 69, 168,
205, 209, 213
scheduling of television programs,
54n10, 106–7, 109, 151, 157, 185,
209
SCN (Saskatchewan Communications Network), 113, 118
scrambling. *See* encryption
self-regulation, 35, 149–50, 152, 153,
158, 159
set-top decoder, 43, 48, 74n3, 159,
180, 181
sex role stereotyping, 16, 155–6
Shaw Communications, 125n20, 135,
166, 168, 234–6
Shaw Direct (Star Choice), 166, 168
simultaneous substitution, 45, 54n10,
105, 106–7, 111n8
Sirius Canada, 116, 166–7
social groups. *See* broadcasting,
social issues
Société des auteurs de radio, télévision et cinéma (SARTEC), 86
SODEC (Société de développement
des entreprises culturelles du
Québec), 78, 133, 138, 140
sound recording, 4, 129, 138, 194, 195
specialty television services, 48–50,
59, 63–5, 70–3, 75nn14–15, 77, 79,

84, 95, 103–5, 109, 110, 110n7, 116,
124n14, 146–47, 150, 154, 157, 160,
160n1, 161n4, 161n12, 166, 179;
180–3, 186–7, 188–9, 191, 197–8,
202, 209, 211, 214, 218, 253
spectrum (frequencies), scarcity of,
7, 8, 35, 146, 205, 238; radio frequency, 7, 8–11, 13, 18, 18n1, 18n4,
27, 28, 30, 78, 163, 164, 173, 188,
197, 205, 238, 240, 244n13
Spry, Graham, 27
streaming technology, 62, 198, 199,
200
subscriber fees, 14, 72, 110n7, 154,
188, 189, 190
subsidies, government, 14, 105, 225,
228
Supreme Court of Canada, 5, 13, 28,
43, 55n18, 92, 172, 178n9

tax credit, Canada. *See* Canadian
Film or Video Production Tax
Credit (CFVPT)
tax credit, Quebec, 133, 139, 140
tax credits, 14, 15, 77, 101, 102, 126,
131, 132–3, 134, 138, 139–41, 228
Telecommunications Act, 1993, 4–5,
10, 12, 17, 77, 78, 169, 219, 240–1
Telefilm Canada, 13, 19n6, 50–1,
55n17, 102, 110n3, 126, 134, 135,
137–8, 225, 233, 237, 255, 256
telegraph, 20–3, 39nn2–3, 46, 79
Telelatino, 146
Télémedia, 220, 222n15
telephone, 9, 10–11, 21, 24, 39n2, 46,
58, 60, 79, 173, 175, 203, 204
telephone, cellular, 9, 10–11, 58, 175,
203, 204
Télé-Québec, 78, 112–13, 118, 119–21,
154

Télévision Quatre-Saisons (TQS).
See V
television, conventional (over-the-
air), 7, 18, 44, 45, 49, 51, 53, 54n10,
63–5, 71–4, 75nn13–14, 75n16, 95,
103–7, 116, 122, 146, 150, 154, 157,
160n4, 161n5, 163–4, 166, 177n1,
185, 188–90, 190n2, 198, 200, 209,
211, 216, 217–18, 222n11, 253; digital, 15, 50, 59–60, 64, 74n3, 75n15,
104, 160n1, 161n4, 164, 167–77,
180, 181–8, 191n13, 197, 253;
digital cable, 15, 50, 59–60; digital
satellite, 15, 59, 60, 167–72, 197;
violence, 16, 149, 154, 156–8. *See
also* digital technology; pay television services; television, pay;
TFO (Office des télécommunications
éducatives de langue française de
l'Ontario), 112, 118, 122, 243
trade, international, 17, 223–31;
international agreements, 13, 53,
197, 223–31, 257; international,
barriers to, 16, 17, 210, 223, 226,
231n3
transfer of (management) control,
128–9, 131, 214, 216, 217, 220, 221n2
transfer of ownership, 73, 85, 128–9,
131, 139, 141n2, 208, 214, 253
treaties, official international co-
production, 100, 102, 136
TSN (The Sports Network), 49, 50,
181, 203, 209
TVA network, 12, 37, 73, 105, 154,
209, 214, 217, 244n12
TVO (TVOntario), 78, 112, 118, 119,
121–2

U.S. border stations, 10, 32, 33, 44,
45, 177

undertaking, broadcasting, 11–12,
24, 28, 32, 41, 43, 45, 53, 76, 79, 81,
85, 90, 94, 114, 127, 144–5, 148, 158,
163, 169, 170, 175, 179, 180, 187,
195, 198, 199, 202, 203–8, 213, 216,
219, 220, 235, 239, 241–3, 247–50;
broadcasting distribution (BDU),
12, 45, 53, 83, 84, 85, 87, 95, 96, 106,
109–10, 111nn15–16, 117, 119, 122,
134, 139, 142n8, 142n11, 144–5,
163, 167, 169, 179, 180, 182, 185–7,
188, 190n1, 197–8, 219, 220, 235,
239, 243, 250, 253, 254; network,
12, 249; pay audio programming,
166, 253. *See* distribution, DTH
(direct-to-home) satellite
UNESCO (United Nations Educational, Scientific and Cultural
Organization), 17, 230; Convention on the Protection of Cultural
Diversity, 17, 230–1
Union des Artistes (UDA), 86

V (formerly TQS), 73, 154

variety television programs, 51, 65,
66, 104, 105, 108, 111n9, 130, 136,
194, 238, 242
VCR (videocassette recorder), 60, 65,
66, 160
vertical integration, 16, 131, 209,
210–11, 212, 216
Vidéotron, 123, 135, 139, 209, 214,
235, 236, 244n12
violence on television. *See* television
violence
Vipond, Mary, 22, 26, 29
von Finckenstein, Konrad, 220, 235,
241

Wi-Fi, 11
Wireless Telegraphy Act, 1905, 21–2
work, artistic, 193, 194, 195; cinematographic, 194, 195, 196, 197;
dramatic, 193, 194, 195, 196, 197;
musical, 193, 194, 195
Writers Guild of Canada (WGC), 86
WTO (World Trade Organization),
228–9, 230–1